Seed Corn of the Confederacy

The Story of the Cadets of the Virginia Military Institute at the Battle of New Market

by
James Gindlesperger

 Burd Street Press

This Burd Street Press publication
was printed by
Beidel Printing House, Inc.
63 West Burd Street
Shippensburg, PA 17257-0152 USA

In respect for the scholarship contained herein, the acid-free paper used in this book meets the guidelines for permanence and durability of the Committee on Production Guidelines for Book Longevity of the Council on Library Resources.

For a complete list of available publications
please write
Burd Street Press
Division of White Mane Publishing Company, Inc.
P.O. Box 152
Shippensburg, PA 17257-0152 USA

Library of Congress Cataloging-in-Publication Data

Gindlesperger, James, 1941-
    Seed corn of the Confederacy : the story of the cadets of the
Virginia Military Institute at the Battle of New Market / by James
Gindlesperger.
        p.   cm.
    Includes bibliographical references and index.
    ISBN 1-57249-056-X (alk. paper)
    1. New Market (Va.), Battle of, 1864. 2. Military cadets-
-Virginia--History--19th century. 3. Virginia Military Institute-
-History--19th century. I. Title.
E476.64.G56   1997
973.7'371--dc21   97-6747
                                                         CIP

973.73

Gin   PRINTED IN THE UNITED STATES OF AMERICA

2001\02   Gift

To the Memories
of the
New Market Cadets
and
all others who have known the horrors of war

"Put the boys in, and may God forgive me for the order."

Major General John Breckinridge, C.S.A.

Table of Contents

Illustrations

Maps

Acknowledgements

Although those about whom the following pages are written have long been gone, the author has attempted to bring them back to life and give them personalities one more time. Any success in this endeavor is due to the help and assistance of many people, to whom I owe much.

Anyone who undertakes a project of an extended duration knows that its completion is more easily attained if there is support, encouragement, and patience displayed by the family throughout the process. I am no exception, and I owe my family a debt of gratitude. Thanks are especially extended to my wife and travel companion, Suzanne, who came to look on the cadets with as much admiration as I have.

Thanks also must be extended to Lieutenant Colonel Keith Gibson of the Virginia Military Institute, and to his staff, particularly Judith Haviland at the VMI Museum and Barbara Blakey at the New Market Battlefield Historical Park. I appreciated not only their hospitality, but also their friendly and helpful attitudes. Their support and encouragement must be acknowledged as well, for without it the project would not have proceeded nearly as easily. I also appreciate their endorsement of the idea for the story and their permission to use many of the photos found throughout this book.

As always, the employees of the National Archives provided invaluable assistance and their efforts must be publicly acknowledged. In the same vein, the employees at the Library of Congress who assisted and made suggestions had much to do with the final result, and to the National Park Service I am indebted for much of the background information used to put together the story of the Shenandoah Valley.

Much of the research material was located by Geri Kruglak of the Interlibrary Loan Department at Carnegie Mellon University. Geri, who had an ancestor with the VMI cadets at New Market, went out of her way to acquire even the most obscure source of material, and was successful more often than not.

Many other fine organizations and institutions must also be recognized for their gracious assistance. The VMI Archives, the Stonewall Jackson House in Lexington, The Hall of Valor Museum at the New Market Battlefield Historical Park, The Museum of the Confederacy, The Civil War Library/Museum, the Alderman Library of the University of Virginia, the Connecticut Historical Society, the Commonwealth of Massachusetts State Library, and the Pennsylvania State Archives all provided valuable assistance, and much of the critical reference material which they furnished did a great deal to fill out the details of the battle. If I have missed anyone, I extend my sincere apologies.

And finally, I am indebted to those friends who read the manuscript and offered suggestions, and to those whose interest and encouragement kept the project on track. Your help and kind words are deeply appreciated.

Introduction

The pages which follow accurately describe the actions of the cadets of the Virginia Military Institute at the Battle of New Market, Virginia on May 15, 1864. No attempt is made to portray this story as an elaborate account of the battle in its entirety; other authors have done an admirable job in that area. While this story discusses the entire battle, it more greatly details those portions of the battle in which the cadets were directly involved. The segments of the battle, and the events leading up to it, in which the cadets either had limited involvement, or were not included at all, are chronicled in lesser detail. For a complete account of the battle, regimental histories are recommended, or one of the many books devoted to the overall battle itself.

Prologue

The Valley, they called it. Its official name was the Shenandoah Valley but to everyone who lived there it had always been simply the Valley. Even both governments had taken to using the popular appellation. Now, in 1864, whether it was an official in Washington or Richmond talking, nobody asked which valley was referenced when someone mentioned the Valley. Unless stated otherwise, there was no question in anyone's mind.

The Valley was a verdant stretch of ground bounded on the east by the Blue Ridge Mountains and on the west by the North Mountains of the Alleghenies. About 140 miles in length, the Valley extended southwest to northeast from just north of Lexington to the Potomac River. Nestled between the two mountain ranges, few places in this country could boast of more natural beauty than the Valley. Fewer still had been ravaged as much by the effects of the war.

The Shenandoah Valley took its name from the Shenandoah River which flowed through it. By one of those quirks of geography, the river ran from south to north, so that to go down the valley required one to travel north. Conversely, if one wished to go up the valley, he would, in fact, turn to the south.

For the first two years of the war, one name had stood out when the Valley was discussed. Lieutenant General Thomas "Stonewall" Jackson and the Valley were synonymous, one and the same. One was rarely mentioned without the other. General Jackson had made the Valley his own personal battleground, creating tremendous problems for the Union armies in both 1862 and 1863, and those who lived in the Valley in the spring of 1864 spoke his name in hushed reverence.

Striking quickly, then fading back into the hills, Jackson had long stymied the Union armies. Familiar with the area, he knew the shortest routes from town to town, knew which gaps offered the most protection, and knew how to use the terrain to his advantage. He had also received no small amount of help from the local citizenry, who placed him nearly on the same plane as Robert E. Lee himself.

But Stonewall was no longer a part of the Valley. No longer a living part, anyway. He had been killed a year earlier at Chancellorsville, shot accidentally by his own troops. The grief among the residents of the Valley had been, and still was, for that matter, beyond description. They had lost one of their own. It had never occurred to anyone that Stonewall wouldn't always be there. But now he was gone. It had only seemed natural that his body be brought home to the Valley for burial, and he had been laid to rest in his beloved Lexington.

Since his death, the Valley was no longer the same. Union troops entered with a new confidence, knowing that Stonewall was no longer just around the next bend. To be sure, the Valley was still not uncontested. The unmarked graves in the fields attested to that. But it wasn't the same anymore.

Jackson's successors, Lieutenant General Richard S. Ewell and Major General Jubal A. Early, had tried to preserve the Valley. They had been successful at Winchester, scant weeks after Stonewall's death. They had controlled the Valley long enough for the Confederacy to use it to move into Maryland and Pennsylvania, only to use it again as a retreat route after the Battle of Gettysburg. And perhaps most importantly, they had been able to stave off the Union forces, keeping the Valley under Richmond's control into the winter lull.

But, competent as they may have been, Ewell and Early did not inspire the confidence that Stonewall did. Men who are legends have a way of making things difficult for those who follow, and Ewell and Early had to contend with this added burden. To the inhabitants, the control of the Valley was tenuous without Stonewall. In the Union's mind, the Valley could finally be taken. The failures of 1862 and 1863 had been due, in large part, to Jackson, and his death all but assured that these failures would not be repeated. And as the confidence levels of the invaders increased, the apprehension of the Valley's inhabitants did likewise.

Those who lived there were aware of the strategic importance of their Valley. Beyond its lush beauty, the land was also rich and fertile; so fertile that many referred to the Valley as the "Granary of Virginia." Many of the Valley's residents were pacifist Quakers or Dunkers. Their refusal to fight kept them on the farm, and many in Richmond believed the pacifists made a bigger contribution to the war effort by farming than they would have as soldiers. Much of the grain, cattle, salt, and lead consumed by the Confederacy came from the Valley. In fact, the primary lead mines for the entire Confederacy lay in the Valley, as did some of the chief iron forges and furnaces, important for the horseshoes they provided the cavalry and for the raw material they provided the military foundry in Richmond. When other parts of the Confederacy would boast of the regiments they had sent to General Lee, the residents of the Valley merely smiled smugly, knowing that not only had they also organized regiments of their own, they had fed and equipped those regiments, as well as those of the remainder of the South. But the Valley had felt the full fury of the war, and her rich stores had been despoiled by both armies.

In addition to being rich in minerals and grains, the Valley had one other attribute which magnified its importance: railroads. Railroads which could be used to move goods and supplies to General Lee's Army of Northern Virginia. Railroads which could be used to move the army itself, if need be. In fact, three major railroads ran through the Valley. The Baltimore and Ohio connected Washington with the west. The Virginia and Tennessee did the same for Richmond. A second Confederate railroad, the Virginia Central, ran between the two. A number of smaller feeder railroads, such as the Winchester and Potomac and the Mannassas Gap Railroad, had already been decimated by the war and no longer held much importance.

All this information was not lost on those in Washington. After all, the Valley had once been part of the United States. Perhaps taken for granted, it was not missed until after the secession. Now, there were many on President Lincoln's staff who would like to have the Valley back in the fold. The realists among them knew, however, that it could not be. Not as long as the rebellion remained to be put down, anyway. Thus it was apparent to even the most casual observer that both armies had reason to covet this beautiful stretch of land between the two mountains.

The strategic importance went still deeper. Deeper than the minerals and railroads. Deeper than the network of good roads that connected important towns, a road network which aided rapid military deployment from one point to another. Deeper than the well-cultivated fields, fields which permitted foot soldiers to march on either side of the road, thereby allowing the artillery and supply wagons to move more quickly and with less hindrance on the smoother road surfaces. No, the real strategy resulted from, and was dictated by, the geography of the area.

To move an army from the Valley into the eastern portions of Virginia, and ultimately to either Washington or Richmond, it was necessary to pass through gaps in the Blue Ridge Mountains. The terrain was simply too rugged to allow efficient troop movements in any other fashion. East-west routes through the Valley were dictated by the location of these gaps, and control of the gaps became vitally important. Not only could the controlling army utilize the gaps for troop movements, but the controller could also seal off those gaps and use the mountain range as a shield while moving troops from one end to the other, unseen by and unknown to the enemy. Hence, the army which controlled the gaps also controlled the all-important

Valley, and conversely, by controlling the Valley, one could move practically at will through the gaps.

One of the most significant of these gaps was New Market Gap, which cut through the Massanutten Mountain, a ridge extending through the heart of the Valley for a distance of some 50 miles. The Massanuttens divided the Valley into two smaller valleys, and unless the New Market Gap was controlled, it was necessary for an army to march either 14 miles farther south, to Harrisonburg, or 31 miles north, to Strasburg, to move large bodies of troops through the mountains.

The main road through the Valley was the Valley Turnpike, taking a north-south route through the town of New Market. Extending from Williamsport to Lexington, the turnpike, or pike as it was often called, followed the hills of the Massanutten range, which rose nearly four hundred feet above the road. The Valley Turnpike was originally an Indian trail, and later it became a part of the Great Wagon Road from Philadelphia to the Carolinas. Its macadamized surface permitted travel in adverse weather, a characteristic which resulted in many of the Valley's Civil War battles taking place along its route. Anyone following this turnpike from one end of the Valley to the other would, of necessity, pass through the town of New Market.

In the spring of 1864, the Union's Department of West Virginia, which encompassed the area including the Valley, was commanded by Major-General Franz Sigel. Born in Germany, he had graduated from the German Military Academy. He had resigned from the German army in 1847 and fought in the ill-fated revolution the next year, after which he had fled to the United States by way of Switzerland and England. Sigel had taught school in New York for a while, also serving in the militia at the same time. The opening salvo of the Civil War had found him in St. Louis, serving as Director of Schools. Joining the Union army, he had taken part in some minor skirmishes and had quickly become a hero to his fellow Germans, who made up a rather significant portion of the population in the area. Despite more reversals than successes, he was looked up to by the German community; so much so, in fact, that he had united the Germans on the Union side. These German soldiers identified more with Sigel than with their own regiments, and their reply, when asked what regiment they belonged to, had usually been a simple one: "I fights mit Sigel."

Sigel temporarily had commanded a division at Fredericksburg, but when returned a few days later to his corps, he took offense. This reduction in responsibility had rendered a stinging blow to his Teutonic pride, and he soon resigned for reasons of "poor health."

Early in 1864, pressure from the German community had led several West Virginia politicians to submit Sigel's name to President Lincoln as a potential commander of the Department of West Virginia. President Lincoln, recognizing the strength of the German vote in the upcoming election, had agreed, and Assistant Adjutant General W. A. Nichols issued General Orders Number 80, assigning Franz Sigel to the command of the Department of West Virginia. With the issuance of this order, Sigel now found himself back in the services of the Union, commanding the department which included the Valley.

Also in the Valley, in the town of Lexington, was the Virginia Military Institute (VMI). Referred to by proud Southerners as the West Point of the Confederacy, the Institute had been established in 1839, its location based on the presence of an arsenal. By the start of the war, VMI was the jewel of Southern military facilities, and was becoming known throughout the country as a highly respected training school. Few historic families of the South were not represented in the student body of VMI, and the cadets were affectionately nicknamed the Seed Corn of the Confederacy by none other than Jefferson Davis, president of the Confederate States of America.

The Institute had already contributed to the war effort in more ways than merely training future army officers, however. Stonewall Jackson had been a professor at the Institute, teaching natural and experimental philosophy, and if his loss was deeply felt in the Valley, it was felt even more at the Institute. If anything, his stature had grown since his death, as legends are wont to do. Another, Captain W. H. Morgan, an assistant professor of languages, had been killed at the Battle of Cedar Mountain in 1862. Two other professors, Major General R. E. Rodes, professor of applied mechanics, and Lieutenant C. D. Crittendon, another assistant professor of languages, would pay the ultimate price before the war was to end. At least six other professors had already been wounded in battle, with more to share their fate before the war would draw to a conclusion.

In 1861 the cadets themselves had been sent to Richmond to serve as drillmasters for new recruits, and several times they had been called out for various skirmishes. However, they had never been an active part of any of the fighting, returning each time in a dejected mood after still more inactivity on the battlefield. Frustrated by their lack of opportunities to serve the cause, the cadets had held a meeting of the student body in the early months of 1864 and had voted to offer their services to General Lee. Lee, obviously touched, had responded that he appreciated their gesture but that he preferred that they stay in Lexington. He had offered some hope to the would-be combatants, though, saying he would call on them if he saw the need. Nobody, neither the cadets nor Lee himself, could foresee that the need would not be long in coming.

Union Lieutenant General Ulysses Grant opened the campaign in the spring of 1864 by developing plans to, among other objectives, destroy the New River Bridge on the Virginia and Tennessee Railroad, cutting off Richmond's rail access to the Western Theater. The plan also called for harassment of the Virginia Central Railroad system at Staunton.

Staunton was regarded by many as being second in importance only to Richmond. With its huge commissary stores and railroads, much of the Confederacy's supplies inevitably passed through the town. If the Union could capture Staunton, its loss could be fatal to Richmond. With this part of the campaign taking place in the Valley, the responsibility for the successful fulfillment of Grant's plan fell on the shoulders of Franz Sigel.

Sigel's secondary purpose in this campaign was to keep the Confederate troops occupied, thereby elevating the chances for the success of Grant's movements against Lee. This secondary purpose gave rise to comments by both Grant and Lincoln which, while not grammatically eloquent, described Sigel's role in the campaign well: "If Sigel can't skin himself, he can hold a leg whilst someone else skins."

Understandably, Robert E. Lee had no intentions of allowing any of this to happen. Receiving intelligence reports of the planned activity in the Valley, he sent troops under General John C. Breckinridge to resist the Union advance. Breckinridge had been the vice president of the United States under James Buchanan, a United States senator, and an unsuccessful candidate against Lincoln for president. However, although he was not a secessionist and had, in fact, spoken out against slavery, he no longer held any allegiance to his former government. A vocal opponent of Lincoln's war policies, he had alienated authorities in his home state of Kentucky to the point where he was declared disloyal to the Union. In danger of arrest, he had cast his lot with the Confederate States of America. For his part, Sigel, knowing that Breckinridge had been dispatched to offer resistance to Sigel's troops, said to those around him, "If Breckinridge should advance against us, I will resist him at some convenient location."

That convenient location would turn out to be New Market, and that resistance would be necessary soon enough. Thus, the stage was set for yet one more bloody engagement in the Valley, one of 326 incidents over the course of the war. The battle to come would find the youthful cadets of the Virginia Military Institute pitted as unlikely opponents for the battle-hardened Sigel. As if driven by fate, the two were about to become intertwined in history, their names forever linked.

1

"Dat you, Mr. Stanard?" the old black man queried, his back to the door.

"It's me, Judge," came the answer from the young man, as he surreptitiously slinked through the doorway. The young cadet only knew his host as Judge. Neither he nor any of his friends had ever heard the old black man's real name.

"I swear, Mr. Stanard, y'all are gonna get us both in trouble one 'a dese fine days," Judge commented, letting his breath out in a long, hard sigh. "I seen y'all sneakin' down the path and I said to myself, 'Dat dere's gotta be Mr. Stanard. I ain't seen 'im for coupla weeks, and ain't nobody crazy 'nuff to come down here dis hour 'a night 'cept Mr. Stanard.' Dat's what I said to myself, sho' 'nuff."

The young cadet smiled, his eyes twinkling. Jacqueline Beverly Stanard, known to his friends as Jack, was well known to the old black man. The 19-year-old Stanard had been here many times, and his list of demerits at the Institute was there for all to see as proof.

"Well, Judge," he said slowly, peeking cautiously around the corner of the window to be sure nobody had seen him enter, "I haven't seen y'all for some time now, and I know y'all must miss me. Besides, that there bread 'a yours is worth gettin' in trouble for."

"Not to me, it ain't," muttered Judge. "Y'all know ya ain't allowed to come down to da bakery. Gen'al Smith, he finds out, we both in trouble."

"You worry too much, Judge," said Stanard, laughing. "I'll just give Old Specs a loaf and he'll smile and thank me and tell me to be on my way," he said, using the nickname the cadets had bestowed on the Institute's superintendent behind his back, for his ever present spectacles.

"Jes' like dat," Judge mumbled to himself.

Judge busied himself by kneading a large ball of dough. He spread some flour on the table, wiping his hands on his more than ample belly. Judge did the baking for the cadets at the Virginia Military Institute, and, although he always protested, he could not resist slipping a loaf or two to the many cadets who made the late night visits. Stanard was one of his best "customers."

"What y'all doin' down here dis time 'a night, Mr. Stanard," Judge asked, already knowing the answer.

"I just came to liberate a few loaves of fresh bread from the fair Commonwealth of Virginia, Judge. Y'all don't mind that now, do you?" Stanard answered, saying just what Judge had known he was going to say. Stanard inhaled deeply, savoring the aroma emanating from the large brick oven.

"Y'all know I ain't allowed to do that, Mr. Stanard. Why do y'all keep comin' down here an' askin? I swear, one 'a dese days, Gen'al Smith's gonna run outta places to write down all your demerits an' he's gonna start givin' 'em ta me," Judge protested.

Stanard sat down beside the table, still smiling broadly. "I keep comin' down and askin' 'cause I know y'all will give me a loaf or two, that's why. Y'all know it, too. Oh, we both know how outta sorts y'all are gonna try to make me believe you are. And we both know y'all are gonna tell me how many demerits I have. By the way, I'm up to 114 right now, in the event y'all were keepin' a tally. Most of 'em 'cause 'a your bread, I might add. And we both know y'all will either swear at me or tell me the Good Book don't permit stealin', dependin' on your mood this evenin'. Then y'all will give in and take one of those fresh loaves over yonder there and hand it to me and tell me to git."

Judge looked up. "Not dis time, Mr. Stanard. Leastways, not that last part. Ain't gonna give y'all none tonight."

"Why not, Judge?" Stanard asked, playing the game. He knew it was just a matter of time until the baker gave up and ended the charade by handing him the loaf he wanted.

"Ain't right. Da Good Book say so, jes' like y'all said. And Gen'al Smith say so, too. He say y'all get five more demerits and extra guard duty. And if y'all got 114 y'all jes' can't affor' no more," answered Judge.

Stanard laughed softly. This was going exactly as he knew it would. Tonight Judge was in one of his pious moods; he was using his Good Book argument.

"That's why I'm repeatin' my fourth class year, Judge. Old Specs has so many demerits to give me he just can't squeeze 'em all in. Told me he needs an extra year, so I'm just tryin' to oblige. Y'all could do your part by givin' me a loaf or two, don't y'all agree?"

Judge chuckled to himself. He knew Stanard was right. He was going to give him the bread he wanted. Eventually. Judge wasn't going to make it easy, though. Stanard would have to work for it.

"No, sir. Ain't gonna do it. Done it before, but ain't gonna do it no more," Judge protested.

"Now, looka here, Judge," Stanard retorted. "If a bunch a' Yankees came in here right this very minute and asked for all your bread, every loaf now, mind you, y'all would give it to 'em, wouldn't you? Then why won't y'all give just one loaf to a good ole Southern boy like myself, one who's fightin' to keep the Yankees outta our bread."

Judge turned away from Stanard before the youth could see his involuntary grin. "Ain't no Yankees gonna come in here an' ask for no bread, Mr. Stanard. An' y'all ain't never fought the Yankees yet, not fer bread or nothin' else. I'll give y'all this much, though, y'all ain't never used that arg'ment before."

Stanard laughed. "I just thought that one up, Judge," he admitted. "But it could happen, yuh know. That's why the Yankees are down here in the first place. Came for some 'a your bread."

Judge shook his head slowly, still grinning. "Dey ain't never heard 'a Ole Judge's bread. Y'all are makin' dat up."

"Am not," said Stanard quickly, sensing a weakening in Judge's resolve. "Why, I hear tell that the smell 'a your bread gets clean to Washington when the breeze is jest right. Even President Lincoln wants a loaf, some folks say."

Judge could contain himself no longer. Letting out a laugh, he turned and looked at Stanard. "Y'all always know jes' what ta say, don't yuh?"

"I do my best, Judge," answered Stanard, standing and waiting patiently for the coveted fare.

The black baker picked up a fresh loaf in one of his large hands, still laughing.

"Here," he said, handing it to the youth. "Take it. And y'all be sure ta tell Gen'al Smith I only gave it to y'all ta keep da Yankees from gettin' it."

"Don't worry, Judge. Old Specs won't ever know I was here." Stanard strode to the door, peering cautiously through the window before exiting. "Thanks, Judge," he said. "I do appreciate it."

"I know y'all do," answered Judge. "Jest y'all be careful gettin' back to yer qua'ters, y'all hear?"

"I'll be fine," said Stanard, stepping outside. "And thanks again." He softly closed the door behind him, too soon to hear Judge chuckle.

The old man grinned as he watched the young cadet wend his way up the path to the barracks. "Pres'dent Lincoln," he muttered, shaking his head all the while. "Pres'dent Lincoln."

*   *   *

Stanard reached the barracks without incident. Tapping on the darkened window, he waited for an unseen hand to open the sash.

"How'd y'all do?" softly queried a disembodied voice. "Did he give it to you?"

"Got it, just like y'all knew I would," replied Stanard in a whisper. The hands reached out and relieved Stanard of the still warm loaf of bread as he hoisted himself through the window.

"I don't want any part of this," said another voice. "Y'all are gonna get extra guard duty and demerits for all of us."

The sound of a match being struck was soon accompanied by a soft glow near the center of the room. The match was touched to a candle and the room filled with a warm light.

"Get that under the table," Stanard said quickly, in a mild panic. "Y'all want Specs in here to share this bread?"

Stanard's roommates scrambled to get the candle beneath the large oak table, around which had been arranged a curtain of blankets to shield the candle's glow from the eyes of a passing sentry. Five hungry cadets maneuvered their ways under the table and closed the blankets.

"Still warm, jest the way I like it," said Archibald "Squirrel" Overton, the accomplice who had opened the window to readmit Stanard.

"Squirrel, you'd like it if it was a week old," said another of the roommates, Willis Harris. Harris was Overton's seventeen-year-old cousin.

Squirrel giggled as he tore a piece of bread from the loaf. "Prob'ly, Willis. Prob'ly."

Stanard tore a piece from the loaf and handed it to the cadet on his left, John Wise. The eighteen year old also grabbed a handful of the warm bread and passed it to his cousin Louis, the fifth cadet to share the room.

"Wait a minute," protested Louis, the eldest of the group, at age twenty. "I know I heard John say he didn't want no part of this. Now he's got his hands right in there with the rest of us."

John smiled, unable to reply with a mouthful of the warm bread.

"You shouldn't even be under here," Louis went on, making a show of trying to retrieve the bread from his cousin's hands. The two wrestled playfully as Louis tried to push John from beneath the table.

"Quiet!" cautioned Stanard sternly. "You knock that candle over and we'll have more trouble than a few demerits."

The two stopped shoving each other as Overton reached for another handful. "Ole Judge give y'all the usual arguments?" he asked.

"Of course," said Stanard, swallowing. "But it always ends up the same, don't it?"

"As long as he hands it out, who cares what he says?" said Willis. "He always gives me the same argument, too. I just let him go on, then take my bread and leave."

"He ain't a bad feller, Ole Judge," said Squirrel. The rest mumbled agreement.

"Been around here forever, I hear," Louis said between bites. "Reckon he bakes about as good a loaf of bread as you'll find in the Valley."

"No argument here," agreed Stanard. "Someone else can take a turn next time, though. I'm kinda loaded up with demerits right now."

"When did that ever start to bother you?" asked John. "Y'all even piled 'em up when you were gone."

The others laughed. John had referred to Jack's resignation from the Institute in mid-winter, a resignation that had lasted only eight days.

"I know," said Stanard. "Ole Specs was so used to givin' me demerits he never missed a beat while I was gone. I ain't even sure he knew I wasn't here. Just kept on writin' me up. I swear I had more demerits when I got back than I had when I left."

The rest laughed as loudly as they dared in the dimly lit space under the table.

"Y'all ever eat bread this good when you lived in the Governor's house, John?" Squirrel asked. Wise's father had served as Governor of Virginia from 1856 to 1860, after serving as an envoy to Brazil for several years. Wise had been born in Brazil, something he reminded the others about from time to time, telling them that none of the group had been born as far south as he had.

"Never," replied John. "Fact is, if we had known about Judge we'd have grabbed him away from Old Specs before he knew it, just so's he could make bread for us."

"Chinook says cadets have been sneakin' out and runnin' the blockade to get Judge's bread ever since the Institute was opened," offered Louis. Chinook was Louis's older brother Henry. Henry had graduated from the Institute a few years earlier, standing ninth in his class. He had joined the 46th Virginia after graduating but had been captured and paroled. He was awaiting his exchange by serving as an assistant professor of mathematics and Latin at his alma mater. The origin of his nickname was unknown.

"You mean Old Chinook did this, too?" asked Squirrel incredulously. Even though Henry was only twenty-two years old, his status as an instructor made him appear much older to the cadets.

"Must have," said Louis. "Judge told me once that Chinook was one of the best at gettin' down there and back without gettin' caught."

Willis laughed. "Old Chinook a bread thief," he said, almost to himself, thinking of Henry's nearly legendary puritanical habits. "Don't that just about beat all?"

"I don't think I'd mention it to him until you've learned how to calculate angles a little better, Willis," said Stanard, finishing off his handful of bread, then reaching for more.

Willis looked at Stanard. "Was that Jack I just heard tellin' me I can't figure out angles? The same Jack who already failed mathematics, geography, and French? As I recall, Private Stanard, just this mornin' you was makin' the fool of yerself in front of the whole class when Chinook asked y'all how to estimate artillery ranges. Wasn't there an angle or two involved in that little debate?"

The others laughed, recalling Jack's dilemma.

"He just caught me by surprise, is all," Stanard said sheepishly. "I coulda figured it out if he gave me a little more time. And I never failed French, either, by the way."

"A little more time?" laughed Squirrel, ignoring Stanard's clarification regarding his French class. "We'll all be gray beards 'fore y'all ever figure out how to aim a 12-pounder. That's why Chinook said y'all better consider the infantry as your callin' when he told y'all to sit down."

"Well, I don't reckon I'm gonna have to be much of a student when I get to fightin' the Yankees, anyway," said Stanard. "As long as I can shoot straight I ain't gonna have to know one single thing about angles."

The others drew quiet for a few moments. Then Louis spoke.

"Y'all reckon we'll ever get to fight 'em?" he asked. "I mean, we've had a lot of close calls but none of us ever got a chance to even see a Yank. I'm just gettin' a little tired 'a gettin called out and then havin' to come back to the barracks without seein' the elephant."

The others nodded agreement.

"I don't think I've ever felt as bad as I did when General Rosser came here and gave us that flag," said Willis. "I guess he thought he was doin' the right thing and all, and it was nice of 'im. But it sure made me feel bad."

Harris had brought up a subject that had struck a nerve with every cadet at the Institute. General Thomas Lafayette Rosser's Brigade had wintered only a few miles from Lexington, and before departing for the spring campaign Rosser had come to the Institute and presented a captured flag to the corps of cadets. It had been accepted politely, but many had misinterpreted the general's gesture as one of mocking the corps for its lack of experience.

"I don't want other regiments goin' out and capturin' our flags for us," agreed John. "Jest give us a chance, we'll capture some of our own."

"Ever wonder what it's like, fightin' the Yankees?" Willis asked of no one in particular.

"It's just about the best feelin' ever, I'd guess," said Stanard.

"John Early told me there ain't nothin' like it," said Louis. Early, a nephew of Confederate General Jubal A. Early and a classmate of the five, had already seen his share of fighting. He had started his military career at the age of only 13, carrying provisions and supplies to those who were doing the actual fighting. He had been at First Manassas and often regaled the cadets with tales of the fighting, even though he didn't actually arrive on the field until the battle was over. He had served as a courier at

Gettysburg, though, and his experiences there served him well as a story teller. The battle got more fierce with every telling, as if it needed any embellishment. The younger Early played a more important part each time the story of the three day battle was related, also, and the cadets always listened enviously. With youthful exaggeration, Early always related how he had come close to death several times, but that he had performed his courier duties unflinchingly. His stories never failed to attract an eager audience. The fact that much of what he said was made up did not diminish the attraction.

"He is the lucky one, isn't he?" said Stanard with a trace of envy in his voice.

"I'd give anything to have been with John and General Lee up at Gettysburg," said Louis softly. "I'd have done my part, I'll tell you. If General Pickett had asked me to charge them Yankees I woulda done it without a word. The bluebellies woulda had to kill me to stop me."

"They prob'ly woulda, too, Louis," said Willis.

"I don't care," Louis said defensively. "I woulda been proud to die like that. Ain't no better way to die than while yer tryin' to kill a Yankee."

"I ain't so sure, Louis," said Stanard. "I mean, I don't mind dyin' if that's what it's gonna take to push the Yankees back up north, but I ain't real keen on it."

Louis brushed bread crumbs from his chest before replying. "Not me, Jack," he finally said with youthful bravado. "I'll die tonight if I have to, as long as I do it fightin'. I'm just tired of sittin' here and hearin' about everyone else havin' all the fun."

"Y'all wouldn't get none of this good bread if y'all was out in the field, Louis," joked Stanard, trying to restore the earlier lighthearted mood.

Louis frowned, saying nothing. The need for becoming a real soldier, one who actually carried a gun and fought, weighed heavily on him.

"More for us, then," remarked Squirrel matter of factly.

"Yeah," agreed Willis. "Why didn't y'all bring two loaves, anyway?"

Stanard punched Willis in the shoulder playfully. "Ole Judge wasn't in a real givin' mood tonight, or I woulda. Soon as he started tellin' me what the Good Book says I was afraid I was gonna get a preachin' to."

"Judge can preach to me all he wants," said John. "Long's he comes through with some bread when he's done, that is. Little preachin' don't hurt nobody."

"Guess not," agreed Stanard. "I just didn't want to be gone too long. I was pretty hungry. I figured if Ole Judge got to preachin' I might be there all night. Mighta started eatin' the bread right there."

"Good thing for y'all that you didn't, then," said Squirrel. "We mighta had to come down there after you. What do y'all think, Louis?" He poked Louis in the ribs with his elbow.

Louis, still brooding about his lack of battle experience, said nothing.

The other cadets looked at one another. It was not like their friend to be so sullen.

"What's troublin' y'all?" asked Stanard, genuinely puzzled.

Louis maneuvered his position in preparation to exit from beneath the table. Pushing the blanket back, he gazed at his friends with a determined look before answering.

"Y'all can spend the war sittin' under a table eatin' bread, if that's what y'all want to do," he finally said. "But I'm gonna fight somewhere. They gotta let us fight. This war's gonna be over and we're all still gonna be sittin' here trying to figure out artillery angles and learnin' how Napoleon lost at Waterloo. How are y'all gonna be able to go home and face your folks? What are y'all gonna say when people ask y'all what you did to help win the war? Just answer me that! What are y'all gonna tell them?"

"Reckon I'll tell everyone I stole bread," Stanard answered obligingly, a wide grin spreading across his countenance.

The others laughed. All except Louis, that is.

"Y'all can laugh all you want," he said with fire in his eyes. "I'm gonna get some sleep." He crawled from under the table and slammed the blanket shut angrily.

"Dream about the war, Louis," said Squirrel. "Dream all you want, 'cause dreamin's as close as any of us is ever gonna get to fightin' the Yankees."

2

"Telegram from General Grant, sir," the young aide called out.

"Good," responded General Franz Sigel in his thick, guttural accent. "Perhaps this will be our orders for the spring campaign."

The relative inactivity of the winter months always brought boredom to Sigel. Although not spoiling for a fight, he was still anxious for the maneuvering to resume in the spring. After all, he was a soldier. He recognized the need for the administrative work, and he also saw the necessity for the winter lull in the fighting. But, just as the warming temperatures of March caused the sap to flow in the huge maple trees outside his window, it also seemed to get his own juices circulating more rapidly. Others in the Union army may be better organizers or tacticians, but few matched Sigel's desire and pride.

Rising from his chair in the cramped office, he snatched the telegram from the aide and quickly tore it open. Anxiously, he perused its message. Sigel was disappointed when he realized that the telegram did not contain any hint of what he would be doing militarily in the coming months. Instead, the message informed him that General Ord, an old nemesis, would be coming to visit him. Sigel, trying to be optimistic, hoped that the message represented the next best thing to the actual spring campaign plans. Perhaps General Ord would be bringing the plans with him.

Sigel walked slowly to the window, absentmindedly tapping the telegram against his open palm. He contemplated the possibilities as he walked. Small in stature, his blue eyes squinted as he neared the window. The sun beamed brightly into the room, flooding the office with its light. It offered no warmth yet, but in a few weeks that would change.

9

He gazed out into the encampment, mentally speculating on what Grant's spring campaign might entail. Outside, several soldiers gingerly stepped over huge puddles which had formed in the muddy lane where the snow had melted.

Perhaps there would be a push toward Richmond in the weeks ahead. Maybe the coming months would see an end to the war. There had already been some near misses. Some would call them lost opportunities. Whatever was to come, Sigel hoped that he could be a part of it. Unfortunately, his participation was not a certainty.

On a personal note, Sigel knew he had not shown much promise so far. He had shown a propensity for favoritism to any officer of German descent, a habit that had not endeared him to many of his non-German officers. He had also heard rumors that Grant even considered him inept. Certainly, he was not proud of some of his performances. Wilson's Creek, for instance. Some said he was beyond inept at that fight. Negligent . . . that was the description he heard most often. Even though it had been more than two years since he had contributed greatly to the Union's defeat there, it was still brought up from time to time when a rival general wanted to get him angry.

In his own mind he had actually become a martyr as a result of Wilson's Creek, and he hoped that the idle winter months had dulled Grant's memory. Maybe he would get a fresh start with the new campaign. Arguably the most popular German in the United States, at least he still had the support of his countrymen under his command, if not the support of the people above him.

Sigel watched the melting snow form small rivulets on the window, flowing down the glass to a point below his vision where they joined to form larger streams that reappeared near his door. The resulting mud was something Sigel hoped he wouldn't have to contend with in whatever assignment Grant had for him. Sigel likened the mud to the political battles he had been forced to fight to gain his command. Both the mud and the battles were inconveniences to contend with, obstacles to be overcome.

He had been in command only a few weeks. Perhaps Grant viewed this as Sigel's last opportunity. The infighting that had been necessary for Sigel to gain this command was still fresh in his mind as he now contemplated the coming meeting with General Ord. His angular jaw set firmly, he realized that he was getting angry already, without even hearing Grant's proposal.

He would give Grant a chance. All he asked was the same in return. Given the opportunity, Sigel knew he could redeem himself for Wilson's Creek. He would make Grant glad that Sigel was in charge of this department. "Just tell me what you want, General," he thought. "You'll have no problems in the Department of West Virginia."

*   *   *

"General Sigel, how have you been?" the voice boomed as Major General E. O. C. Ord strode smartly through the door. He threw off his coat and placed a long tube on the floor beside a chair.

"Fine, thank you, General," said Sigel, saluting smartly, trying not to stare at the tube. He strode confidently toward the door to welcome his guest. He didn't want to give off any signals that he was intimidated by Ord's presence, or apologetic for his own less than inspirational war record. Ord and Sigel had never been close friends, and had quarreled more than once. Now, Sigel would have to be cordial, at least until he learned the purpose of the visit.

"Are you pretty well settled into your new duties, General Sigel?" Ord asked, making small talk before getting to the real reason he had come.

"Yes, sir," said Sigel, in his thick German accent. "There's much to do, but I think everything is going along reasonably well."

"That's good, that's good," said Ord, drawing a deep breath as his eyes scanned the office. "I know your men have been inactive for some time, but I have confidence that you are just the one who can bring them back into fighting shape."

Sigel contemplated the significance of Ord's words before answering. Was he really expressing confidence, or was this his way of getting Sigel to drop his guard? Sigel mentally berated himself for his paranoia.

"Well, sir," Sigel began, "as you know, my people are pretty well spread out. Protecting the B&O, you know." The Baltimore and Ohio Railroad was the shortest line of communication between Washington and Cincinnati, and its protection was essential. To Sigel had fallen that responsibility.

"I understand," said Ord, nodding in agreement. He chose to say no more, waiting to hear what Sigel was leading up to.

Sigel obliged. "It isn't easy getting the men together to drill, what with them all spread along the railroad," he said in broken English. "But I do what I can under the circumstances."

"I'm sure you do, General," replied Ord.

The visitor stood, stretching as he did. Sigel watched as Ord tried vainly to loosen muscles which had became taut from the long ride.

"You have any coffee, General?" Ord asked as he sat down again.

"Yes, sir," answered Sigel. "I'll have my aide bring some in."

Sigel went to the door and signaled an unseen aide.

Within minutes the aide entered with two cups of the steaming brew. "It may not be very good," said Sigel to his guest, "but I guarantee that it's hot and strong."

"This will be fine," Ord replied as he took a sip. Sigel was right, he noted. It was strong. And not very good.

Sigel took a drink from his cup, then set the coffee on the table beside him. He had never acquired a taste for coffee, not even good coffee, for which this would never be mistaken.

"I'll get to the point, General," said Ord. "I've brought plans for the spring campaign from General Grant. I'd like to share them with you. You'll be an important part."

"I was hoping you'd say that, General," Sigel said. Finally, the real discussion could begin. This small talk was not what he wanted to hear.

Ord retrieved the tube which he had placed on the floor, retrieving a rolled piece of paper from inside. As Ord unrolled the paper, Sigel recognized it immediately as a map of the Valley. Ord motioned to Sigel to move closer to the map as he spread it out onto a small table.

"General Sherman is going to break up Johnston's army, if possible, and General Grant is going to be moving against General Lee. He will need support in the Valley," Ord said, as he tried unsuccessfully to flatten the paper to keep it from rolling up. Finally, in exasperation, he placed a book on either side to hold the map in position.

"What kind of support?" Sigel queried.

Ord pointed to the map. "General Grant wants an army of no less than 8,000 infantry, three batteries of artillery, and 1,500 picked cavalry to move southward," Ord began. Sigel listened attentively. This could be bigger than he had thought.

"He wants a two-pronged expedition made through the Valley. I am going to take one column and move toward Covington, Virginia. As I go I will try to destroy as much of the Virginia and Tennessee Railroad as I can. The ultimate destination will be the supply depots at Lynchburg." Ord traced his route on the map. Sigel's eyes followed Ord's finger.

Ord continued, pointing out another route. "General Crook will take a second column and move on the railroad south of Charleston. Once he has destroyed as much of the railroad as he thinks practical, he is going to move on the saltworks at Saltville. When he's done there, his next target will be the lead mines at Wytheville. If he can get even one full day without resistance, we think he can put both those places out of the war for good."

Sigel contemplated what he was hearing. His name had been conspicuously missing from the plans thus far. "And me?" he asked, trying not to sound tentative.

Sigel had not been far wrong in his assessment of Grant's opinion of him. Grant did have reservations about Sigel's abilities, large reservations, and he had expressed them to his staff in their discussions of how much he actually wanted Sigel involved in the coming campaign. After much thought, he had finally arrived at something he thought Sigel could handle. Sigel would lead a third column.

"Staunton, General," said Ord, looking at Sigel to see how he took the assignment. "You are to take some troops and go to Staunton to meet

General Crook and me. You'll bring us fresh supplies. Along the way you are to destroy communications lines and stores. You'll also be providing protection from an invasion down the Valley."

Sigel nodded. It wasn't as much responsibility as he had hoped for, but at least he was gong to be a part of the campaign. If he performed well, there may be additional responsibilities later.

"This expedition as a whole will also serve another purpose," Ord was saying, bringing Sigel back from his thoughts. "It's going to divert some of Lee's troops away from the main thrust, and it will keep him from being reinforced through the gaps in the mountains. If we can keep the enemy in our front and away from General Grant's, he'll be happy. And I think you'll agree that it is best to keep General Grant happy."

"He can depend on me, General," replied Sigel. "Tell the General I'll do my part."

"Thank you, General Sigel," Ord responded. "That's what I was hoping to hear you say."

"We must travel as light as possible," Ord continued. "We'll live off the country, but General Grant emphasizes that he'll tolerate no indiscriminate marauding. Do you understand?"

"Yes, sir," Sigel replied assertively.

"You should take only what is necessary for the troops, unless you can capture supplies from an armed enemy. Receipts must be given for anything liberated from private citizens, so the owners can be paid."

"You can count on us, General," said Sigel, not knowing what else to say.

"I'm sure I can," Ord said absently, already thinking of what he wanted to say next.

"We will probably get some resistance," he went on. "The Confederates have a new man in the Valley, too, you know. I guess you could say he's your counterpart. He's going to want to impress his superiors, just as I'm sure you'll want to impress everyone at headquarters."

Sigel winced inwardly. Ord was more perceptive than he had realized. Ignoring the obvious challenge, he asked, "Who's their new man, General?"

"John Breckinridge," came the reply. "The old vice president."

Sigel smiled. "A politician," he said softly.

"Don't underestimate him, General Sigel," Ord cautioned. "We're getting reports that he is already drilling his men twice a day. He's been giving his officers training classes and cracking down on deserters, too. Sounds like he means business."

"I won't underestimate him, General," responded Sigel. "But I'm not sure how effective a politician's going to be as a fighter. He never got his hands bloody in Mexico, you know."

"I know," agreed Ord. "But he's got Echols, Imboden, and McCausland under him, don't forget, and they're all good men."

"We'll see," said Sigel. "We'll see."

The two generals continued their discussion on the campaign for another hour. Both cups of coffee grew cold. Sigel didn't mind.

As the discussion drew to a close, Ord rose to leave. There was much to do in the coming days, and he wished to be on his way so he could start.

In closing, Ord extended his hand and said, "I don't think I have to tell you how important the coming months will be, General. This won't be an easy time."

Sigel accepted Ord's handshake, although he would have preferred not to. "I know that, General Ord," he said, trying to sound cordial. "But I promise you this. By the end of the summer, the Valley will be ours."

*   *   *

Sigel began brooding over the campaign plans almost as soon as the door closed behind Ord. He had hoped to be playing a more visible role. Escorting a wagon train was not what he had expected to be doing when he was given his recent command, but he would have to be satisfied with what he had been assigned to accomplish. For now, anyway.

His bigger problem was the inclusion of General Ord in the campaign in the first place. Sigel did not care for Ord, and the German suspected correctly that the feeling was mutual. But Sigel was aware of Ord's friendship with General Grant, and he knew enough not to protest to Grant about Ord's proposed involvement. If Grant didn't like Sigel very much to begin with, such a protest would be enough to ruin any chance Sigel may have to work his way into the general in chief's good graces.

Sigel resolved to do what was necessary to accommodate Ord, but little else. In fact, Sigel would not mind coming up with an alternate plan which would eliminate Ord from the picture without offending Grant.

A confrontation with Ord was not long in coming. Within a few days he was complaining to all who would listen that Sigel was not giving him enough men, even though General Grant himself had directed Sigel to do so.

Sigel was in no mood to argue with his old nemesis. The more he considered his assignment in the coming campaign, the more he seethed. All the plum assignments were going to others, as if Sigel himself did not even exist. Sigel's mood grew darker by the day. The fact that Ord didn't like something Sigel was doing was the only thing that made the German smile. Ord's complaints fell on deaf ears. He would have to work with the men Sigel assigned him.

The situation with Ord reached its pinnacle when he told Sigel in a less than tactful way that Sigel would have to meet him with fresh supplies at some point. Sigel adamantly said he would not. The argument grew in intensity, as each man insisted that his wishes be carried out. Sigel won the argument, and Ord immediately wired Grant and asked to be relieved of his command. After much discussion, Grant gave in and accommodated Ord's request.

This sudden change called for a modification to the original plans. Grant dispatched Lieutenant Colonel Orville E. Babcock to meet with Sigel.

"What do you suggest, General Sigel?" Babcock queried as the two tried to devise a workable plan.

Sigel scratched his chin, appearing to be deep in thought. He already had a plan in mind, but he wanted Babcock to think that what he was about to say was spontaneous. As one would expect, Sigel's new plan would bring him more visibility.

"See what you think of this," he finally said. "Why don't we form two columns instead of three? General Crook can take 10,000 men and follow through what was originally proposed. The only thing I would add to that would be to assign Averell to Crook, with about 1,000 cavalry. He knows the area and I think he can be a big help to Crook."

Brevet Major General William Averell was indeed a capable leader. Babcock knew him well. He nodded in understanding.

"Go on, General," said Babcock, intrigued and unaware that Sigel's plan had been thought out days earlier. He listened closely, trying to ignore Sigel's deep accent while concentrating on the plan.

"We could let Averell take command of Crook's cavalry, too," Sigel was saying. "That would let Crook concentrate on his infantry and Averell could run the cavalry. Crook could start by destroying the New River Bridge on the Virginia and Tennessee. From there, he can destroy the whole railroad in the direction of Lynchburg. While he's doing that, Averell can go on to Saltville and harass the mine. When he's finished, he can start tearing up the railroad from Saltville back to the bridge. That way, by splitting up, Crook's column can get more done in less time. When they're finished, there won't be a Virginia and Tennessee Railroad!"

Babcock contemplated the plan. It seemed to have merit. Then he remembered the second part of Sigel's plan. "You mentioned a second column, General. Who would lead it and what would it do?" he asked.

Sigel had already decided that his best avenue to regaining his respectability was to win a decisive victory somewhere. Guarding a wagon train full of supplies would hardly provide that opportunity. But an engagement with somebody, perhaps even Breckinridge himself, might. Fighting and winning a battle had therefore become the driving force in the formulation of his plan. Of course, he couldn't tell Babcock that directly, but if he could make it sound as if he just wanted to do something to help the campaign achieve success, it would probably convince Babcock.

"I will lead it!" Sigel enthusiastically replied. "I will go to Staunton and harass the Virginia Central Railroad before Crook and Averell move out. There are many loyalists in Staunton. I will try to enlist their assistance. The enemy will have to engage me somewhere. If he should advance against us, I will resist him at some convenient place. And while he's engaging me, Averell and Crook will be free to destroy the Virginia and Tennessee! This will deprive General Lee of a main source of supply."

Babcock frowned. A confrontation would most likely be between Sigel and Breckinridge . . . what would be the outcome? Babcock shared Grant's less than enthusiastic opinion of Sigel. Could the German defeat Breckinridge?

Sigel, chagrined by Babcock's hesitancy, stood quickly, knocking his chair over. "You don't think my plan will work?" he blustered.

"It's not that, General," countered Babcock. "I'm just weighing everything in my mind. As a matter of fact, I think it could be a good plan. Just give me a minute or two to think it over."

Sigel picked up the fallen chair. The plan was a good one. It would give the Union what it wanted. And it would give Sigel what he wanted. Why would Babcock have to think about it?

"I like it!" Babcock finally said, to Sigel's relief. "And I think General Grant will approve it, as well. I'll try to clear it with him. Why don't you proceed accordingly, unless you should hear otherwise from General Grant?"

"Danke," said Sigel, lapsing into his native tongue.

"You're welcome," responded Babcock. "Just make it work, or both of us will have some very difficult explaining to do."

"It will work," insisted Sigel. "You must convince General Grant that it is a good plan."

"I'll try," said Babcock. "You should proceed as if you have his approval. You will be notified as soon as he makes his decision, but I don't believe he will change anything from what you are suggesting."

Sigel smiled. The groundwork for his return from mediocrity had been laid. Now he knew it would be up to him to follow through.

*   *   *

For several days Sigel drilled his troops as if the battle may come tomorrow. He ordered his aide-de-camp, Colonel David Strother, to have all their desks and papers sent to the rear. Nothing must interfere with the movement of the troops when the orders came, as he was sure they would.

True to his word, Babcock had been able to convince Grant of the merits of Sigel's plan. The general had needed little convincing. Rebel deserters had reported massive troop build-ups on the part of the Confederacy. Rumor after rumor came to Grant's attention. At one point, even James Longstreet, Lee's top general, was said to be on his way to the Valley.

**Major General Franz Sigel, commander of
the Union forces at New Market**
Courtesy of Hall of Valor Civil War Museum

Grant approved Sigel's plan, ordering him to start the expedition by May 2, and telling him that cutting the New River Bridge and destroying the railroad would be the most important thing the expedition could accomplish.

Sigel's army numbered nearly 9,000 men and 28 guns. The men had been drilled. They had been prepared. There was no reason to doubt their effectiveness. By the end of April, all was in readiness. It was time.

Finally, Sigel gave the order. "Turn over your tents and be very ready to march," he told his officers. The campaign was under way.

3

"Don't move a muscle, you stinkin' Reb, or you're a dead man!"

The voice was accompanied by an arm around the throat of the intended victim.

"Come on, John," the victim said, struggling against his unseen assailant. "Why do you always have to be doing things like that?" Virginia Military Institute cadet Moses Ezekiel had just returned from his last class and had entered his room, only to be jumped on by his roommate. This was an act which was beginning to become a routine occurrence. Despite its precision-like regularity, however, Ezekiel never failed to be surprised when it happened, for some reason. This was a fact that was not lost on his attacker, John Cabell Early, a nephew of the famed Confederate General Jubal Early.

Early relaxed his hold on his roommate, laughing at his friend's obvious consternation. Ezekiel tossed his book onto the large table in an angry gesture and straightened his jacket. Seeing that Ezekiel was angry made the prank all the more enjoyable.

"I thought you were sick," exclaimed Ezekiel. "Sick people should be conserving their energy instead of jumping on people!"

Early had only recently returned from a furlough necessitated by illness.

"I'm feelin' a lot better now, Moses. Especially with all this here exercise I'm gettin' jumpin out from behind doors. Besides, y'all should be glad I do that to you now and again," said Early. "Keeps y'all on your toes."

"I don't need you to be jumpin' on me from behind doors to keep me on my toes," protested Ezekiel.

"But you do, don't you see?" said Early. "If I had been some ole Yank hidin' behind that there door y'all would be dead right now. I'm just doin' my duty as a good roommate. Someday y'all are gonna thank me."

"We don't see all that many Yanks inside the rooms here at the Institute," said Ezekiel, his anger slowly beginning to subside.

"That's probably 'cause they know I'd be here to jump on 'em if they showed up," replied Early.

"Yeah," responded Ezekiel. "I'm sure the Yanks talk about you all the time around their campfires at night."

"Wouldn't surprise me none," said Early. "I can hear 'em right now, warnin' each other about me in one of those squeaky New England voices."

Ezekiel shook his head in mock amazement.

Early took on his version of a New England Yankee, effecting a nasal tone and speaking as properly as he thought a New Englander might. "Be careful, my friends," he mocked. "If you should happen to visit that esteemed military school in Virginia, the Virginia Military Institute. As you all know, John Cabell Early, that well-known hero of Gettysburg who gave all us Yankees so much trouble in Pennsylvania, is a student there."

Ezekiel snorted. "Yeah. And he might jump on you from behind one of their doors!"

To himself he thought, "Well-known hero of Gettysburg, indeed!"

"The element of surprise, Moses. The element of surprise. Never underestimate it. Don't you pay attention in tactics class?" said Early.

"I do pay attention in class, and I don't underestimate the element of surprise, my Gettysburg hero friend," said Ezekiel. "I just don't want you to do anything that might injure my hands."

"Oh, your hands," laughed Early. "I had almost forgotten about your hands."

"These are the hands of an artiste," countered Ezekiel, holding his hands in front of his face and pretending to gaze on them admiringly. "Someday, when I'm a famous artist maybe I'll paint your portrait."

"I can barely wait," said Early sarcastically.

The two cadets were more than simply roommates. In their time at the Institute they had become close friends, and with a third roommate, Thomas Garland Jefferson, they had become a nearly inseparable group. The banter had become part of their daily ritual, and both enjoyed it more than either cared to admit.

Early sat down at the blacking stool and began to polish his boots. The spring thaw and accompanying rains had made it nearly impossible to go anywhere without getting muddy. The cadets, however, were not exempted from keeping their boots cleaned and polished, no matter how adverse the conditions became.

Ezekiel sat at the table and began sketching on a small white pad. While he enjoyed life at the Institute and looked forward to being a soldier, art was his first love. The two went about their respective tasks for several minutes, neither saying anything to the other.

The sudden opening of the door caught their attention, and both involuntarily looked up to see their friend and roommate Thomas Garland Jefferson enter. Wordlessly, he walked to the wardrobe and placed his coat and hat inside. When he turned around he saw Ezekiel for the first time, a surprised look crossing his face.

"What are you doing here so early in the afternoon?" he queried.

"I'm allowed to be here," replied Ezekiel. "This is my room, too, remember?"

"I know that," spat Jefferson. "But I'll bet I missed it again, just 'cause you came back too soon."

Ezekiel looked puzzled. "Missed what?" he asked sincerely.

"You gettin' jumped on, is what," answered Jefferson. He turned to Early. "You get 'im?"

"Of course I got 'im," answered Early proudly. "It's my job."

"He got me," admitted Ezekiel. "Like to choked me to death, too." Ezekiel playfully punched Early in the arm.

Jefferson plopped into the chair beside Ezekiel. "I always miss the fun," he said dejectedly.

"Well, I gotta jump on 'im when I get the chance," explained Early. "I can't wait for the likes of y'all to get here before I do it."

"I would have been here sooner, but . . . ," Jefferson said with a twinkle in his eye.

"But what?" Early asked. The smug look affixed to Jefferson's face indicated that he knew something the others didn't.

"But I had to stop at Old Specs's office to drop off some papers for Chinook," Jefferson said, his self satisfied smile growing larger.

"Y'all see Stanard there again?" asked Ezekiel, not looking up from his sketch while referring to Stanard's regular, albeit involuntary, visits to the superintendent's inner sanctum. Some cadets joked that Stanard had a standing appointment. Stanard did nothing to discourage that image.

"Not this time," said Jefferson. "But I did get to hear some interesting pieces of conversation between Old Specs and Captain Preston. Seems like the Yankees are up to something, and there's a good chance they might be comin' our way."

"You expect us to believe that Old Specs and Captain Preston told you somethin' like that?" Early asked incredulously.

"They didn't really tell me that," answered Jefferson. "Actually, they didn't even know I was there. Y'all know how Old Specs's office is shaped so strange?"

"It's called a hexagon, Thomas," said Ezekiel, with a chuckle.

"Whatever it's called," responded Jefferson. "It's still shaped funny for an office. And the way Old Specs and the captain were sittin', they couldn't see me standin' there, what with all those corners and all. When I got there the door was open and I was just about to knock before I took Chinook's papers in when I heard Specs sayin' somethin' about Imboden. I thought he was about to say somethin' about Jacob, so I stopped to listen."

Jacob Imboden was a fellow cadet and the younger brother of the Confederate General John Imboden.

"I would have done the same thing," agreed Early. "I would have thought Jacob was in trouble, and I would have wanted to be the first to spread the word."

"That figures," hissed Ezekiel. He shot a disapproving look at Early and went on. "Jacob's one of the nicest boys we have here at the Institute. Why would you want to spread the word if he was in trouble?"

"I don't know," mumbled Early. "Probably 'cause nobody would believe it, I guess. Now if I heard somethin' about Jack I wouldn't tell anyone, 'cause they'd probably all know already." Stanard's reputation was legendary among his fellow cadets.

"Anyway, do you want to hear what I heard them sayin' about the Yankees or don't you?" Jefferson interrupted.

"Sorry," Early apologized. "Go ahead."

"As I was sayin', I heard Imboden's name. Somethin' told me to wait. Then I heard Captain Preston sayin' somethin' about Imboden talkin' to General Lee, and I don't reckon Jacob does a whole lot of that."

Early and Ezekiel were now listening attentively. General Lee's name had a way of getting people to listen, especially young cadets.

Jefferson appeared pleased that he now had the undivided attention of his two friends. "General Imboden apparently told General Lee that he was expectin' a big raid here in the Valley within the next month."

"The next month?" Ezekiel quickly reacted.

Jefferson stood up before responding. "That's what I heard them sayin'. Said somethin' about some Yankee general named Averell comin' to attack Staunton and Lexington. That ought to put us right about in the middle of it, wouldn't y'all think?" Jefferson strode to the window and peered out, as if expecting to see a line of blue coats riding across the parade ground.

"Certainly would," agreed Ezekiel. "Maybe now we'll finally get a chance to be a part of the war. You hear anything else?"

"A lot more," said Jefferson. "Old Specs told the captain that he heard that General Meade has already sent all his invalids and sutlers back to Washington. He wouldn't do that if he didn't have somethin' planned, right? Captain Preston said his guess was that the Yanks would be makin' some kind of a move as soon as the roads are a little more passable."

Ezekiel and Early looked at each other. This was big news.

"Anything else?" queried Ezekiel.

"Ain't that enough?" Jefferson responded.

"Yeah, it is," answered Ezekiel. "I just wasn't sure if you were done, is all."

The three friends drew silent, each absorbed in his own thoughts.

Then, Early broke the silence. "Y'know, I think I have to agree with Jack Stanard about one thing."

"What's that, John?" asked Ezekiel.

Early looked at his friends, then picked a thread from his sleeve before continuing. "Well," he said, "Jack says all the time that he thinks it's a disgrace for boys our age not to be in the real army. He says we should be out there doin' our part fightin' the Yankees, and I happen to agree with him."

Jefferson looked solemn. "I think most of us feel that way, John," he said softly. Jefferson had sent numerous letters home, as had many of the cadets, first asking, then imploring, that permission be granted to allow him to drop out of the Institute and join one of the regular regiments.

Each of Jefferson's requests, and indeed most of his classmates' requests, had met with the same answer: a resounding and emphatic "NO!"

Most of the cadets had interpreted their parents' refusal differently from its real intent. The cadets believed that their parents probably meant "maybe" rather than "no," and a refusal to allow the cadet to quit school was usually followed immediately by another request, this one worded in an even more beseeching tone. With only a few exceptions, the answers came back identical to the ones which the cadets had ignored. Slowly but surely, the cadets learned that they would have to do more than beg for permission if they were to join the war effort.

"You havin' any luck convincin' your parents that you should be fightin' instead of studyin'?" Jefferson asked Early.

Early looked at his friend, then back at the boots he was polishing. "Not yet," he answered. "But I'm not done tryin', though."

"You have any good ideas about how to do it?" Jefferson asked.

"I thought I did," said Early. "But nothing has worked so far, and I'm about out of ideas, even bad ones."

"I was thinkin' of maybe gettin' myself a bunch of demerits so Old Specs would have to kick me out," said Jefferson. "If I wasn't here at the Institute any more then my folks would have to let me join up."

"You really think that would work?" asked Early enthusiastically.

"Who knows if it would or wouldn't?" replied Jefferson. "I'd say it's sure worth a try though, don't you think?"

"Listen to yourselves," interrupted Ezekiel. "Do y'all realize how stupid y'all sound?"

"What do you mean?" asked Jefferson innocently.

"What do I mean?" repeated Ezekiel. "What do I mean? Look, how many demerits do you think you have right now?"

"I don't know," mumbled Jefferson. "Not very many, I guess. But I could get them! If it gets me to the fightin' I don't mind bein' in trouble with Old Specs."

"How many do yuh think y'all would have to get before Old Specs had enough and asked y'all to leave?" Ezekiel persisted. "Just a wild guess. Y'all don't have to be accurate."

"I don't know," answered Jefferson, still not sure where Ezekiel was leading him. "Forty or fifty probably."

Ezekiel laughed and shook his head. "Forty or fifty!" he said derisively.

"Yeah. Maybe a few more," said Jefferson. "Why?"

"Well, just for the sake of argument," said Ezekiel, "who do y'all know who has more demerits than anybody else in the Institute? Maybe in the whole history of the Insitute?"

Jefferson and Early looked at one another and answered simultaneously, "Jack Stanard!"

"Exactly," agreed Ezekiel. "And do either of y'all have any idea how many demerits he has right now?"

"Probably over a hundred would be my guess," answered Early.

"And isn't a hundred more than fifty?" Ezekiel asked, his voice dripping with sarcasm.

"Yeah," said Jefferson. "What's your point?"

"Figure it out, Mr. Gettysburg," said Ezekiel. Y'all say yuh think fifty demerits will get Old Specs to ask y'all to leave. Jack has more than a hundred right now and he's still here. Doesn't that tell y'all somethin'?"

"Well, maybe I will need more than fifty, then," rebutted Jefferson. "I can get them."

"If Jack can't get enough demerits to get thrown out, there isn't any possible way either one of you will," Ezekiel said, tossing his sketching pencil aside. "The war will be over before that happens."

Jefferson looked at Early.

"He may be right, Thomas," Early said, with more than a hint of dejection in his voice.

"I am right," insisted Ezekiel. "And both of y'all know it!"

Early and Jefferson sat quietly for several minutes. Ezekiel, seeing that his two companions appeared to be ending the conversation, picked up his pencil and resumed sketching.

Finally, Early broke the silence.

"Well," he said, "there has to be some way we can go and fight. We'll just have to find it. And I'm not going to give up until I do!"

4

The old man removed his sweat-stained hat and placed it on a peg pounded into the wall. Slightly stooped with age, he slowly walked across the room and gingerly dropped onto the bench beside the table. His wife looked up from her work, smiled, and wordlessly returned to her task of kneading dough.

"The wheat's beginnin' to look a little better, finally," the man said.

"That's good," answered his wife. "It has been such a bad spring I was afraid we wouldn't even have a crop this year."

The spring of 1864 had not been a good one for farmers in the Valley. Scarcely six weeks earlier a freak, late winter storm had blown in and dumped nearly a foot of snow on the fields. The temperatures then plummeted, struggling to edge much above 0°, even in the warmest part of the day. Then, the rains had come, the resulting mud making it impossible for fields to be prepared for the spring planting, even with the best of horses.

Farmers throughout the area commiserated with one another, but could do little else. Crops eventually got planted, though, and those planted earlier were finally beginning to show signs of growth. Those which hadn't either frozen out or been washed away by the heavy spring rains, that is.

"We're still gonna have a crop," the farmer said. "Probably not as good as last year's, but we're still gonna have a crop."

The farmer and his wife were Jacob and Sarah Bushong. Their farm, situated just outside New Market, between the Valley Turnpike and the North Branch of the Shenandoah River, had been in the family since Jacob's father Henry had cleared the land and built the first house some seventy years earlier. Jacob and Sarah had lived on the farm for nearly thirty years, and as they got older, the farming got more difficult. At the age of seventy-four, Jacob tired more quickly now, and found himself depending on his sons more and more to get even the basic chores done around the farm.

"I talked to the Rice boy over at the mill this mornin'," Jacob said to Sarah, changing the subject.

"Does he have all his crops in yet?" asked Sarah.

"We didn't even talk about crops today," said Jacob. "Everyone's more interested in talkin' about all the Yankee activity they've been seein' up around Mount Jackson and Rude's Hill."

"Yankees?" Sarah asked in a surprised tone. She momentarily stopped kneading the dough, wiping her hands on her apron. "Are they comin' back?"

"Looks like they might," Jacob answered. "Now that the weather's gettin' half decent, it looks like they're startin' to take an interest in the area again."

"Who saw them?" queried Sarah, a touch of concern entering her voice.

"I didn't talk to anyone that saw any Yankees theirselves," answered Jacob. "But the Rice boy said his uncle was up around Meem's Bottom a few days ago and he talked to a fella who had seen a couple of Union regiments."

"Oh, Jacob," said a much relieved Sarah, resuming the task of kneading her dough. "A man talked to a man who talked to another man. That's all gossip, and you know what the Good Book says about that."

"Ain't gossip," said Jacob defensively. "I ain't never knowed the Rice boy to lie, nor his uncle either."

"What about the man who said he saw the Yankees? Can you vouch for his truthfulness also?" said Sarah with a slight smile and a twinkle in her eye.

"Don't know anything about him," admitted Jacob, "But I don't see why he'd go and make up a story about Yankees comin'. People in this valley know what a real Yankee looks like, and that's a fact. Ain't no way he'd make a mistake about whether they was Yankees or not."

"And did he say how many there were," asked Sarah, sarcastically, "Or which way they were going? Oh, let me guess. There were thousands of them, weren't there? And they all are probably on their way to our farm right now, am I right?"

"Didn't hear," said Jacob, with a touch of irritability entering his voice. He hated it when his wife assumed this attitude. "All I know is what I jest told yuh. Folks is seein' Yankees in places Yankees ain't supposed to be, and that ain't a good sign, whether you want to believe it or not."

"Well," said Sarah, placing the dough aside and scraping up the remnants from the table, "if those Yankees were comin' this way they'da been here by now, if they was spotted a few days ago around Mount Jackson.

I'm certainly not going to bother myself about a few bluecoats, and you shouldn't either. I swear, every time you go over to the mill to get flour you come back with the most outlandish stories."

Jacob walked to the fireplace and took down the gun he kept hanging above the mantle. "Well, I ain't gonna take no chances," he said. "You don't know if this story is true or not, nor do I. But it jest might be so, and I'm gonna be ready for them if they try to come on my property."

"You'll do nothing of the sort, Jacob," scolded Sarah. "The last thing those Yankees are afraid of is some old fool standin' out on the lane with an old gun that doesn't work half the time. Now put that thing away!"

"I'm tellin' yuh, Sarah. They's comin' this time," protested Jacob. "And with Stonewall gone, I ain't too sure anyone's around to stop 'em."

*   *   *

Confederate Brigadier General John Imboden was excited. Ecstatic may even be a better description.

"Y'all come on right up the Valley," he was saying to nobody in particular. "We chased y'all out before and we'll do it again."

Imboden had been given the responsibility of the Valley District by General Robert E. Lee in July 1863, a district covering an area west of the Blue Ridge and as far south as the James River in Botetourt County. This particular area had been threatened only minimally by the Union since Imboden had assumed command, and he had been able to defend it with only about 3,000 effectives. A native of the Valley, Imboden used his intimate knowledge of the area to his advantage. He knew most of the leading citizens in his district, most of whom had been of great help to him at one time or another. He also was familiar with the natural features and resources of the area, a familiarity which had served him well on more than one occasion.

Now he was chatting with General Gabriel C. Wharton. A message had just been received that Union troops were showing signs of preparing an advance up the Valley. The Valley. Imboden's back yard, in a manner of speaking. He couldn't wait to match wits with the enemy in such a familiar setting.

"It's going to be interesting to see if they get away from the railroad tracks," Wharton said, a hint of sarcasm in his voice.

The Federal troops in Imboden's area had shown a strong propensity for staying close to the Baltimore and Ohio Railroad system. Whether they were actually defending it from Confederate marauders or simply using the potential danger as an excuse had long been a matter of conjecture and consternation among Union officials. Imboden had never really concerned himself with the reasoning behind the habit. He had just been pleased with the predictability of the Union troops.

He laughed at Wharton's statement.

"If they do, we'll find out what kind of map readers they are, won't we?" he stated.

Imboden looked again at the message his aide had given him. It was from a Captain Bartlett of the Signal Corps on Massanutten Mountain. The message said that two bodies of cavalry, each one about 1,000 men strong, had left Sigel's headquarters. One column was going across North Mountain westward on the Moorfield Road. The other was headed eastward through Front Royal and toward Chester Gap in the Blue Ridge. Local citizens had told some of Imboden's scouts that the columns were to meet General Sigel at New Market. Imboden contemplated the meaning of the message.

"How do you see this, Gabe?" he asked his trusted friend.

"I'm not sure, John," was the answer. "One thing's sure, they're a'comin', ain't they?"

"That they are, Gabe," Imboden agreed. "I'm just tryin' to figure out what this Sigel is doin'. Comin' in two columns like this might mean that he isn't sure if his flanks are safe or not. That would mean he isn't sure where we are. And it's gonna take him a few days to get that information."

"Y'all don't think we should jest let 'im come on up the Valley, do yuh?" Wharton asked incredulously.

"Course not!" snapped Imboden. "We'll jest let 'im come up far enough that he won't be able to expect any help from his base. Then we'll hit 'em."

"I like that," admitted Wharton. "Where do you think we oughtta hit 'em?"

Imboden didn't answer immediately. Then he asked, "What's the name of that pass on North Mountain we were talkin' about the other day?"

"The Devil's Hole?" responded Wharton.

"The Devil's Hole," repeated Imboden. "Right."

"Y'all think that's where we oughtta attack?" Wharton asked.

"Nope," answered Imboden. We'll let 'em get through there first, then seal it off. We can let 'em come clean into Hardy County. If we can't capture 'em, we'll drive 'em back through Romney, across the Potomac, and all the way into Maryland."

"Who do y'all want to send?" queried Wharton.

"Tell Colonel Smith to take his 62nd Virginia, along with the 18th Virginia Cavalry, McNeill's Rangers, and two of McClanahan's guns. Don't tell anyone other than Colonel Smith what we're plannin', though."

"How are we gonna explain movin' that many men out?" Wharton wanted to know. "The Federal scouts are all over the countryside and one or two of 'em are bound to see 'em movin'."

"Jest spread the word that we're movin' the camp a few miles closer to North Mountain, and that we're lookin' for better grazin' for the horses. Any Federal scouts that see us movin' will think that's all we're doin'.'"

"There's two columns, John," Wharton reminded his friend. "What about the other one?"

"Major Gilmor can keep an eye on them," answered Imboden. "This message says the second column is the 1st New York Cavalry, and they ain't in a particular hurry. Gilmor can intercept them where they least expect it. Even if he can't defeat 'em, between Colonel Smith and Major Gilmor we oughtta be able to delay Sigel for a while. We've been givin' 'em fits on the railroad and we'll do it again here!"

Imboden and his troops had spent a great deal of time and effort over the past several months frustrating the Union soldiers along the railroad. Striking swiftly at those areas in which the Federal forces were weakest, he had destroyed track, rolling stock, and even a few bridges. An added bonus was the capture of a number of detachments. Imboden's name was not a popular one among those responsible for guarding the railroad. He was especially despised by Franz Sigel.

"I keep hearin' Averell's name mentioned by the scouts," Imboden said to Wharton. "Maybe he's gonna come back and try again."

"Let 'im," replied Wharton. "We'll be ready for 'im this time."

The two were referring to a raid which the Union's Brevet Major General William Averell had made the previous December. Hitting the Virginia and Tennessee Railroad with some 4,000 cavalry, he had succeeded in destroying several storage depots before returning to his base at New Creek. Even that success had been tempered, however, by the fact that Imboden's mere presence in the area had forced Averell to take an indirect route behind the North Mountain range. The added time required for travel had reduced the amount of time Averell's raiders had to complete their objective, and thus reduced their effectiveness.

"What about this Sigel?" asked Wharton. "You know anything about 'im?"

"Not much," admitted Imboden. "German. New man. Not much experience in the Valley. I hear he's a little indecisive at times. We can use that to our advantage. Other than that, you probably know as much about 'im as I do."

"Well, it sounds like we might get to know 'im a little better, doesn't it?" Wharton commented.

"Looks like it," agreed Imboden. "Last I heard he was movin' into Winchester with more than 8,000 infantry and 2,500 cavalry. Sounds like he means business."

"I hear he's bringin' three or four field batteries, too," offered Wharton. "Any idea what his objective is?"

"Nope," answered Imboden. "Not yet. I don't think he's after New Market, though. I think that's jest where they're all gonna meet up. Personally, I'd guess his objective might be Staunton, but that's just my opinion. With all those regiments he's bringin' up the Valley, though, one thing's certain. We're gonna need all the help we can get. We can't hope to hold 'im off with only 3,000 men, as good as they are. I'm gonna get in touch with General Breckinridge and ask for some reinforcements."

"From where?" asked Wharton. "General Lee's gonna have his own problems in the next few weeks, and with all due respect, John, he'll probably have some priority over your request. Neither General Lee nor General Breckinridge are gonna have anyone to spare."

"I've been thinkin' about that," said Imboden, scratching his chin. "I have a little brother who's been itchin' to get into the fightin'. He's down in Lexington at the Institute, and he's been tellin' me in his letters that the cadets can't wait to do their part. General Lee has been against usin' 'em, but the way our manpower is strectched, I think I'm gonna ask General Breckinridge to consider sendin' 'em to me. "

"The Institute!" exclaimed Wharton. "They're just boys, John."

Imboden nodded in agreement. "You're right, Gabe. Just boys. But that's all we got left. Young boys and old men. All the able bodies are already fightin'. Not much of a choice, is it?"

Wharton shook his head. "I don't know, John. You want to take the responsibility of leadin' a bunch of 15 year olds into a battle?"

"Not really," agreed Imboden. "But if what my brother tells me is true, those 15 year olds are as ready as any veteran. I've seen 'em drill, and I know they march as good as any man."

"Marchin's one thing, but doin' it while someone's shootin' at yuh is somethin' else," protested Wharton.

"No matter," said Imboden. "We need their help, and they've already offered it, so I know they won't turn down the chance. Besides, it'll be nice to see my little brother again."

*   *   *

"Jacob! You'd best come out here," Sarah Bushong shouted with a note of urgency in her voice. She had just come out of the hen house with her apron full of eggs when she spied a lone horseman approaching. As he got closer, Sarah could see that it was a soldier, and he appeared to be wearing blue.

Jacob came out to see what Sarah was shouting about. As he closed the door behind him he looked in the direction Sarah was looking, trying to see what it was that had her so concerned. Almost immediately Jacob saw the man on horseback, and he sensed that something was wrong.

"Mornin' to both of you," said the horseman cheerfully as he reined his mount to a stop, scattering chickens in all directions. He was obviously a Union soldier, but Jacob wasn't sure what kind, or how important he might be. The insignia on his hat probably meant something, but Jacob never could understand those emblems, nor did he even want to.

The Bushongs returned the greeting politely but said nothing further.

The soldier remained on his horse, a beautiful stallion. It pranced nervously as the man struggled to keep the animal under control. "Yankees never did know how to ride a horse," Jacob muttered to himself.

"I'm Lieutenant Adams," the man said in introduction.

Jacob merely nodded, saying nothing.

"You folks live here, do you?" asked the soldier.

"Thirty years," said Jacob in answer, not wishing to appear too cordial.

"You have any stock you'd like to sell?" Lieutenant Adams queried.

"What kind of stock, and how much of it?" Jacob asked, ignoring the sharp glance shot in his direction by Sarah.

"Oh, whatever yuh got, I guess," the lieutenant replied in a friendly manner, much as would an old friend who had happened to stop by. "Chickens, a cow or two, mebbe some horses."

"Nothin's fer sale," Sarah interjected curtly.

"Well now, ma'am, you may want to reconsider that," said the soldier with a smile. "I'm authorized to give you a receipt that you can turn in for real greenbacks. Not that fake money folks seem to use down here."

"We don't need yer greenbacks," Jacob said belligerently. "Nor do we want them. Folks in this valley is poor, thanks to this war, but we look out for each other. We all get along jest fine. What we can't get with our fake money, or by tradin', we do without."

"A few greenbacks would make you a rich man in comparison, then, wouldn't it?" asked Lieutenant Adams, sarcastically.

"Riches don't interest me none," said Jacob. "And like my wife says, we ain't got nothin' to sell, anyway, even if they did."

Jacob looked closely at the soldier's face. The man's eyes were bright blue, his cheeks ruddy. A full beard, somewhat unkempt after several days in the field, hid what may have been a handsome face. For the first time since the soldier rode up, his smile disappeared.

"Well," said the lieutenant icily. "General Sigel's comin' along not too far behind me with several regiments, and I'd hate to see nice folks like yourselves lose yer stock and not get nothin' in return."

"I don't expect to lose no stock as long as you Yankees act like gentlemen," said Jacob.

The smile returned to the horseman's face. "Really, now?" he asked. "And what makes you think every one of General Sigel's boys is a gentlemen?"

Jacob and Sarah stared at the man, saying nothing. Jacob's mouth twitched slightly, as it often did when he was angry.

"Them boys is mighty hungry," Lieutenant Adams continued. "I'm tryin' to buy some things for them to eat, but if I can't find nuthin' for them, I can't guarantee they won't just take whatever it is they see. Gentlemen or no, a hungry man's gonna do what he has to do to get food. I see some mighty fine lookin' roastin' chickens here, and that cow over yonder looks like it would make a fine meal for a small company of men. I'd like to see that you get a receipt, just so's you can get a little money from Washington, but if you don't want one, that's fine with me. Them boys are gonna eat whether you have a receipt or not. You can't expect a hungry man to march all day with nothin' to eat."

"Nobody asked y'all to come marchin' through here," Sarah said, unable to contain her anger any longer. "Why don't y'all go back home and let us be? Surely there is plenty of food for Mr. Sigel's boys up north, isn't there?"

"Ain't my decision to make, ma'am," replied the soldier in as pleasant a tone as he could muster. "Our orders are to come up the Valley and that's just what we're gonna do. You don't have to like it, or even accept it, but it's gonna happen."

"Y'all ain't the only soldiers in the Valley, yuh know," Sarah shot back. "Our boys ain't that far away, and they'll push y'all back down the Valley jest like they did last year, and the year 'fore that."

"Things is different now, ma'am," countered the lieutenant. "This ain't 1862 or 1863 no more."

"I don't see any difference," Sarah challenged. "You Yankees don't belong here, jest like y'all never belonged here, and that's a fact. Y'all run into any of our boys, they'll be chasin' y'all back up the turnpike as fast as that pretty horse you're sittin' on can run."

"I don't expect that's gonna happen any time soon, ma'am," said the soldier, leaning down from the saddle until his head was just above Sarah's. "Yuh see, the big difference is Stonewall isn't around to help yuh no more."

Sarah's eyes flashed, and she could feel her face and neck turning hot. Jacob's hands opened and closed repeatedly at his side as he struggled to control himself.

Lieutenant Adams sat upright in his saddle once again and touched his index finger to the brim of his dusty hat in a half-hearted salute. "Sorry we couldn't do business, folks," he said as he spurred his mount.

Jacob placed his arm around Sarah's shoulder as they watched the Union soldier depart, drawing her closer to him. "Sarah," he said, "gather the chickens while I get the pigs and cows. I think we'd best move them all into the house fer now, leastways till the Yankees go on through."

5

"Sir, we've come across some information that you should probably take a look at!" the messenger, a young captain from Pennsylvania, said to General Sigel in an excited tone.

The Union general had just ridden into Woodstock and he was still in the process of setting up a temporary headquarters. His troops had taken the town with only a minimum of resistance. In fact, the march to Woodstock had been more eventful than the actual taking over of the town. All along the route the Union soldiers had encountered sniper fire and periodic ambushes from Lieutenant Colonel John S. Mosby's rangers. Never quite sure where or when Mosby and his men would appear, it had been a tense trip for the Federal soldiers.

"What kind of information, Captain?" inquired Sigel.

"Some kind of telegraph messages, sir. When we got into the telegraph office we started going through the messages to see if there was anything we could use. Apparently the telegraph operator ran off at the first sign of trouble, without securin' anything. When we first read them we weren't sure if what we were seein' was the real thing, but it turned out it was. I'm pretty certain you're gonna want to see this for yourself, sir." The young captain appeared to be very pleased with the information he had brought to his general.

Sigel followed the captain to the nearby telegraph office where he found several soldiers milling about just outside the door. They respectfully stood at attention as he passed.

Once inside, Sigel had to strain to see where he was walking. The cluttered room was lit with only a small candle, around which several officers had huddled to read numerous dispatches which the telegraph operator had left on the desk when he fled. At his approach, two of the men stepped back a pace, creating an opening for Sigel to enter.

"What have you found?" Sigel demanded impatiently. The march had left him hot, tired, and irritable. Mosby's sharpshooters had done nothing to improve his humor, either. The news at this point had better be as good as the young captain had indicated.

"Well, sir," said one of the officers, "there are several dispatches here from Vice President Breckinridge. If they're true, we know just what he's doin' and what he's gonna do."

Sigel shot the man a look of contempt. "He's not the vice president any more. He's just another traitor!"

"Sorry, sir," the man said sheepishly. "I guess I'm jest used to callin' him the vice president. It jest slipped out."

"Well," snapped Sigel, "you make very sure that it doesn't slip out again. Not while I'm around, anyway."

"Yes, sir," the officer mumbled, trying to blend into the shadows.

Sigel angrily snatched the stack of papers from the officer and leaned toward the candle. The first telegraph message piqued Sigel's attention at once. It was a dispatch from General Breckinridge to General Imboden saying that 4,000 men were en route for Jackson River Depot. It went on to note that the quartermaster should plan to furnish transportation for Breckinridge, his staff, and sixteen horses.

"Very interesting," said Sigel, to himself as much as to the men who had gathered around him. Breckinridge was moving, and he was bringing a rather large contingent of soldiers with him. His plan remained to be seen, but somehow, Sigel thought, it may involve the Union general. He read the message a second time to be sure he had missed nothing, then placed it on the bottom of the stack and read the next.

This one drew a soft chuckle from Sigel as he read it closely. The message from Breckinridge directed a Captain Davis to do everything he could to learn the strength of Sigel's forces.

"He doesn't know how many men we have, even though we have been traveling through Breckinridge's own territory for several days. Perhaps the people who live here are not as friendly to him as he thought," Sigel mused.

Those gathered around the general laughed softly. They had no way of knowing the extent of the network of partisans in the Valley who were furnishing information to both Imboden and Breckinridge.

"Here's another dispatch to our good friend, Captain Davis," said Sigel as he read the third message. "General Breckinridge wants Mr. Davis to inform him if I make any movement toward General Grant's army. Why does he think I would even consider such a move? He must fear that we are going to reinforce General Grant! General Breckinridge is going to find out soon enough that our purpose is not to do any such thing, won't he?"

Murmurs of agreement arose in response to Sigel's question, rhetorical though it was.

Sigel frowned as he began to read the fourth message, however. His amusement over the content of the first three dispatches was quickly dashed as he read another telegram from Breckinridge to Davis, this one saying that General Lee was driving the enemy at every point. This was bad news indeed. It also explained, at least in part, why Breckinridge was so concerned that Sigel would make a move toward Grant.

Sigel had previously dispatched Colonel William Boyd and the 1st New York (Lincoln) Cavalry on a mission to go to New Market and secure the Luray Road and the gap through the Massanuttens. In Sigel's mind, Breckinridge's concern justified that action. Apparently Breckinridge had also thought of the gap. If Boyd could get to the gap first and control it, Sigel, if he was of a mind, could do just what Breckinridge feared most: move through the gap and either reinforce Grant or strike Lee on his flanks. Even if he had no plans to make such a move, there was nothing wrong with letting Breckinridge think he may do it.

"We will have to stay here in Woodstock until we hear from Colonel Boyd," Sigel said to his men after digesting the information he had just read. "There is no need to hurry. If we leave now we'll just have to contend with that outlaw Mosby, anyway. We are only one day from New Market, and Breckinridge is at least two days away, so we can still get there before he does."

Sigel directed his officers to have their men drill while they were waiting. "No reason to have men just sitting around," he thought.

Predictably, this was not received well by the men. However, although it was done with great reluctance, it was done. Sigel also sent out patrols several times a day to determine the locations and strengths of the enemy. Invariably these patrols found themselves ambushed and harassed by the men under Mosby's command. The purpose of the patrols was questioned by those who were assigned to go out, but Sigel insisted that they be done, even though the daily skirmishing continued unceasingly. In their spare time some of the men debated which was worse: going out on patrol to get shot at or staying in camp and drilling incessantly. They came to no conclusive answer.

To add to Sigel's consternation, he received a telegram from Brigadier General B. F. Kelley indicating that Imboden had totally routed Colonel Jacob Higgins and his cavalry, upon whom Sigel had depended for protection of his flank. Sigel swore in German when he read the dispatch. Confederate General John Imboden had seen to it that Sigel would not have those 500 men at any time in this campaign! The cautious German was convinced that he would need every man in whose hands he could place a gun, and the loss of Higgins and his men infuriated him.

Meanwhile, still fearing the possibility that Sigel may have been planning to move eastward toward Grant, Imboden directed that his troops be moved to the New Market area. This would allow better protection of the gap, preventing Sigel's plan from reaching fruition if, indeed, that ever was his plan. Imboden camped at Rude's Hill, some four miles north of the town of New Market. The added elevation gave him the opportunity to observe any Union activity in the immediate area while still allowing him to reach New Market rapidly should the need arise.

On May 13 (Friday the thirteenth, to be specific, which would prove to be portentous for Boyd) Colonel Boyd and his men reached New Market. Their arrival did not go unnoticed.

Alerted by his scouts, Imboden attacked Boyd, routing the Union troops. Many of the Union soldiers were captured, along with several horses which were badly needed by Imboden's troops. Those Union men who weren't captured were driven off into the Massanuttens in total confusion, roaming through the thick woods in small groups. Imboden wired Breckinridge of the skirmish, pointing out gleefully that Boyd himself was ". . . wandering in the mountain tonight."

With the loss of Boyd coming on the heels of the loss of Higgins, Sigel found himself with nearly a third of his cavalry gone and his flanks exposed. Perhaps worse than that, Imboden controlled New Market!

Continuing to get reports that he faced only Imboden, despite the contrary information he had received from the captured dispatches from Breckinridge, Sigel decided that the time was right to move from Woodstock. Under the misconception that Imboden was his sole opponent, however, he made a fateful decision. Even though it would mean splitting his army into two segments, he decided he would take both New Market and Mount Jackson, believing that controlling Mount Jackson would allow him to monitor enemy movement in all directions. It was also one of the strongest defensive positions in the Valley.

The morning of May 14 found Sigel in the headquarters of Major General Julius Stahel, commander of the First Cavalry Division. The two, both Germans, were discussing Sigel's ill-planned strategy in their native tongue, when a knock on the door was heard. Stahel, under Sigel's direction, had summoned Colonel August Moor, commander of the First Infantry Brigade, another fellow German. Their countryman had arrived.

After exchanging pleasantries, Colonel Moor was directed by Stahel to take infantry, artillery, and 1,000 of Stahel's cavalry to determine the relative strengths and positions of Imboden at Rude's Hill and New Market.

"Do you have a preference as to which regiments I take?" Moor asked.

In response, Sigel assigned the 1st West Virginia and 34th Massachusetts Infantries, four guns from Captain Alonzo Snow's Battery B of the Maryland Light Artillery, and two guns from Captain Chatham T. Ewing's Battery G, 1st West Virginia Light Artillery. For cavalry support, Stahel had suggested sending Colonel John E. Wynkoop, commander of the Second Cavalry Brigade, with detachments from the 20th Pennsylvania Cavalry and the 15th New York Cavalry. Sigel had agreed.

"You will be joined at Edinburg by the 123rd Ohio Infantry and 600 men from the 1st New York (Lincoln) Cavalry, the 1st New York (Veteran) Cavalry, and the 21st New York Cavalry. These will all be under the command of Major Timothy Quinn. He has already been made familiar with our objective," said Sigel.

"I am not familiar with this area, General," Moor said. "Would it be possible for you to get me some maps?"

"Unfortunately," said Stahel, "we don't have any maps here, and there is not enough time to get them."

"Why have I been selected to lead the expedition, if I may ask?" inquired Moor.

"I believe you are the best man I have available, Colonel," said Sigel, abruptly.

"I appreciate your confidence, sir," said Moor. "But, as I mentioned, I do not know this area, and the men you have assigned to me are not even my own men. I know nothing of their strengths and weaknesses, whether they will fight or not, or even if . . . "

Sigel cut him off in mid-sentence. "You will be the commander of this expedition, Colonel. I will listen to no more words of protest!"

Moor stood in silence, knowing that it would be fruitless to argue further. On the other hand, Sigel knew better than to ask Moor if there were any more questions.

Finally, after an uncomfortable silence, Moor asked, "Will there be anything else, General?"

"Just keep me abreast of any new developments, Colonel," was the response.

Exiting Stahel's headquarters, Moor questioned in his mind the wisdom of splitting the army into two units. Others agreed, some going so far as to say that Sigel was courting destruction.

Whatever the feelings of Moor and the other officers, however, the Colonel had his troops ready to move within two hours. When he left camp, a full one third of Sigel's forces in the Valley went with him.

By 3:00 p.m. cannon fire could be heard coming from the general direction of Mount Jackson, indicating that Moor had indeed discovered the enemy. Sigel sent the 18th Connecticut Infantry to Edinburg, in the event Moor would need them for support.

The cannon fire lasted throughout the rest of the afternoon and well into the evening. As he listened and contemplated his next move, Sigel received several disturbing reports. Contrary to what he had chosen to believe up to this point, he was informed that Imboden was not the only force in front of him. General John Breckinridge was reported to be on his way to join forces with Imboden, with the reports saying that he may be bringing as many as 15,000 Confederate troops and 19 guns! This, if true, would be a force to be reckoned with.

The unconfirmed entrance of Breckinridge into the scenario bothered Sigel a great deal. Staff members reported seeing him pacing back and forth in his headquarters, his hands clasped behind his back and his head bowed, deep in thought. Sigel concluded that the addition of Breckinridge was part of a Confederate plan to defeat Sigel in the Valley, allowing Robert E. Lee to advance through the gap and use the Valley as a direct route for an invasion into the north. Sigel also believed that an alternate plan, should Breckinridge be unsuccessful in his effort to defeat Sigel, would see Breckinridge diverting across the Blue Ridge and launching an attack on Grant's flanks. Either way, Lee would benefit. Neither situation was desirable in Sigel's mind, and he would do everything in his power to see that neither succeeded.

Then, after several anxious hours, came good news to temper the news about Breckinridge. Word was received that Moor had pushed Imboden out of New Market and was now occupying the town. This was the news that Sigel had been waiting for. Pleased with the way things were progressing, he made plans to march to Mount Jackson early in the morning.

*   *   *

Imboden and Breckinridge had never met. Now, Imboden stood outside Breckinridge's headquarters, dreading having to tell his superior that New Market was in danger of falling. After all, this man had once been the vice president of the United States! Even though neither Imboden nor Breckinridge considered themselves citizens of that country any longer, a former vice president of any country still commanded respect, and first meetings should be under more favorable circumstances. Taking a deep breath, he knocked on the door. At the sound of Breckinridge's answer, Imboden entered. The greeting was cordial and the two officers appeared to get along well immediately.

"I haven't eaten yet, General," said Breckinridge, after a brief update in which Imboden assured Breckinridge that, even though the Union was slowly gaining ground, Imboden's men were fighting valiantly and would continue to do so until their last breath. "Would you care to join me? We can talk while we're eating."

Imboden agreed, and the two discussed plans for the next few days while enjoying their lunch. Before the meal was finished, however, a courier arrived.

"Sir, the Federals have just pushed our boys off Rude's Hill," he said breathlessly. "We're formin' a line of battle outside of town to try to hold them back."

"Thank you," Breckinridge said calmly, no hint of alarm entering his voice.

Dismissing the courier, Breckinridge turned to Imboden. "Do you think your boys can hold New Market till dark?" he queried.

"We'll try, sir," was the emphatic answer. "If it can be done, we'll do it!"

"Good," replied Breckinridge. "Do all you can to hold the town until dark, then fall back three or four miles. I have reinforcements coming and we'll join you there."

"Where are the reinforcements coming from, sir?" asked Imboden.

"I thought you might be interested in that," the former vice president said with a smile. "I'm bringing Echols, with the 22nd Virginia and the 23rd Virginia Battalion. I also was able to call up the Rockbridge Reserves and the boys from Virginia Military Institute. I understand you have a brother there, am I right?"

"Yes, sir," said Imboden. "My youngest brother, Jacob."

"Well, I don't plan on using the cadets, but if I have to it's good to know they're available," said Breckinridge.

"They say they are ready, General," said Imboden.

"That's what I've been led to believe," Breckinridge answered. "If nothing else, at least you'll get a chance for a family reunion."

"It'll be a bigger reunion than you think, General," replied Imboden.

"Oh, really?" Breckinridge exclaimed, a note of surprise creeping into his voice.

"Yes, sir," said Imboden proudly. "I have three other brothers here at New Market already."

"There are four of you here right now?" blurted Breckinridge.

"Soon to be five, according to you," Imboden countered. "My brother George is the colonel of the 18th Virginia Cavalry, and I have two other brothers in the same regiment. Frank is captain of Company H and James is a sergeant major. If Jacob gets here, we'll have a grand old time."

Breckinridge laughed. "I hope we can make it a happy reunion for you, General."

"Beatin' the Yankees will make it happy enough, sir, especially if none of us gets hurt in the process," Imboden replied.

"That's the plan, General," said Breckinridge.

"Mine too," Imboden responded. "And you can count on the Imboden family to do our fair share of bringin' it about!"

"I'm sure of that," Breckinridge answered. "I won't be worryin' about the Imbodens doin' their part. Y'all have done a good job already."

After the two generals laid plans for how Imboden would hold New Market for a few more hours, Breckinridge, unaware that Sigel had captured his dispatches at the telegraph office in Woodstock, said, "We have one thing in our favor, and that's the fact the Sigel probably doesn't know

I'm comin' with more troops. That will give us the element of surprise. If you can hold New Market until tonight, we'll join forces after dark. And early tomorrow morning, I'll hit him so hard he'll have to fall back to Maryland. And General Lee will not have to worry any further about an attack on his flank through the gap!"

Breckinridge had no way of knowing that the element of surprise he hoped for, and needed so badly, had long ago been lost!

6

It was a perfect late spring-early summer type of evening. The kind of evening a person would like to save and use again on some stormy evening in the future. It was only fitting that the weather had been perfect on this day, because this had been a special day for the Virginia Military Institute. In fact, it had been a special day for the entire town of Lexington. It was May 10, 1864: the first anniversary of Stonewall Jackson's death. Somehow, a year had come and gone. To a person, the citizens of Lexington agreed that the past 365 days had been a blur. Much had happened, and it still didn't seem possible that it had all happened without their beloved Stonewall.

To commemorate the day, a special ceremony had been held at the cemetery in town where Stonewall had been laid to rest. The cadets of the Virginia Military Institute had played a major role in that ceremony, with an honor guard chosen to raise a flag over Stonewall's grave. The ceremony had been solemn but impressive, and the cadets had been proud to have been a part of it. Following the ceremony, the cadets had been given the rest of the day free. A day to do with what they chose. There were few of those in the life of a cadet, and when one came along it was cherished by all.

Now, it was evening. The eventful day was drawing to a close. The cadets were on duty once again. The evening dress parade was scheduled to take place on the emerald green parade ground. The people of Lexington gathered to watch, as they often did. The cadets enjoyed performing in front of the townspeople, particularly on an evening like this one, a perfect spring evening that saw hordes of pretty young ladies as part of the admiring throng.

Following the dress parade, the evening gun was fired and the colors were brought down the staff. The day was finished, the crowd dispersed, and the cadets slowly retired to their rooms to reflect on the day they had just experienced.

Sometime after midnight, Jack Stanard awoke with a start. What had interrupted his sleep? As he tried to clear his head he was shaken by John Wise.

"C'mon, Jack. It's the long roll!" John was saying excitedly. "Wake up! Let's get moving!"

The long roll. The call to assemble. At this hour? Stanard briefly considered going back to sleep, mentally computing how many demerits that would earn. Then he thought better of it and quickly bounded out of bed. Already, Louis Wise was running out the door.

Stanard quickly followed, running down the interior stoop to the stairs leading down to the quadrangle. As he ran to the parade ground with his classmates, their footsteps crunched on the gravel walkways, a sound that seemed strangely out of place considering the hour. As he ran, Stanard thought to himself, "What's it gonna be this time? A fire, like the last time? Or maybe we'll be sent somewhere to guard a baggage train while the real soldiers get to do some fightin'!"

He soon realized he was not the only cynic in the corps, as several cadets running beside him were also grumbling out loud. "At least I'm complainin' to myself," thought Stanard. Stanard was not all that fond of military life as it was, and long rolls in the middle of the night had a great deal to do with establishing that opinion, infrequent as they may have been.

Reaching his assigned location Stanard could see several of the officers standing near the statue of George Washington. One was holding a lantern as high as he could, while the others were using the light from the lantern to read a piece of paper held by one of their number.

Half asleep and not in the mood for listening to speeches, the cadets nonetheless reacted automatically to the commands given by the first sergeants. "Fall in, A Company!" the first commanded sharply. Those in A Company quickly fell in and snapped to attention. One by one the commands were given to B, C, and D companies, all responding in identical fashion. The companies were then side stepped together, and the roll was called.

As the last name was called, Adjutant Cary Weston stepped forward and held the mysterious paper near the lantern. He cleared his throat and ordered the cadets to parade rest. He then began the speech which every cadet would remember for the rest of his life.

"I have a dispatch from General Breckinridge to read to you," Weston began. The corps was deathly silent. He looked at the row of sleepy faces gathered in the darkness in front of him, then went on.

"This dispatch is addressed to Superintendent Smith, but since he is not feeling well I have been authorized to read it to you in his place." Weston looked down at the paper, paused momentarily, then read the dispatch. "Sigel is moving up the Valley. Was at Strasburg last night. I cannot tell yet whether this is his destination. I would be glad to have your assistance at once with the cadets and the section of artillery. Bring all the forage and rations you can. Have the reserves of Rockbridge ready, and let them send at once for arms and ammunition, if they cannot be supplied at Lexington."

The adjutant looked up at the assembled corps. "This dispatch is signed by Major General John Breckinridge."

The cadets were awake now! Each wanted desperately to react to this long awaited announcement, but until they were dismissed they would be unable to do so. They all listened carefully to every word uttered by Weston, hoping that the pounding of their hearts didn't drown out his words. Weston himself was just as excited, and he struggled to maintain his decorum.

"Because of General Smith's illness, he will be unable to accompany us," the adjutant was saying. "Colonel Gilham will go in his place and serve as acting superintendent until we return. Major Ship will lead us on the field. The first sergeants and Captain Minge will detail eight artillerists from each company. It will also be necessary to keep some of you here at the Institute to serve as guards. The first sergeants will also select those of you who must remain."

With that last statement, 280 hearts dropped as each cadet hoped against the odds that he wouldn't be one of those chosen to stay behind. They had waited so long for this opportunity. How could they live with the knowledge that they had come so close to finally getting a chance to fight, only to be selected for the home guard detail?

"Now," Adjutant Weston went on, "Major Ship has a few words he'd like to say."

Major Scott Ship[1] stepped forward. A large man with a booming voice, he had graduated from the Institute just a few years earlier, in 1859. He was only twenty-four years old, but looked forty. A no nonsense man, he had served as an assistant professor of Mathematics, Tactics, and Latin at the Institute following his graduation, but had dropped mathematics from his duties after one year. He had been present with his fellow cadets at the execution of John Brown, a fact which impressed his students immensely. Well liked by the corps and now serving as commandant of cadets, Ship was about to lead them into battle!

---

[1] Ship changed the spelling of his name to Shipp in 1883, and it appears that way in some publications. The 1864 spelling will be used throughout this work.

He glanced at the young faces gathered in front of him. They were so innocent, so young, so full of romantic ideas about war. They wanted to fight. Ship had spent his entire sixty-day leave with Company H of the 4th Virginia Cavalry the previous summer, and he had an idea what war was about. But these young men, these boys, had no idea what they were about to get into.

"This is the opportunity you all have been waiting for," he began. "I know you will give a good account of yourselves if you are called on to go into battle. You have prepared well. Now it is up to you to show what you have learned. We will be marching at daybreak, and we have been ordered to report to General Breckinridge at Staunton. You will take sufficient rations for two days' march. We will replenish supplies along the way. Now, you have much to do and not much time to do it. Prepare well, and try to get some sleep. You will have a long march in the morning."

The adjutant took over again as Ship walked away. Ship, too, had many things to do.

Then, in his best voice, the adjutant announced, "Parade . . . Dismissed!"

The sergeants then side stepped the cadets to their respective company parades, where the selection processes began. First, the sergeants, with the help of Captain Collier Minge, selected those cadets who would serve in the artillery. The nineteen-year-old Minge was the highest ranking cadet, and would be in charge of the artillery. The criteria for selection of the cadet artillerists were simple: either be an experienced horseman or know a little about gunnery, or both. As the cadets' names were called they could hardly contain their elation. Being chosen for the artillery meant they could not be chosen for guard duty. They would definitely be going on the march! Two second lieutenants, Frederick Claybrook of Company D and Levi Welch of Company B, were placed in charge of the three-inch rifled guns the cadet artillery would take with them. Both first classmen, they had studied gunnery, and their knowledge could be put to use. First Corporal Otis Glazebrook of Company D, who stood first in his class, and Third Corporal Patrick Henry of Company B, were selected to be the gunners. The gun crews were then quickly selected, one of which included Lewis Davis of Company C, the youngest cadet at the Institute, just four weeks past his fifteenth birthday.

Those whose names had not yet been called held their collective breaths, knowing that the next group of names selected would be those who would not go, those for whom the chance to fight for the cause would be gone. Each cadet silently whispered a prayer that it would be someone else whose name was called.

Then it began. Some of the names called were not unexpected. Martin Wood, a nineteen-year-old private in Company D, had received a leg wound at Antietam and had great difficulty marching, even for the daily drills on the parade ground. Although he would have preferred to have gone along, he knew he would not be able to keep up with the others, and did not protest his selection. Others, however, did not take the news as well. Sixteen-year-old Francis Johnson, a private in Company D, was one of those. Johnson's father, Robert Ward Johnson, had been a United States senator when the war broke out. He now sat in the Confederate States senate. The younger Francis knew his father would be disappointed that Francis had not been in a battle when the opportunity had presented itself. More than to please his father, however, Francis sincerely wanted to be a part of the corps which went to join up with Breckinridge.

"No!" he shouted when he heard his name. "Please take me along. Please!" He began to sob, heartbroken at the idea of not being with his friends in their hour of glory. Although he begged and pleaded, he was unsuccessful and remained on the list. While all felt great pity for Johnson, none volunteered to trade places with him.

All names having been called, the sergeants gave some last minute instructions. "You will report to the parade ground at 4:00 a.m. with blankets, full haversacks, and canteens," they had said. Then the corps was dismissed.

Immediately a loud cheer went up, as the cadets released the pent up emotion that had been building from the moment the adjutant had read General Breckinridge's dispatch. They were finally going to be able to call themselves real soldiers. Their time had finally come!

Excitedly the cadets made their ways back to their rooms, extending sympathies along the way to those who had been selected for guard duty. Many of the young men who would not be going were beside themselves with despair. Inconsolable, they sought solace in each other. One cadet selected for guard duty, however, sought out his roommates. Right now, he needed their support more than anything. That cadet was John Cabell Early, roommate of Moses Ezekiel and Thomas Jefferson.

Trying not to show his feelings, he quickly swiped at the tears running down his cheeks as he approached his two friends, hoping they would not notice the streaks. Forcing a wry smile, he said, "Well, at least two of us will be able to go."

"This isn't fair, John," exclaimed Jefferson. "There are others here who are sicker than you."

"I know," agreed Early. "But the sergeant said he didn't think I'd be able to keep up, what with just comin' back to the Institute after bein' sick, and all."

"You can keep up," said Ezekiel. "I know you can. Let me go tell the sergeant how y'all are strong enough to jump on me every day and wrestle with me. Let me tell 'im!"

"No, Moses," Early said in a tone of resignation. "He's probably right. I am still a little weak. I probably wouldn't be able to keep up with the rest of you, like the sergeant says."

"No," Jefferson blurted out. "You can do it. We'll take care of you. When y'all get tired we'll help you. We can carry your gun for you, or your knapsack. We can even put our arms around you and help you walk if we have to. Y'all have to be allowed to go with us, John. It won't be right to make you stay back."

"Thanks, Thomas," said Early. "I appreciate that. I surely do. But it wouldn't work that way, don't y'all see? If the two of you had to slow down to help the likes of me, then all three of us wouldn't be able to keep up. This way, you two can go and march with the rest of the boys. Mebbe y'all can shoot a Yankee for me."

The three had reached their room by now. Ezekiel and Jefferson were elated that they would finally be going to fight in the war, but they were both sad for their friend. They both knew how much he had wanted to go along. Wordlessly, the three entered the room. One of them threw himself on his bed. The other two, with mixed emotions, sadly began their preparations for the march.

The use of young boys was not without precedence, particularly after three years of war. The availability of fighting men in the Confederacy was rapidly dwindling, and manpower was gathered up wherever it could be found. To be sure, at this point in the war there was scarcely a regiment, or perhaps even a company, in the Confederate army which didn't have at least a few boys under the age of eighteen. The Parker Battery, an artillery company from Richmond commanded by Captain W. W. Parker, was almost exclusively made up of boys between the ages of fourteen and eighteen. They were fondly referred to as The Boy Company, because only the officers, and possibly a few others, were of age. McClanahan's Staunton Horse Artillery was another unit which was overloaded with boys seventeen to twenty years of age, but they were battle-hardened veterans, having already ridden with J. E. B. Stuart.

The boys of VMI ranged in age from fifteen to twenty-five, with an average age slightly under eighteen. That Virginia Military Institute was even able to remain open at this stage of the war was a tribute to General Smith, Old Specs. With conscription taking all able-bodied males between the ages of eighteen and forty-five, most colleges throughout the South found their student body gone to war. Smith recognized what was about to happen before it reached critical proportions, and he acted quickly to lower the age of admission to sixteen. On many occasions, that age limit was stretched to allow even younger boys to attend. These boys under the age of eighteen could not be drafted, which stabilized the student body, and the Institute was able to maintain its capacity of 300 cadets. Under state law, however, they were considered part of the reserves, a militia unit which could be called out at any time in the event of an emergency, whether real or perceived.

The Rockbridge Reserves, who were being called out at the same time as the cadets, were also a militia unit. Numbering less than 1,000, the Rockbridge Reserves consisted nearly entirely of boys under the age of sixteen and men older than forty-five. These were unskilled and undisciplined soldiers, armed with personal shotguns and hunting rifles, but they could be used as guards to allow other soldiers, soldiers who were more fit, to fight. If either the Rockbridge Reserves or the cadets of Virginia Military Institute were to see any actual fighting on this callout, it would almost certainly be the cadets.

Few of the cadets slept that night, or even tried to, even though they still had several hours until their appointed time. The corps, being a military institute, was already fully equipped, having ammunition, tents, knapsacks, rifles, and other accouterments. That equipment, however, still had to be gathered and loaded onto wagons. Several of the cadets who were not going along were detailed to this task. Early, unable to bear watching his roommates pack their gear, threw himself into this work, trying to take his mind off his bitter disappointment. It didn't stop the hurt, but it made him feel more a part of the proceedings.

In addition to the two days' rations each cadet was taking along, General Smith had ordered five hundred pounds of bacon and one hundred bushels of corn to be loaded, plus as much beef as he could find transportation for. The cadets would also have access to sixty-four barrels of flour once they reached Staunton.

Jefferson and Ezekiel, for their parts, were busy with their own preparations while Early was helping load wagons. Carrying Austrian muskets, they each had drawn their allotment of forty rounds of ammunition. Would they have the chance to fire their weapons? At this time it was anybody's guess, but simply drawing the ammunition had made the callout feel like the real thing.

When each cadet had completed his packing, he turned to other activities to fill the hours before it was time to report. Some gathered in small knots and speculated on what the next few days would bring. Other cadets wrote letters home, excitedly telling their families that they were finally going to be real soldiers. By the time their families received the missives the battle would be over, but none of the writers gave any consideration to that. One thing was certain: nobody was able to go back to sleep.

Breakfast was by candlelight, although little was eaten. The excitement of the impending march had dulled appetites, and many of the boys stuffed the remaining biscuits and rolls into their knapsacks. After all, like teenage boys of any era, even though they were not hungry at the moment, they would certainly get hungry on the march.

Finally, it was time to assemble. As they had done just a few hours before, they formed into companies and the roll was called. Then, Scott Ship stepped forward for last minute instructions. The sun was just beginning to make its appearance over the nearby mountains.

"There has been a last minute change of plans," he began. Each cadet had reason to believe his heart may have stopped momentarily. What was he saying? Were they not going now, after all this preparation? Those boys who had been assigned the task of guarding the Institute in the absence of the corps silently felt a sense of jubilation. Maybe they weren't going to miss out on anything after all.

Ship continued. "We have been unable to gather a sufficient number of horses on such short notice, and we cannot immediately take the artillery pieces along. This will delay the artillery's departure by a few hours. However, they will still be going." The collective sigh of relief was almost audible when the cadets realized they would still be joining Breckinridge.

"The artillery will leave as soon as the horses are brought in and hitched up. They have orders to rejoin us by nightfall, wherever we may be. Those of you assigned to the artillery may fall out of ranks at this time."

The boys whose duties called them to be artillerists obediently fell out. They reassembled a short distance from the main body of cadets.

When all were in place, Ship resumed his message. "You boys are all aware of the proud tradition which has been established here at the Virginia Military Institute." He paused, scanning the faces in front of him before continuing. These boys who had sat in his classroom were about to take the ultimate test. It would be far more crucial than any exam he had ever given, or could ever hope to give. But this exam was one each cadet simply had to pass! A second chance may not come.

"Many brave men have gone on before you, graduating from here to take their places on the fields of battle," he continued. "They have made the entire South proud, as well as this fine institution. Today, you are being called on to continue that proud tradition. We don't know if you will be called on to fight, but if you are, I trust that you will all do your duties. Remember where you are from. Remember what you have been taught. Remember what you have been trained to do. And do it well."

Ship continued to survey the young faces staring back at him. They were obviously anxious to get started. He would hold them back no longer. "Musicians, take your positions!" he ordered.

Immediately James Henry Crocken, Jacob Marks, and Richard Staples assumed their places in the front of the ranks. None of the three was a cadet, but they had all been a part of the corps for so long that they considered themselves cadets, or at least honorary cadets.

At Ship's signal Marks and Staples began the cadence on their drums. Crocken, with his fife, would join in at regular intervals. The cadets were stepping out!

A loud cheer rose from the ranks as one voice. Those who were staying behind bravely tried to choke back their tears. Some were not successful. Their tears of disappointment quickly changed to tears of anger, however, as those marching off to battle began to jeer those left behind.

"We'll tell the Yanks y'all said hello!" yelled one cadet, accompanied by the laughter of several of his companions.

"Keep the Yanks out of my room!" shouted another.

The mocking shouts rang out for as long as the cadets could see their ill-fated friends. Then, tiring of the game, they turned their attention to one another until Ship turned in his saddle and shot a stern look at those in the front ranks. They quickly got the message.

Still, with spirits high and showing the exuberance of youth, they stamped their feet on a small, wooden bridge as they crossed Woods Creek near the edge of the Institute's campus. The resulting bouncing caught several cadets off guard, much to the amusement of their friends.

Then, as the Institute disappeared behind them, they gave out one last cheer. They were no longer students. They were on their way to becoming soldiers! Little did they know that several of their number were seeing the Institute for the last time.

Major General Francis H. Smith, superintendent of Virginia Military Institute, at the time of the battle

Courtesy of VMI Museum

7

The sun was slowly rising toward its zenith when the cadets began their march toward the Valley Turnpike. Reaching the pike the boys turned north and set a steady pace. The mood was light hearted, and they appeared to be enjoying every step they were taking. Disciplined, they marched as one. However, Commander Ship had relaxed the rules and the young soldiers joked and laughed heartily as they marched.

Beside the road the buttercups thrust their yellow petals skyward. On the road, the steady beat of the drums set a fine cadence for the cadets to follow, and even the horses at the front of the brigade appeared to be enjoying the moment.

By midmorning the novelty of the march had run its course, however, and the lively banter of the cadets decreased. Almost immediately it was replaced by the age-old hobby of soldiers everywhere: complaining. And if there was one topic the cadets were good at complaining about, it was their fighting history, or rather, their lack of a fighting history. Having graduates and professors who had fought valiantly did not count. These young men had been called out before like this, only to find that their services were not needed when they reached their destination.

"I don't care if General Breckinridge did sign that dispatch," complained Private James McCorkle of Company B. "Y'all are gonna find out when we get to wherever it is we're goin' that the general is gonna want us to watch over a baggage wagon or look fer some deserters. Ain't no way on God's green earth the general is gonna let us fight the Yankees."

At the age of twenty-three, McCorkle was the only member of Company B, except for officers, who was no longer in his teens. As such, his opinions commanded the respect of his younger colleagues.

John Roane, a wide-eyed fifteen year old who was the second young-est cadet on the march, peered at McCorkle. "You really think so, James?" he asked.

McCorkle looked at Roane intently before answering. "I know so, John," he said, snapping off a sprig of tall grass from the side of the road and placing it in his mouth. "Y'all haven't been here long enough to re-member, but those of us who have been at the Institute fer a while know what I'm talkin' about."

"I know what yer sayin', James," responded Franklin Gibson. "We've had a bunch of false alarms in the past, but fer some reason I have a feelin' this might finally be the real thing."

"The real thing?" McCorkle blurted. "I'll believe that when the time comes, and not a minute before!"

"Mebbe yer right," Gibson answered softly. "But don't say I didn't tell you so if we really get into a fight."

"Well," McCorkle retorted, opening his canteen and taking a long swallow, "only thing I can say is it's gettin too hot to argue about somethin' we'll have to wait to see about, anyway. I hope y'all are right and we finally do get to do some serious fightin', but I still say it's a false alarm and we'll all be goin' back to the Institute in a day or two just like we always did before, grumblin' about everyone else gettin' to do the fightin' but not us."

"We'll see," said Gibson. "Meanwhile, somebody tell Tutwiler there's another creek comin' up ahead."

Those around Gibson laughed uproariously, while several others passed the word back into the ranks that the corps was approaching a creek.

"Creek, Tutwiler!" shouted one.

"Time to get yer shoes off, Edward," chortled another.

The derisive remarks were being directed at a young private in Com-pany D who was having obvious problems with the hot road surface. The heat which was being reflected by the pike's macadam was already rais-ing blisters on many of the cadets' feet. However, seventeen-year-old Ed-ward Tutwiler was feeling the effects more than most. At each creek he had found it necessary to stop and soak his sore feet, then run to catch up with his friends just before they marched out of sight.

"We'll be in Staunton if yer lookin' fer us, Edward," laughed one of his companions.

Tutwiler took the pointed remarks in good humor, despite his obvi-ous discomfort. "I'll still outwalk y'all," he answered to nobody in par-ticular. "Even with bloody feet!"

In reality, however, Tutwiler was not the only cadet experiencing problems with the hot road surface. More than once Colonel Robert Louis

Madison, the corps surgeon, dismounted from his horse, offering it to some unfortunate cadet who was having difficulty walking.

"I swear, Colonel," laughed Ship, after Madison had dismounted yet another time, "I think you've done more walkin' than some of the boys have!"

"Maybe so," the colonel responded with a chuckle. "But walkin's still a lot easier than fixin' up a sore foot."

"Maybe we should give the boys a short breathin' spell," suggested George Ross, the assistant surgeon.

"Especially them drummers," added Jonathan Woodbridge, the cadet sergeant major, in reference to the nearly constant cadence which had aided the corps in maintaining its pace. "Their fingers gotta be close to droppin' off."

"Reckon y'all are right," admitted Ship, holding up his hand as a signal to those following him to stop.

As the word filtered back through the ranks to fall out alongside the road, Tutwiller came running up to his place in rank after yet another wade in a nearby stream.

"Everyone gets a rest 'cept you, Edward," said Charles Crockett, a seventeen year old who had been marching directly in front of Tutwiler. "Y'all go on ahead and we'll take a turn sittin' in the creek fer a while!"

Crockett's remark was received by a loud guffaw from those around him. Even Ship, who had come back through the ranks to check on those near the rear, could not suppress a laugh. He shook his head and looked at Tutwiler, who was seated on a stump taking his shoes off so he could rub his aching feet.

"How you ever gonna be able to chase Yankees, Edward?" he asked.

"Don't worry, sir," responded Tutwiler cheerfully. "I'll be able to hold up my end when the time comes to chase Yankees."

"Only if they're runnin' through a creek," responded Crockett, to another round of laughter.

Tutwiler said no more, perhaps realizing that he was outnumbered and had no chance to better his tormentors in a match of wits. He remained seated on the stump, wordlessly rubbing his feet and wondering how much farther they would be marching before they stopped for the night.

As the boys rested at the side of the road the conversation turned to what it would be like to actually get into a battle.

"Y'all reckon it's gonna be scary?" asked one.

"Won't scare me none," responded another with typical youthful bravado.

"Y'all are gonna be scared jest like the rest of us, and that's a fact," said the first.

"Ain't a one of yuh that knows what y'all are gonna feel like," said a young cadet who had been seated on the opposite side of the road.

The first two cadets looked at him suspiciously. This boy had only been a cadet for less than a week, and was not yet known to many of the cadets in his company. In his short stay at the Institute he had already developed a reputation for being quiet, speaking little, and then only when spoken to.

"Some of yuh are gonna be scared, and some won't," he went on. "Some won't be scared till the shootin's done, then y'all will get so weak in the knees y'all are gonna have to sit down. Everyone's different. And I'm here to tell y'all that yuh flat out won't know how y'all are gonna feel till it happens." The speaker was Thomas Clendinen.

"And I guess you do?" asked a tall, thin boy seated beside him.

"A little," was the response.

"How do you come to know so much about fightin'?" asked another cadet in a challenging manner.

"I done my share," said Clendinen, who, at the tender age of seventeen had already spent nearly two years as a prisoner of war. "Spent a little time in a Yankee prison fer my trouble. Only got released a few weeks ago, right before I came to Lexington."

"Y'all were a prisoner?" asked Tutwiler from his stump.

"Fer a while. Wasn't too bad, I reckon, but even marchin' in this heat beats sittin' in a prison," said Clendinen, wiping the perspiration from his neck with a red bandanna.

Before any more questions could be asked the booming voice of Commander Ship could be heard ordering the cadets back into rank. Clendinen had time to say no more. In the space of one short conversation during a break along the side of a road, however, he had become an instant hero in the eyes of his fellow cadets. He had seen the elephant.

The march resumed, weary feet kicking up dust into throats already parched by the exertion in the mid-May heat of Virginia. The longer the corps marched the quieter they got, until the only sound that could be heard was the beat of the drums and the metallic clanging of tin cups and canteens in perfect rhythm with the cadence.

At midafternoon Ship called another halt. To the gratification of the foot weary cadets, this stop was not just another break. The commander ordered the boys to set up camp, a command that was met with more than one sigh of relief as knapsacks were unceremoniously dropped to the ground. Soon the woods were ringing with the sounds of axes cutting firewood and the youthful voices of the cadets shouting to one another. In a matter of minutes the scent of smoke, followed shortly by the pleasant odors of cooking food, wafted through the trees.

As the young soldiers lounged around the campfire after a well-earned meal, a soft rumble was heard in the distance.

"Is that artillery?" asked one of the cadets wistfully.

"Sounds more like thunder to me," answered a friend.

The answer came within minutes, in the form of the first raindrops. As the rain fell more heavily the boys rushed for cover.

"Maybe the rain'll cool things off for tomorrow's march," someone said.

It would not do much to relieve the heat, but the cadets would soon find they would have no more problems with the dust for the rest of this expedition. As the thunder rolled and the rain fell even harder, the artillery arrived at the camp. The corps was intact once again.

*　　　　　*　　　　　*

When the cadets awoke early the next morning, they quickly realized that, although they were no longer at the Institute, the strict discipline was not going to relax entirely. Colonel Gilham and Commander Ship allowed the boys a short time to cook breakfast, then ordered them into rank once more, the artillery falling in behind the last row of Company D.

Almost immediately the complaining began anew. The rain continued to fall, as it had done most of the night. There had been little sleep. Now, the rigors of the previous day's march appeared in the form of sore feet and aching muscles. The lighthearted mood of yesterday had been replaced by the realities of being a soldier.

"Y'all are gonna have to find a bigger creek today, Tutwiler," one of the boys in Company C remarked. "There's gonna be a lot more of us joinin' yuh!"

What had been dust yesterday was mud this morning. For a while the boys dodged puddles on the road. Then, shoes soaked through and covered with mud, there was no longer a reason to go around or step over them. They simply marched through the puddles as if they weren't even there.

Soon, however, the mood lightened once more. Someone near the back tossed a pine cone forward, the missile striking Stanard in the back.

"Five demerits for gettin' in the way of that pine cone, Jack," someone shouted. Even Stanard was amused.

"I've got 'em fer a lot less than that," he responded good-naturedly, to a chorus of laughter.

The march continued, the conversations less animated than those of the previous day. Today, with the realization that they may be going into battle, most of the conversation centered around war. What it must be like. How it must sound. Or smell. Or feel. However, the conversations were not morbid. This simple fact had not yet settled into their minds: some of their number may die.

As the cadets marched past homes and farms along the route, the occupants often rushed outside to wave or shout words of encouragement. Children ran to the road to watch them, often marching along for a short distance. Some of these children carried a stick over their shoulder, holding it in much the same manner as the cadets held their guns. All in all it made the march seem shorter, and it was difficult to determine who enjoyed the spectacle more, the spectators or the cadets.

At midmorning the cadets approached a battle weary group of soldiers resting beside the road. One of the veterans squinted at the cadets as they neared, as if to get a better look.

"What do yuh make of that?" he asked, nudging the soldier lying beside him, his hat pulled down over his eyes.

The second soldier raised the brim of his hat and watched the cadets draw nearer. To the disheveled soldiers, no two of whom were dressed alike, the sight of the corps in their matching uniforms and precise strides must have been a magnificent display.

However, to the men who had fought and been blooded, it also raised some animosity. They were in no mood to see young boys, resplendent ones at that, join their ranks.

"Looks like we got the kiddie corps a'comin with us, Amos," the first soldier said in a voice deliberately raised to a level which the cadets could hear.

Amos watched the cadets for several seconds before answering. "Appears that way, Jedediah," he finally remarked loudly. Then, directing his comments to the cadets, he shouted, "Do yer mommies know y'all are out here playin' soldier with the big boys?"

Henry Wise, captain of Company A, quickly took charge of his company, warning them to refrain from responding. "Just keep marchin', boys. Eyes front!"

The cadets tried to ignore the jeers and comments coming in their direction from the side of the road. It took all their willpower, but the discipline which had been a part of their routine at the Institute proved to be the difference. They maintained their composure, and the entire corps passed the veterans without any further incident.

"Who do they think they are," demanded Stanard, after the cadets had passed beyond the veterans' hearing distance.

"Don't worry about them," cautioned Wise. "Just do yer job and ignore them."

If Wise could have foreseen the future, he could have also told Stanard that this was only the first of several encounters the cadets would have with veteran regiments over the next several days. The boys were not about to be welcomed with open arms by any of the regular regiments.

And the rain continued to fall.

                    *   *   *

"Staunton—two miles," Ship shouted back to the cadets as he passed the sign post.

A cheer immediately went up. The day's march was nearing its end. The cadets would be meeting up with General Breckinridge in Staunton.

Earlier in the afternoon Ship had gone on to Staunton ahead of the corps, hoping to receive more explicit orders from Breckinridge. Breckinridge had told Ship that there would be no lengthy delay at Staunton. After an overnight camp, the march would continue down the Valley.

The cadets had been looking forward to their arrival in Staunton. They had already tired of marching, and for a time, at least until Ship relayed Breckinridge's latest instructions, Staunton represented the end of their trek. When Ship had told them that they were going to continue at least one more day, their hopes had rapidly deflated. More marching! This was not the message they had hoped their leader would bring back.

The town of Staunton represented more than simply a destination, however. Several of the cadets had made plans for their evening hours after they reached Staunton.

The town was the home of several girls' schools, and many of the boys had set their sights on meeting the young ladies who attended these institutions.

Others had different plans. Private Carrington Taylor of Company C was a native of Staunton, and he planned to visit his mother. He had convinced several of his friends to go with him, and a home cooked meal was to be their reward.

As the corps approached the town they saw other regiments camped beside the pike. If any of the boys had harbored thoughts that their earlier encounter with the veteran regiment was an isolated incident, those thoughts were quickly dispelled.

Many of the veterans along the road stopped in mid-task when the cadets passed, staring at them intently. Many said nothing, and for those the cadets were truly grateful. Others, obviously more opinionated about the use of the cadets, spoke out.

"Where y'all from?" one of the men shouted to the passing cadets in what appeared to be a friendly tone.

"Virginia Military Institute," came the proud reply from several of the boys at once.

"Virginia Military Institute?" the man shouted back. "That there's a school fer girls, ain't it?" His friends responded with a chorus of laughter.

"Welcome to Staunton, girls!" shouted another soldier in a high-pitched falsetto voice.

Ship took command of the situation at once, ordering the corps to remain silent and continue marching. As before, the cadets were models of self-discipline.

With the town in sight, a group of soldiers who gave the appearance of having been in the field since the beginning of the war began to serenade the cadets, singing "Rock-A-Bye Baby" at the top of their voices. Not only could they not carry a tune very well, their less than subtle message was not well received by the cadets. While the singers and their friends laughed uproariously at their attempt at humor, the cadets clenched their fists, pursed their lips, and did their best to ignore the men. Staring straight ahead, the boys held their anger in check, forcing themselves to remain quiet.

Reaching the outskirts of town in a light rain, James Crocken raised his fife and began to play "The Girl I left Behind Me," and the boys picked up their steps. Nearly exhausted after two days of marching, and feeling the effects of the all-day rain, they were energized by the song, and they marched proudly into the town.

Spying an open area, Ship called a halt and directed the boys to set up camp. Before dismissing them, he stood before them and spoke in what, for Ship, passed as a soft voice.

"You boys did well today, and I'm proud of all of yuh," he said. "You didn't say a word to those soldiers that was makin' fun of yuh, and I know how hard that was. It was hard fer me, too. But y'all did good. Believe it or not, they're on our side, and if they're called on to fight they'll fight as hard as any soldiers ever fought. So don't think too harsh of them. They're jest havin' their fun. If all goes well we'll get our chance to show them how a VMI cadet can fight."

The cadets listened intently. They knew Ship was right, but it still would have felt good to tell the soldiers just what they thought of their jokes and their songs.

"Now," Ship continued, "there's a lot goin' on here, with all these troops in town, and it ain't all good. So, just to make sure we don't have any problems, I'm gonna have to restrict everyone to camp while we're in Staunton."

That was less than welcome news for those who had plans for their evening. As the boys prepared camp, Carrington Taylor made his way to Jack Stanard, John Wise, and Louis Wise. The four were disappointed for a few minutes at the thought of missing out on a good meal at Taylor's home, but then decided that Ship wouldn't really miss them if they slipped away for a few hours. "We'll run the blockade," Stanard had said, and they did.

Later in the evening, after a fine meal at Mrs. Taylor's, Stanard excused himself and moved into an adjoining room. "I think I'll take a few minutes and write my mother a letter," he explained.

While the others sat and enjoyed a pleasant conversation with Mrs. Taylor, regaling her with stories about life as a cadet, Stanard sat at a desk to begin his letter. Hesitant to write anything which would alarm his mother, he decided to let her know where he was and why he was here, but opted to omit any details which could give her concern. He would be back at the Institute by the time she received the letter, anyway, so why write something which would upset her?

"My darling Mother," he wrote. "No doubt a letter from this place will take you greatly by surprise."[2] He told of the call from General Breckinridge and the march to Staunton. He mentioned the Union army and the fact that they were advancing up the Valley, but decided not to tell her any more than that. Instead, he changed the subject, telling her how his feet hurt and thanking her for a package he had received just before leaving VMI. After some small talk, he closed with a prayer for her good health.

The letter finished, Stanard set the pencil aside and read what he had written. Satisfied that it would not overly alarm his mother, he folded it and placed it in his pocket, where it would be safe until he had an opportunity to mail it. He then went back into the parlor to join his friends and some of the girls of Staunton who had stopped by when they learned that young Taylor had returned home, and had brought some of his friends.

The evening passed by all too quickly, and soon it was time for the cadets to make their way back to camp. They still had to figure a way to get back into camp without arousing suspicion. They filled their haversacks at Mrs. Taylor's insistence, placing some cakes and dry clothing inside. Bidding the girls farewell, and thanking Mrs. Taylor for her hospitality, John and Louis Wise, Jack Stanard, and Carrington Taylor stepped outside.

"Y'all take good care of Cary for me," she said happily to the other three.

"We'll do that, Mrs. Taylor," responded Stanard.

With a wave, the comrades passed through the gate and began their trek back to camp, arriving a short time later to discover that their absence had not been detected.

"No demerits this time, Jack," Louis Wise had joked.

---

[2] The complete text of Stanard's letter can be found in Appendix D.

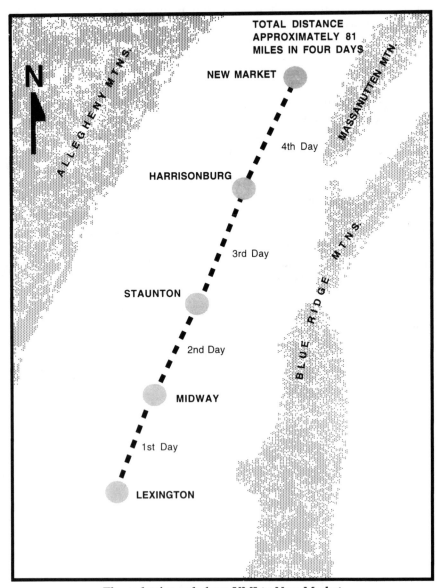

The cadets' march from VMI to New Market

Map by Author

8

It was now the morning of the third day of the march, May 13, 1864. The cadets had wakened at dawn to see that the rains were still falling. The sky was the color of lead and there was no indication that the weather would be clearing up any time soon.

At Breckinridge's direction, the boys of VMI fell into line behind Echols' Brigade, and another day of marching began. It was just starting to turn daylight.

As the cadets marched with the rest of Breckinridge's army, they observed the first signs of what was to come. Several times they were forced to march on the side of the road to allow travelers to pass. These people were fleeing Sigel's advance, and did not hesitate to tell anyone who would listen why they were leaving.

"An army of 15,000 men, that's what I heard they have," said one old farmer from his seat on an old buckboard. "I ain't gonna give 'em a chance to take nothin' of mine. I got it all on the back 'a this wagon and I'm leavin the Valley till things is safe to come back."

The farther the boys marched, the more civilian activity they saw. First in twos and threes, then by the dozens, the displaced inhabitants of the Valley passed the cadets in every type of conveyance imaginable. Beautiful carriages wended their way along the crowded turnpike behind broken down wagons that appeared unlikely to make it another mile. All had one thing in common: each one was filled to capacity with personal belongings.

Behind the wagons came the livestock. Farmers driving their cattle, their pigs, their sheep, and occasionally even their ducks and geese. Now the cadets had to contend with not only the constant rain and mud, they also had to march through the manure left behind by the animals. This was not what they had expected just a few nights ago when they were overjoyed with the news that they would be marching to join General Breckinridge. The life of a soldier was no longer as glamorous as it had first appeared.

Then, the full impact of the war became apparent. By the middle of the morning they saw their first wounded soldiers. Covered with mud, many of them had mere stumps where legs had once been, or an empty sleeve that once had housed an arm. There was no joking in ranks any longer. Soberly, the boys made their way down the turnpike, averting their eyes when the wounded passed.

A colonel on a mangy appearing chestnut mare rode past the cadets at a full gallop. Reaching the rear of the artillery, he wheeled around and returned to the front, confronting Ship.

"Double your columns!" he shouted to Ship, over the noise of a passing carriage. "Make sure you have no stragglers!"

Ship gritted his teeth in anger. "These are the cadets of the Virginia Military Institute!" he shouted back. "And you will find, sir, that the cadets of the Virginia Military Institute do not straggle!"

The colonel, surprised by Ship's unexpected response, did not have an immediate answer. Then, he sputtered, "Well, y'all jest see to it that they don't."

"I'll be sure to do that!" Ship shot back sarcastically.

The colonel glared at Ship for several seconds, then reared his horse and rode off toward the rear of the column, presumably to find a friendlier audience.

With the rain continuing to fall, the cadets marched another mile, then took a welcome break to allow Ship to confer with some officers from Wharton's Brigade, which was marching just in front of them.

As the boys slumped wearily to the ground, several of the men from the Twenty-Third Virginia Battalion of Echols' Brigade also stopped to rest, not more than twenty yards away. No longer trustful of any regular soldiers, the boys eyed them warily without speaking.

The veterans spoke quietly among themselves for several minutes, none of them giving any indication that he had even seen the cadets. Then, one of the men of the Twenty-Third glanced in the direction of the resting cadets and caught Private Philip Wood staring at him.

"Never seen a real live soldier up close, boy?" the man said.

Embarassed, the fifteen-year-old Wood hurriedly broke eye contact, averting his gaze toward the ground.

"I was talkin' to y'all, son," the man persisted, walking toward Wood. The cadets tensed, not knowing what the stranger had in mind. One thing they were sure of, though, Wood was not going to fight this man alone!

"Y'all don't have to be scared, boy," the man said. "Nobody here's gonna hurt yuh. I was just wonderin' if yuh ever seen any soldiers this close before, is all."

Wood looked at the man, than answered in a shaky voice, "No, sir."

"Well, then," said the man with a laugh, "take yerself a good look." He held his arms out at his sides and slowly turned in a circle. "Don't look no different than any other man, I reckon," the man went on. "Ceptin' we prob'ly don't smell as good."

His friends laughed.

"That's a sure fact," one of them remarked, walking over.

Slowly recognizing that these men meant to cause them no problems, the boys gathered around and began talking to them.

"Y'all are the first ones to talk respectful to us," said Wood.

"That a fact?" a thin, wiry corporal said. "And why do yuh reckon that may be?"

"Don't rightly know," answered Wood. "They just haven't been very friendly."

"Well, we're not that bad," said the corporal. "We're all fightin' fer the same thing, is how I sees it. Don't make no sense to me to make someone mad at yuh when yuh might need 'im to save yer hide some day."

The man's friends murmured their agreement.

The ice broken, the boys began asking questions.

"Y'all ever see a real Yankee?" asked John Wise of a man standing next to him.

"More'n I care to remember, son," he said with a big smile, revealing several missing teeth. "And some of them were closer than I care to remember, too."

"What are they like?" quizzed Stanard. "They good fighters?"

"The ones I seen ain't no slouches," the man replied, as his friends chuckled. "Mebbe I seen the wrong ones, but the ones I seen fought purty good, as I recall."

"They good shots?" Stanard persisted.

The man drew himself up proudly, then said, "Not as good as we are!"

A man in a checkered shirt interjected, "They's a lot better foragers, though, wouldn't yuh say so, Joseph?"

Joseph, the corporal, nodded his agreement. "That there's the gospel," he replied. "Don't matter where we go, either. Anytime we happen to be followin' the Yankees through an area they's no food left anywhere. I swear they don't even leave us the bark on the trees!"

"Ain't none too smart, though," said the man in the checkered shirt. "I was talkin' to some 'a them prisoners we seen yesterday. One 'a them told me they was on the march last week and the brigade in front 'a them wasn't payin no mind to their campfires. Next thing they knew, they had the woods on fire in a buncha places."

The men laughed. "Sounds like Yankees," one said.

"Not only that," the speaker struggled, almost convulsed with laughter, "fer the next two hours them boys had to go through fire on each side 'a the road. Burned their horses' tails and legs somethin' awful!"

Even the most staid cadets were now laughing out loud at the self-imposed misfortune of the Yankees.

When the laughter died down, Wood asked a question that had been plaguing him since he had seen the first wounded men walking to the rear. "Y'all think there's many out there waitin' fer us?" he asked.

Joseph smiled. "They's more of them than they is of us, and that's a fact. 'Course, their generals is tellin' them they's more of us, so I reckon it depends on who y'all decide to listen to!"

The cadets, unsure of themselves, hesitated, then joined in when the men of the Twenty-Third laughed again.

"Only difference is, we all speak the King's English," Joseph went on, pleased to see that he had an interested audience. "Some 'a them Yank regiments, well, I hear tell that some 'a them don't have no two men speakin' the same language. Their officers have to give commands in Dutch, German, French, Irish, . . . jest name it!"

"Heard that myself, personal," offered a sergeant.

"I did, too," agreed another man.

Just as Stanard was about to ask if Yankees were really eight feet tall, as he had heard, Ship gave the command to fall back into ranks.

"Y'all take care of yerselves, boys," said Joseph as the boys lined up.

"Thank yuh, sir," answered Wood. "We'll be sure to do that."

And with that, the cadets marched off, leaving behind the first friendly regiment of regular soldiers they had met on this march. The conversation had lifted their spirits and they talked animatedly among themselves until the effort of the march made it too difficult to talk any more than was necessary.

The mud and manure were now making the walking very difficult. Footing was becoming quite slippery, and marching took a great deal of concentration now. In addition, strict attention was necessary to avoid being struck by one of the steadily growing stream of fleeing carts and carriages.

Finally, the day's march came to an end. The cadets found themselves setting up camp somewhere just south of Harrisonburg. Their campsite was a small clearing in the woods.

After eating, they huddled around their fires, trying to dry their soggy clothing, when a cavalry detail passed. They rode by slowly, having in tow several surly looking Union prisoners who did not appear interested in walking any faster than necessary. One of the guards gave a greeting to the nearest cadets, then said, "Y'all wanna stay away from them high trees over yonder, what with all the lightnin' we're gettin'. Jest heard someone sayin' that lightnin' hit right smack in the middle of the Twenty-Third

Virginia Battalion back the road a piece. Hurt a corporal real bad. Some other fellers was hurt too, I heard, but they ain't as bad."

The cadets looked at one another. There was no way of knowing if it had been the same men they had talked to earlier in the day, but the Twenty-Third didn't have all that many men to start with. And the corporal who had been struck. Was it Joseph? They would never find out. But the boys went to sleep that night with heavy hearts.

*   *   *

Saturday, May 14, 1864 dawned much the same as the previous two mornings had: with the rain still coming down and the cadets still soaked to the skin. Their uniforms, while still looking better than anyone else's they had seen on the march, were beginning to show the effects of the weather. And they were getting heavy as they absorbed the water.

The groups of wounded soldiers passing toward the rear became more frequent. The estimates of the enemy's superior numbers, however, were the one thing that remained constant. No matter who was doing the estimating, the result was always the same: the Union had far more men up front than did Breckinridge's army. "You've got hot work in store for yuh, boys," one of the wounded men had shouted to the cadets as they passed.

The ranks of the cadets had thinned by three boys who had become ill on the march and had been left behind in Staunton. Everyone else, including Tutwiler, was still marching, and the cadets were all ready to do something different. They didn't care what it was, as long as they could do it sitting down.

"We gonna march er fight Yankees?" became the cry.

Except for the unrelenting rain, the day's march was uneventful. There were no more encounters with any of the regular regiments, no additional illnesses, no more itinerary changes. As it had been doing for three days, the long column continued its relentless march northward. Sooner or later they would have to run into Sigel.

The evening encampment found the cadets, as a group, unhappy. The fun had passed long ago. Marching in a driving rain for three days on muddy, manure-strewn roads will foul even the best of moods, and there was no denying that the mood was foul this evening. Right now, the target of the cadets' ire was the food. The attitude being what it was, the focus of their aggravation could have been almost anything, but the food presented itself as a convenient target.

"What is this stuff?" inquired Louis Wise, holding it up and examining it closely.

"Raw pork," came the answer from Samuel Atwill.

Wise, in an uncharacteristically bad humor, responded, "I don't eat nothin' raw!"

Atwill, his attitude reflecting the effort of the past three days, snapped, "Well, cook it then and quit gripin'!"

Private John Howard looked at Atwill as if he had just committed heresy. "I've always made it a point to avoid any kind of cooking whenever it was possible," he said crabbily. "If I wanted to be a cook I wouldn't have gone to the Institute."

Atwill stood up. Turning to Wise, he said, "Then you can cook the stuff," and turning back toward Howard, he continued, "And you can eat it the way it is!" Atwill stomped off, presumably to find more amiable dinner partners.

Howard watched Atwill walk away. Looking at Wise, he said, "Guess it ain't possible to eat pig sides raw, is it? Reckon I'm gonna have to cook it, but I jest want y'all to know, it ain't somethin' I'm gonna like doin'."

Although most of the other boys also spent considerable amounts of time complaining about their evening meal, all were ravenously hungry and, despite the complaints, there were no leftovers to be found when the meal was finished.

As the day drew to a close, John Wise took his turn as corporal of the guard. One by one the cadets crawled under soggy blankets and tried to get comfortable. Wise drew himself closer to the fire and involuntarily shot a look skyward as if to see if there was any end to the rainfall. There didn't appear to be.

Long after the last cadet had gone to sleep, or tried to, Wise heard a soft rustling behind him. Turning around, he spotted Stanard approaching.

"Jack!" he exclaimed. "What are you doin' awake. Y'all run the blockade again without tellin' me?"

"No," Stanard replied solemnly. "Jest couldn't sleep. Thought I'd keep yuh company for a while."

Wise had been occupying himself by watching what appeared to be campfires in the distance, just about at the limits of where a man could see. He had been wondering if they were friendly. Having someone to talk to would be a welcome diversion.

"Glad to have the company," Wise responded. "If y'all are havin' trouble sleepin' I highly recommend that y'all ask to be corporal of the guard. I guarantee y'all will have trouble keepin' yer eyes open. There's somethin' about havin' to stay awake that makes a person sleepy. Did yuh ever notice that?"

Stanard uncharacteristically refrained from saying anything. Wise immediately suspected that something was bothering him, but decided not to ask what it was. Stanard would tell him if he wanted Wise to know.

And he soon did. Stanard absentmindedly poked at the fire with a stick, sending a shower of sparks upward, where their ashes disappeared into the inky darkness. "You been givin' much thought to the battle, John?" he asked after a few minutes.

"What battle?" asked Wise, innocently.

"The battle we're headin' for," answered Stanard.

"No," said Wise. "I can't say that I have. I mean, I've thought about it a little, I reckon, but I haven't tried to guess what I'm gonna do, or how I'm gonna react. Like Clinedinst says, yuh can't plan those things, anyway. Yuh just do 'em. Besides, we're probably not gonna be put into the fight anyway."

"Yeah, I guess," Stanard said quietly. He was unusually somber.

"We've been well trained," said Wise. "We know tactics. We know how to shoot. And we know how to follow orders. There isn't much else we have any control over."

"Y'all are right, I reckon," said Stanard. "But I've been gettin' this funny feelin' over and over for the past couple of days."

"What kind of funny feelin'?" Wise inquired.

Stanard looked at his friend and roommate. "John, I think I'm gonna get killed in this battle."

Wise appeared shocked. He had not expected this kind of a comment from anyone, let alone Stanard. Not happy-go-lucky Jack. Nothing ever seemed to bother him. Wise had often thought that Stanard should probably let things bother him a little more sometimes. Maybe he wouldn't have so many demerits. But this was too far the other way. Being serious was one thing, but Jack was being too grim now.

"That's ridiculous, Jack," Wise scoffed. "You aren't gonna get killed. Why would you even think such a thing?"

"I don't know," said Stanard, a tear glistening at the corner of his eye in the yellow glow of the fire. "I can't explain it. It's just this feelin' I've been gettin'. It pops into my head even when I'm not thinkin' about it. Y'all can call it ridiculous, or y'all can call it fate. Whatever it is, and whatever y'all believe in, I just can't get it out of my mind. I keep thinkin' I'm gonna die in this fight, and it scares me real bad."

"Well," said Wise, "you aren't gonna die, so quit thinkin' about it. We have a lot of things we're gonna do yet, you and me, once we get back to the Institute. Besides, Old Specs still has some demerits he needs to give you."

Stanard smiled ruefully. "I hope y'all are right. "

"I am right," Wise said emphatically. He may have said it, but he wasn't sure he really meant it. Stanard was obviously bothered by this feeling. It wasn't something he was making up, or just talking about to be dramatic. Wise could tell that he really believed it. And this presented a concern to Wise.

Preoccupied, Stanard continued to poke at the fire with the stick. Try as he might, he was unable to shake the mental vision he had of himself lying on the battlefield.

"Why don't you try to get some sleep, Jack," Wise finally said, unsure of what else he could say. "Y'all are gonna feel a whole lot better in the mornin'. That is, if this rain ever stops."

Stanard looked at him, then tossed the stick aside. "Maybe that'll help," he agreed, and rose to leave. "Some of the boys found an old church over yonder. We crawled through the window to see if it would keep out the rain. The roof ain't much, but it beats sleepin' outside. I got there too late to get one of the pews, though, so I'm gonna have to sleep on the floor."

"Y'all want to trade places?" Wise asked mischievously.

"No, I reckon not," answered Stanard. He looked around. "I don't see much shelter here, either."

Wise forced a wry grin and nodded.

"Y'all are a real good friend, John," Stanard said awkwardly. "Thanks fer listenin'."

Wise slapped his friend on the back. "Get some sleep," he repeated softly. He didn't trust himself to say more.

Stanard departed, and Wise walked around the fire several times to try to sort out his thoughts. Stanard's fear of his impending death on the battlefield haunted him. What if he was right? Wise tried to push the thought from his mind, but it kept coming back. Even if Stanard was wrong, and logic dictated that he was, Wise felt concern because his friend was troubled.

Wise pulled his collar up around his neck to try to keep some of the rain from running down his back. As uncomfortable as Wise was in his wet clothes, coupled with the thoughts of Stanard which kept creeping out of the recesses of his brain, it was highly unlikely that he would have to worry about falling asleep, no matter how tired he felt.

Several hours passed, and the most activity Wise had seen was an old raccoon which had wandered into the camp. Wise had watched him for several minutes before he had melted into the shadows beyond the reaches of the light given off by the fire.

It must have been some time after midnight when Wise heard the steady pounding of hoofbeats approaching on the turnpike. The horse stopped somewhere beyond the reaches of Wise's vision. Then he heard the voice of one of the sentinels calling to him.

"Corporal of the guard!" he heard.

Rushing to the sound of the voice, he noticed a soldier standing beside the sentinel. The man introduced himself as an aide to General Breckinridge, and he said he had orders to be given to Commander Ship. Wise ran to where he remembered the commander to be sleeping and quickly wakened him. Ship tried to get his sleepy eyes to focus as Wise quickly relayed to him the news that General Breckinridge had sent an aide with orders.

Ship pulled on his boots and ran with Wise to the sentinel's post, stumbling several times in the dark over unseen and unknown objects. The aide began speaking even before Ship reached him.

"Commander Ship?" he inquired.

"That's me," answered Ship. "What kind of information do you have?"

"Orders from General Breckinridge, sir," the aide said sharply. "You are to bring the cadets north to New Market as quickly as you can. General Breckinridge will meet you there and explain."

"Are we the only ones he's called for?" asked Ship.

"No, sir!" said the aide. "Everyone's gettin' the same message. There's been a lot of skirmishin' goin' on there for the past couple of days and it looks like it's about to get serious. The general needs everyone!"

"We'll be leavin' as soon as we can get everybody ready!" replied Ship over his shoulder, already starting back to the main part of the encampment.

Turning to Wise as they went, he said, "Rouse everyone. Tell them to be ready to march at once. We'll assemble on the pike. And tell them to be quiet! No drums, no loud talking, no noise of any kind. We don't want to be the ones to let the Yankees know we're gettin' ready to move."

Wise rushed to get the cadets moving. It didn't take much, despite the fact that they had only had a few hours sleep. As quietly as they could, they gathered all their gear and ran to the pike.

"I should have guessed this," grumbled Stanard. "First night I get to sleep inside and we have to move!"

When all were assembled, Ship mounted his horse so he could be seen. "We've been given orders to move at once to New Market," he began. "There has been fighting going on in that area for several days, and I have been informed that General Breckinridge expects it to get worse. He wants everyone, includin' us, to get there as soon as we can. Now, I don't know what we're gonna get into once we're there. Maybe nothin'. But we may be called on to fight. I know a lot of y'all have been lookin' forward to this for a long time. It looks like we may finally get our chance to show what a VMI cadet can do. If that happens, I have confidence that you will do your job well."

The darkness prevented him from seeing more than a few of the boys in the front ranks, but he knew they all looked the same. Those in the front were tense and grim. Ship instinctively knew the rest wore the same expressions.

"Before we leave, I think we should have a word of prayer," said Ship. "Colonel Gilham, will you do us the honor?"

The acting superintendent, seated on a horse immediately adjacent to Ship's, said in a barely audible voice, "I would be honored, Mr. Ship. But I truly believe that Mr. Preston should have that honor tonight."

Turning to Preston, Ship said, "Would you, Frank?"

Preston nodded and stepped forward. Preston was an instructor of English, Latin, and Tactics at the Institute, having taken on that position when he was wounded so badly at Winchester that he had lost an arm. He had begrudgingly accepted the likelihood that he would never see battle again, and now, standing here on a dark road in the middle of the Shenandoah Valley, with the rain pelting him in the face, he realized that he may get one more opportunity. He raised his only arm reverently and began to pray.

"Kind Heavenly Father," he began, as the boys bowed their heads reverently. "We are about to march into the unknown. We don't know what lies up the road in New Market, but we expect it isn't going to be good. We ask your protection for these fine boys. We ask that you also watch over their homes, their mothers and fathers, until they are all re-united with their families. Bless our young country, Father, whether we are on our way to victory or defeat. And if any of our number should die in the coming battle, we ask that you take us into eternity with you. May we all be safe in the coming battle, and may we show mercy to our enemy. Amen!"

Many of the boys in the front ranks could be seen wiping their cheeks on their sleeves when Preston finished.

"Nice prayer, Frank," Ship said softly. Then, to the cadets, he said, "Let's get goin'!"

As the corps marched away from their campfires, the night became as dark as pitch. The boys could barely make out the shadows of those in front of them, as the clouds obscured the moon and stars entirely.

One of the cadets whispered to the boy on his right, "If they are going to pray over us, maybe they think we're gonna get into a fight after all."

His friend agreed, then added in a soft voice, "Y'know somethin' else? This is Sunday, and all of Stonewall's big victories were on Sundays. Mebbe that's a good sign!"

The boys marched in silence for the remainder of the night. By dawn they were within a few miles of their destination. They halted and stepped to the side of the road. The rain was now torrential. They would wait there for nearly two hours.

Occasionally, in the dim light of the gathering dawn, they could see flashes, followed by the unmistakable roar of artillery. Although the day had scarcely started, the two sides were fighting already!

Finally, when it appeared that the sky was as light as it was going to get, the word was passed down that it was time to move again. Obediently, the boys followed the men of Wharton's Brigade down the Valley Turn-pike, moving closer with each step to the village of New Market and the sound of the guns.

There would be one last encounter with the regular soldiers before the cadets reached New Market. Passing the men of Wharton's Brigade, who had stopped for a short rest, the veterans cheered them on with a shout of encouragement.

"Go get 'em, VMI!" one man yelled.

Then, with the gallows humor known only to those who have been in battle and faced death before, the veterans began to chide the boys for the serious expressions each was wearing.

Brandishing a pair of scissors high above his head, one man marched alongside the cadets and inquired, "Who wants a lock of hair cut off to be sent home after yer killed?"

Another shouted, "You boys like rosewood or pine fer yer coffins?"

Their friends looked on in amusement, and the cadets quickly realized that they probably did look far more serious than the situation actually called for. After all, unless today was different, they weren't even going to get close to the actual battle.

Slowly they slogged through the rain and mud, passing mile markers indicating that they were within five miles of New Market. Then four. Then three, two, and one.

Behind them the boys heard cheering. As the sound drew closer they moved to the side of the road to allow the recipient of the cheers to pass. Soon, an entourage appeared, led by a tall, handsome man with a large, dark mustache. He rode so smoothly and fluidly that he gave the appearance that he was simply an extension of his horse, a beautiful blood-bay thoroughbred. It was the general himself, General Breckinridge!

Cadet Charles Randolph, caught up in the excitement, instinctively shouted, "Three cheers for General Breckinridge!"

The general reined his horse and looked down at the cadets. "Boys," he said, " I deeply admire your spirit. But you must be as quiet as possible. We are near the enemy, and they could be anywhere. You must be cautious. We have serious work to do!"

Appropriately chastised, the boys watched the general ride ahead, then looked anxiously at the heavy thickets on either side of the road. If the general was right, the Yankees could be behind any one of those bushes right now! From that point on, vigilance became the watchword.

As they reformed their ranks in preparation for the final leg of the march into New Market, the men under Wharton and Echols hurried past. The cadets quickly fell in behind the last man.

Not a word was spoken. The sound of the skirmishing was growing louder, and finally a gentle breeze brought the acrid scent of gunpowder to their nostrils. Rounding a bend in the road, they saw it! Just ahead on the right were the first houses of New Market.

They followed Echols' men as they rushed up a hill on the left side of the turnpike. Reaching the top they had a good view of the entire area. Off

General John C. Breckinridge, commander of the Confederate forces, at New Market
Courtesy of Hall of Valor
Civil War Museum

to the right they could make out the wigwag motion of the Signal Corps. Through the rain and fog it was difficult to tell whose it was.

Stanard poked his roommate, Willis Harris, with his elbow and wordlessly pointed to a churchyard below them and several hundred yards in front. Harris followed his friend's gaze. There, pointed at the very hill they were standing on, was a six gun battery, the guns scattered among the tombstones. As they watched, a puff of smoke spat out from the muzzle of one of the guns, the smoke ring hanging just above the gun crew in the heavy atmosphere. A second or two later a muffled thud reached the boys' ears, indicating that the cannon had indeed been fired. This was quickly followed by a strange whooshing sound passing overhead as the ball sailed harmlessly past. Although the ball had missed them by a significant distance, the boys instinctively ducked. They were being fired on!

Nearby an old veteran laughed at the boys' consternation.

"Don't worry, boys," he shouted. "They's jest lettin' us know they seen us and they know we're here. They ain't gonna waste no more shots fer a while!"

The man was right. There were no additional shots toward the hill, although the guns remained aimed in that direction, and the cadets watched with slack jaws as the skirmishers for both sides maneuvered below.

This is why they had come. They had wanted to fight, and now they were here. The next few hours would determine if they would really be fighters or, as in the past, spectators once more.

9

"Sarah," Jacob Bushong said with more than a hint of anxiety in his voice, "I think we'd best be gettin' ourselves down into the cellar now."

These were welcome words to Sarah's ears. She had wanted to retire to the safety of the cellar earlier in the day, but Jacob had scoffed at her suggestion. "Won't be no need fer that," he had said. Sarah had disagreed, but did not voice that disagreement to her husband.

The skirmishing that had been going on for the past two days in New Market had made her very nervous. No shots had been heard near the farmhouse yet, but Sarah believed that it would only be a matter of time. After all, she had been seeing Union soldiers scurrying up and down the nearby turnpike every time she had stepped out of the house. First a cavalry regiment, then a few supply wagons. She instinctively knew they weren't just passing through, despite what Jacob had been telling her. An army passing through did just that; they passed through. These soldiers appeared to be in no hurry to leave.

"This never would have happened if Stonewall was still here," she thought.

Jacob, too, had been worried, but he didn't want to alarm Sarah. As a means of reassurance to his wife, he had tried to maintain his daily routine, taking care of the stock, mending fences, and pruning the trees in the orchard. Trying to give the appearance of nonchalance to his spouse, he had refrained from retreating to the cellar for as long as he had dared, but now it appeared to be time. He had just returned from the barn, from where he had seen a Union regiment forming a line of battle just beyond the orchard. Not just an encampment. An actual line of battle. The Yankees were now close to the farm and appeared to be intent on staying for a while.

Jacob had watched in anger as the men had taken their respective positions; anger not only at the fact that soldiers in blue uniforms would be here in the Valley in the first place, but also at the damage to the fragile wheat crop which was now being trampled under the brogans of the invaders. He could only imagine what things must look like in town after two days of skirmishing.

"There probably ain't nothin' left!" he thought to himself.

As long as the soldiers had been in town they had presented no immediate threat to either the Bushongs or their farm. The only consequence of their nearby presence had been that Jacob and Sarah had been sharing their home with their livestock for several days now, making sure the Yankees could not steal the animals. The smell in the house had become less than pleasant, but it was no more unpleasant than the idea that their stock would be used to fill the bellies of the Northerners. There had been no discussion between Jacob and Sarah concerning which was worse. Keeping the stock in the house went without questioning. It didn't merit discussion. After all, if the Yankees got hungry they could always go back down the Valley to get something to eat!

Jacob had stood in the doorway of the barn, watching the men scurrying about on the knoll north of the orchard for several minutes before going back to the house. He did not appear to be in any immediate danger, and the soldiers, if they saw him at all, obviously perceived him to be of little threat to them.

The formation of a line of battle so close to the house could only mean one thing: a fight must be imminent. Jacob Bushong had not been aware that the Confederate army was that close, but apparently they were. The thought of a battle on his property frightened, yet exhilarated, him. As long as he and Sarah were safe in the cellar, he had no qualms about allowing the Confederate army to use his farm, or anything on it, as long as it served to drive the Yankees back down the Valley!

*   *   *

The cadets took in the scene that was spread out below them. Nearly unable to grasp it all in one look, Moses Ezekiel and Louis Wise were mesmerized. Their heads moved as though mounted on swivels. Ezekiel couldn't help thinking that he would like to have the opportunity to sketch the scene that was unfolding in the valley.

"Let us through! Let us through!" came the shout. It was Captain Minge trying to maneuver his artillery guns through the crowd. The cadets quickly stepped aside to allow their companions sufficient room to pass.

With space to get through the crowd the cadet artillerists quickly and professionally joined the rest of the artillery on the crest of the hill and unlimbered, taking a position on the right of the line. Under the watchful eyes of their fellow cadets they set up their guns and aimed toward the battery in the cemetery below. When all was ready the first cadet gun fired, to the accompaniment of a loud cheer from the entire corps of cadets. The smoke ring from their cannon hovered above them like a halo. The shot missed its mark by quite a distance, but it didn't really matter. The important thing was that they were finally shooting at the enemy! The cadets, or the artillerists at least, would never again have to offer excuses to others for never having been in battle!

Private James Larrick turned to his fellow cadets from his position at one of the guns. Larrick, at age 25 the oldest cadet at New Market, gave his friends a smile as big as the Shenandoah Valley itself. Larrick had the unusual distinction of having served in a Virginia cavalry regiment before the war had started, and had been with the regiment at Charlestown, now in West Virginia, to serve with the guards for John Brown prior to his hanging. Ironically, the cadets of VMI had been there during the hanging itself. Larrick had resigned from his regiment in 1862 and enrolled at VMI. Today, he was a real soldier again.

The muffled cracks of gunfire could occasionally be heard from the valley below, and the artillery fire from both sides added to the din. Already the town was bathed in the blue smoke of burned gunpowder, and skirmishers from both sides could occasionally be observed stealthily moving from place to place, using whatever protection the topography and vegetation afforded.

Ship, his beard plastered against his face by the rain, gathered John Wise, Jack Stanard, Washington Redwood, and Pierre Woodlief around him. With the sounds of skirmishing in the background he gave them the orders none of them wanted to hear: they were to stay with the wagons and guard them against looters. If Breckinridge and his army happened to be driven back, their instructions were to abandon the wagons and get to a place of safety. Their crestfallen looks had told Ship that they were, indeed, primed for the battle.

Ship could not be concerned with hurt feelings right now, however. There were too many other duties to be tended to, and the four boys would have to deal with their moods as best they could, without his input. Ship had neither the time nor the inclination to discuss it, and he turned and rapidly made his way to another group of cadets where he appointed several as litter bearers. At least they would be a part of the action, even if they wouldn't be fighting. They only hoped they wouldn't be too busy.

As the four shuffled back to the wagons to take their positions, Stanard was the first to give voice to the feelings the other three were also experiencing. "Marched all this way in a rainstorm just to watch over some stupid wagons!" he complained. "I wouldn't mind so much if we all were watchin' the wagons, but why just us four? Why can't we get to fight like the rest?"

"You're right, Jack," said Woodlief. "Do you have any idea how much we're gonna have to listen to from the others once they find out we have baggage detail? They ain't never gonna let us hear the end of it!"

Giving vent to his frustrations, Stanard picked up a stone and threw it at the nearest wagon. It hit the side and bounced harmlessly away, the noise barely audible over the sounds coming from the valley on the other side of the hill.

Some distance away, General Breckinridge saw the display of emotion. Despite the seriousness of the situation, he could not hold back a slight smile at the sight of the unsoldierly exhibition. General Imboden had said the cadets were ready. The show of frustration he had just witnessed appeared to bear that out. Breckinridge took it as a good sign.

Stanard did not know that Breckinridge had seen his display of emotion. It would not have mattered to Stanard if he had. Although Stanard was not the perfect cadet, he did want to do his part. He may never get a second chance. To have such an opportunity taken from him in this manner was more than he wanted to think about.

Breckinridge, already having forgotten the incident, made his way to the top of the hill. As the men chewed on hardtack and fed their horses, Breckinridge surveyed his position from the crest. He had mapped out a defensive strategy, hoping to entice Sigel's troops to attack him. His current position on this hill, known locally as Shirley's Hill, was a good one for defense. The north branch of the Shenandoah River, to his left, and Smith's Creek, a small stream to his right which was now swollen by the three-day rain, would protect his flanks. The artillery, some one hundred to two hundred feet above the enemy, afforded him a plunging fire, and sporadic woodlots, including a stand of cedars on Shirley's Hill, provided protection from which he could pour enfilading fire on any attackers. He liked what he saw, and he felt no sense of urgency that the Union could dislodge him. At the very worst, he figured, he may have to engage in a prolonged artillery duel. With this position, he would be happy to take his chances with that kind of fight.

Breckinridge felt blessed with the quality of the troops at his disposal. His two small infantry brigades were commanded by John Echols and Gabriel C. Wharton, both more than competent. They led veteran troops, as good as any the South had to offer.

If he had known his opponent's strength at this hour, however, he may have taken a different approach. Sigel, in splitting his army, had only a small contingent of his troops on the field. The 18th Connecticut, 123rd Ohio, and 1st West Virginia Infantries, supported by two batteries commanded by Ewing and Snow, represented Sigel's entire army in New Market at that time. The 34th Massachusetts Infantry was in a position on the next hill, some two miles away and practically hidden by the fog and mist. Julius Stahel's cavalry, also nearly invisible in the haze, stood on the opposite side of the turnpike on the north side of the town. The remainder of Sigel's army was stretched out between New Market and Mount Jackson, some on the march, others merely waiting for orders. Had Breckinridge known this and chosen to attack, it may have been a very short battle indeed.

As it was, Breckinridge had no firm knowledge that it wasn't Sigel's entire army facing him, and he stayed with his original defensive scheme. He called for General Imboden.

"General," Breckinridge said, "I want you to send your cavalry to attack Sigel's position, then retreat back to Shirley's Hill. I want to draw him to us. We will form a line of battle up here and maintain a defensive position."

"Yes, sir," replied General Imboden. Then, glancing toward the Union line now forming, and just visible on the other side of the road at the base of Shirley's Hill, he asked, "Do we know who that is down there?"

"Our scouts tell us that General Moor is down there, but I know little of him," was the answer.

"No matter," replied Imboden, "I'll draw him out."

Imboden's cavalry detachment made several feints at the men in blue, as the cadets, peering over the crest of Shirley's Hill, watched in fascination. None of the cavalry's efforts had the desired effect, however, as the Union soldiers remained in their positions, refusing to accept Imboden's challenge.

Finally Breckinridge had seen enough. He took one last look over the valley, then pulled out his watch and studied it for several moments, as if unsure of his next step. "General," he finally said to Imboden, "We will have to attack them. It is now eleven o'clock, and we can't wait any longer for them to attack us. Call in your cavalry skirmish line."

Turning to Lieutenant Colonel George Edgar of the 22nd Virginia Battalion, Breckinridge said with a hint of disgust, "Well, I have offered him battle and he declines to advance on us. So, I shall advance on him!"

Turning back to Imboden, he said emphatically, "We can attack and whip them here, and I'll do it!" The men around him murmured their agreement, as well as their approval of this bold new plan.

As Imboden recalled his troops, Breckinridge called his commanding officers together. As they assembled, he spelled out his plan.

"General Wharton," he said to the commander of the Second Infantry Brigade. "You will have to take command of the entire line as it lays west of the pike." Breckinridge indicated to Wharton just where he wanted him to position his troops.

As Wharton hustled off to inform his men of the plan and get them into position, Breckinridge turned his attention to a huge man standing to his right. The man was General Echols, commander of the First Brigade. Echols, who stood at six feet four inches and weighed in excess of two hundred fifty pounds, was usually quite jovial, but today he was not his usual smiling self. Plagued by heart problems, he was not feeling well and was not really looking forward to a battle today. He would have preferred to be lying down somewhere, but he knew that could not be. His men needed his presence. A secessionist, he was a graduate of Virginia Military Institute, and had expressed his pride at seeing the cadets from his alma mater on the field. He saluted smartly in spite of his discomfort.

"General Echols, you will follow two hundred yards behind and to General Wharton's right, reaching your troops to a point just across the pike."

Breckinridge indicated with a broad sweep of his sword exactly where he wanted Echols to deploy his troops. Then swinging it in the general direction of the turnpike, he said, "I will have McLaughlin's artillery follow the pike. The reserves will be the VMI cadets and the 26th Virginia Battalion under Colonel Edgar, and they will move with you, to your left and slightly detached, staying behind Wharton."

Echols, with a simple nod of his head, indicated he understood what Breckinridge wanted.

"General Imboden," Breckinridge then said to the cavalry commander, again pointing with his sword in the general direction of the pike. "I want you to take your 18th Virginia Cavalry along with four guns from McClanahan's Battery to the right, east of the pike. If you can, try to cross to the other side of the creek and proceed along the east side toward Mount Jackson. At the point where Smith's Creek enters the Shenandoah, recross the stream and destroy the pike bridge over the river. If we can take New Market, I don't want Sigel to be able to use that bridge as an escape route. If you can burn that bridge we will trap him between us and the two rivers. He's either going to have to surrender to us or risk being destroyed."

Imboden repeated the orders to be sure he had them properly set in his mind, then hurried off to take his position. Imboden liked the part he would be playing in this offensive.

"Mr. Ship?" Breckinridge called.

Ship moved quickly to Breckinridge, saluting sharply.

Breckinridge returned the salute, then gave Ship the orders for which he and the cadets had been waiting so long. "Your boys and Colonel Edgar will constitute the reserves," he said, much to Ship's disappointment. Ship had been hoping for more than reserve status, and he knew the cadets would be dejected when he told them the part they were to play in the coming fight. "Keep your artillery with the main column and take a position about two hundred to three hundred yards behind the line of battle. I want you to maintain that distance as we advance."

"But General," Ship protested, almost pleading, "the boys have waited so long for this. Don't deny them this opportunity. They'll fight hard, sir. I know they will!"

"Mr. Ship," Breckinridge responded, "I do not wish to put the cadets in if I can avoid it. However, I will promise you this much. If the occasion should require it, I will not hesitate to use them freely."

"Thank you, sir," responded Ship, somewhat placated. "I guarantee that the boys will perform gallantly, if asked."

"I'm sure they will, Mr. Ship," answered Breckinridge. "I have the utmost confidence in them. Now, please take your position on Colonel Edgar's right."

A pragmatist, Ship knew there would be no changing Breckinridge's mind. He also did not wish to convey the idea that he could not take orders. He trotted to the corps and relayed Breckinridge's plan. As he had expected, the cadets were not happy being relegated to a reserve function again. However, they accepted it with aplomb.

As the cadets moved into position, the men under Edgar's command could not, nor did they make any effort to, conceal their displeasure at being placed with the boys from VMI.

"Why do we have to wet nurse a bunch of schoolboys when there's serious fightin' to be done?" asked one grizzled old corporal.

"New issue, that's what they is!" said another soldier derisively, spitting onto the ground to emphasize his disgust.

As they had done several times while on the march, the cadets maintained their composure, ignoring their detractors and saying nothing in reply.

Once in position, the troops waited anxiously for Breckinridge's next order. They did not have to wait long. The general ordered the troops to march back and forth on the crest of Shirley's Hill, giving the enemy the illusion that he had many more Confederate troops than there actually were. As they did this in full view of the Union soldiers, the artillery kept up a constant fire.

*   *   *

"Commander Ship," said Captain Minge frantically, "we can't move the guns up the hill. The mud's too deep and we're gettin' bogged down. I'm not gonna be able to keep the artillery movin' with yuh."

The cadets had cheerfully deployed when Ship had told them the plan. Minge had dutifully tried to follow Breckinridge's orders as they were relayed by Ship, but the cadets in his charge had only moved a short distance when it became apparent that the artillery was quickly going to be left behind. Minge wanted desperately to avoid that. The firing of his guns had only served to whet the appetites of the boys for more combat.

Ship looked at Minge, then back at a group of cadet artillerists urging the horses as they struggled in vain to extricate a gun from the axle deep mud. Despite all their efforts, the wheels turned but little. As the horses strained, one lost his footing in the mud and nearly fell on a nearby cadet.

Benjamin Colonna, one of the New Market cadets, attired in the uniform worn by the cadets at New Market. Colonna would become a civil engineer after he graduated, and he was responsible for much of the subsequent battlefield mapping.

Courtesy of Hall of Valor
Civil War Museum

"Captain," said Ship after quickly assessing the situation, " take your artillery down to the main road and join the general artillery column as quickly as you can. If you have to, send three guns on ahead, while you continue to free the fourth. Then, send the fourth one as soon as you have it pulled out. Report to Major McLaughlin and tell him why I sent you."

Major McLaughlin was William McLaughlin, commander of the artillery.

Minge rushed back to his stranded gun, eager to get it down to the pike, along with the other three, before Ship changed his mind. All the artillerists joined in the effort to free the mired gun, and with the help of the horses, soon all four guns were rumbling back down the hill toward the pike.

Entering the pike, they turned left without hesitating and rushed down the road at full gallop. Inspired at seeing their friends making their way to the main body of artillery, the cadets on Shirley's Hill gave them a loud cheer of encouragement, a cheer which was nearly drowned out by the sounds of gunfire before it ever reached the ears of their classmates.

The cadets who remained on Shirley's Hill watched in fascination as the veterans around them prepared to do battle. To the cadets' left the men of the 26th Virginia Battalion, even though serving only in reserve, went through the personal rituals followed by soldiers on both sides when facing danger. Samuel Letcher, a private in Company D, was the last cadet on the left of the line and he had the best view of their actions. Some read their Testaments while others, oblivious to the noise and confusion surrounding them, simply prayed. One soldier made a show of throwing away his playing cards. There was no way to know whether he was ridden with guilt or merely not taking any chances.

Shirley's Hill as it appears today, remarkably similar to its appearance in 1864. It was on this hill that Breckinridge massed his forces, including the cadets of the Virginia Military Institute, the morning of the battle.

Photo by Author

Wordlessly tossing them high into the air, they quickly scattered, taking with them all evidence of ownership. Most of the men, however, did little but toy nervously with the hammers of their guns, probably not even realizing they were doing it.

Occasionally, through the mist and fog, the boys could see flame belch from the muzzle of an unseen gun, telling them that, even though the foe was beyond their sight, he was out there. And he was heavily armed.

This was something which the cadets had not anticipated. It had never occurred to them that they may not be able to see their enemy. Beyond the Union's first line of battle which was visible in the valley below Shirley's Hill, not much could be seen. The cadets, as was the case with Breckinridge, were not aware that there were few additional enemy soldiers to be seen.

"Who do we shoot at if we can't see 'em?" a cadet plaintively inquired to no one in particular.

Hearing him, Ship stated simply, "Look for the flags and shoot on either side. You'll hit somethin'! Jest make sure y'all shoot low."

With the excitement and apprehension which accompanied the cadets' first foray into battle, the slackening of the rain went nearly unnoticed.

10

The tension was beginning to build. Even the battle hardened veterans were starting to show the effects, some flinching at the sound of a shell passing overhead, even though it was nowhere near its intended target. More than once the cadets, in spite of themselves, found themselves crouching a little closer to the ground because they were sprayed with mud from a shell striking the dirt in front of them.

On one such occasion, Thomas Clendinen, the young cadet who had talked to his compatriots on the march about how they would or would not react in battle, broke rank and ran toward the rear.

A lanky veteran with Edgar's 26th Virginia Battalion laughed out loud and elbowed his companion. "Showin' the white feather, jest like I figgered!" he exclaimed.

His friend laughed with him, in spite of the surrounding danger. "Won't be long now," he said. "They'll all be gone and we'll have this line to ourselves."

The first man agreed. "Shouldn't be sendin' a bunch 'a boys to fight with men. They'll turn tail and run ever' time!"

However, before the men could continue with their disparaging remarks about the cadet corps, Clendinen returned holding up a pair of shoes for all his friends to see.

"I got 'em," he shouted. "Had my spare shoes tied to my cartridge box and I jest noticed they was missin'. Figgered they must have fallen off back there where we was standin'."

He took his place back in the ranks, to the chagrin of his detractors in the 26th. As Clendinen fastened his extra shoes back in place, Ship walked past the line of apprehensive young men.

"Just guide on the colors, boys," he was saying over the noise of the artillery duel. Listen to what your officers tell you."

The cadets watched intently as General Imboden conferred briefly with Breckinridge, then rode off swiftly to rejoin his men. Breckinridge then took his turn riding along the line.

"All mounted officers must dismount," he shouted. "You'll make a much smaller target if you fight on foot. Only my staff and I will remain on horseback."

Lucien Ricketts, a sixteen-year-old private in Company C, misunderstood the order. Thinking Breckinridge only wanted officers to dismount, he would remain on his horse throughout the entire battle.

Then came the moment all had been anxiously awaiting, veteran and cadet alike. Breckinridge gave the signal, and his skirmishers moved quickly down the hill. Although the rain was still falling, it had lessened considerably. "Ain't surprisin'," one of Wharton's men had said. "There can't be much water left up there."

On the left of the line, Wharton watched as the skirmishers deftly dodged and wove their ways down the hill as artillery shells burst all around them. Concerned that the heavy artillery fire would wreak havoc on his troops if they were to descend Shirley's Hill in formation, he called his company commanders together.

"Tell your boys not to worry about stayin' in any kind of formation when they're goin' down this hill," he told them. "Jest have 'em run as fast as they can down the hill and we'll reform at that fence down yonder."

As his company commanders returned to their men to inform them of the plan, Wharton worked his way to the rear of his line and sought out Edgar and Ship. Finding them, he shouted to them, "We'll be movin' down the hill in a few minutes. Conform your movements to mine!"

Both Edgar and Ship waved their hands as a signal that they had heard him and understood.

Behind Ship the cadets waited nervously.

Then, Breckinridge dropped his sword from its position over his head, giving Wharton the signal to advance.

Wharton took one last look down his line, making sure all were ready. Then, satisfied that his men were prepared to begin their descent, he gave the signal. With a rousing yell which startled the cadets, Wharton's men dashed over the crest of Shirley's Hill and down its other side. The intensity of the musket fire picked up noticeably as soon as the men disappeared over the crest. The battle was on in earnest.

Breckinridge, watching the advance over the crest, observed that Echols and his troops were still in position. Unaware of Echols' illness, Breckinridge remarked to one of his staff, "Why doesn't Echols move forward? That man is the slowest fellow!"

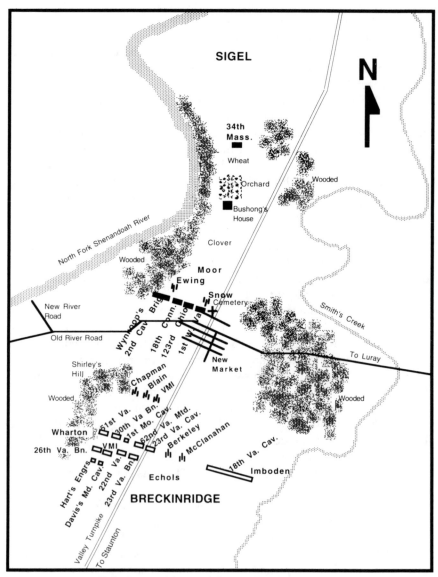

Relative positions of the armies at 11:00 A.M.

Map by Author

Just as Breckinridge uttered the last words, Echols ordered his men to move out. As the cadets watched, Echols passed out of their sight over the top of the hill.

Soon it was their turn. Breckinridge, aware of the apprehension that existed among the corps as they prepared for what, for most of them, was to be their first battle. As the cadets removed their coats, Breckinridge rode in front of their line and repeated what he had told Ship earlier. "Young men," he said, "I hope there will be no occasion to use you, but if there is, I trust you will do your duty!"

Then Ship, anxious to get started, gave his last minute instructions. Shouting to make himself heard over the growing roar of artillery and musketry, he said, "Listen to your officers and obey their orders. If any of us should fall, only the litter bearers are to stop and render aid. All others must continue on!"

Then, after a short pause, he raised his sword and shouted, "BAT-TALION . . . FORWARD! GUIDE CENTER!"

Immediately, Sergeant Major Jonathon Edwards Woodbridge rushed forward and took an advance position, as was his custom when the cadets practiced drilling on the Institute's parade ground.

Seeing this, Shipp quickly ordered him back. "This isn't a drill today, Sergeant Major," he shouted.

Color bearer Oliver Perry Evans unfurled his flag and shook the rain water from it as Woodbridge returned to the rank. At about the same time, the fife and drummers began to play, and the cadets stepped out. They were finally going into battle, even if it was as a reserve regiment!

As they crested the hill, the cadets could see Echols' men just reaching the cover at the base of the hill. Ahead, Union guns roared louder than anything any of the cadets had ever heard. Shells struck all around, showering the boys with mud and debris. Undaunted, they maintained their formation and marched smartly down the north face of Shirley's Hill.

Looking back from their sheltered positions at the base of the hill, the men of the 22nd Virginia could not help but be impressed as the cadets marched in step and in perfect alignment despite the shower of shells directed at them. One of Echols' men stared for several seconds, then remarked admiringly, "Well, I swear if it don't look like them boys is on parade!"

At the other end of the line, however, Gabriel Wharton was less than impressed with the cadets' appearance and apparent bravery in the face of heavy artillery and musket fire.

"Why don't they run down the hill the way we did?" he snapped to an aide. "They were told to conform to my movements!"

It was the last criticism to be levied against the cadets of the Virginia Military Institute by anyone on this day.

*   *   *

Hearing the crescendo of the battle Wise looked up. He had been half kneeling, half sitting against a wheel of one of the baggage wagons, feeling sorry for himself and cursing his luck. Stanard, Redwood, and Woodlief also directed their attention to the top of their hill, watching their friends march sharply over the ridge.

Wise, as were many of the cadets, had been thinking of his family. His thoughts drifted especially to his father, an unusually stern man. After contemplating his situation for several minutes, he reached the conclusion that he would never again be able to face his father if he told him he had sat on a wagon while his friends were fighting.

Slamming his right fist into the palm of his left hand, he decided that, despite his orders, he was not going to sit idly by while his friends were taking part in what may be the only battle they would ever see.

"Boys," he exclaimed loudly, "the enemy is in front of us. Our command is about to go into action! Now, I like fighting no better than anyone else. But I have an enemy at home as dreadful as any before us. If I return home and tell my father I was on the baggage guard while my comrades were fighting, I have no doubts as to my fate. He'll kill me with ridicule, and that's worse than any bullet the Yanks are shootin'! I am going to join the command. Any of you who chooses to remain may do so, but I'm goin' on ahead!"

With that, Wise began to trot up the hill. He was quickly followed by all three of his companions, who ran even faster down the opposite side. They would catch up with their friends at the base of Shirley's Hill, the only cadets who ran down the hill to Wharton's satisfaction all day.

*   *   *

As the cadets marched down the front of Shirley's Hill they passed the first casualties of the battle, several of Wharton's men. Some were lying in contorted positions, others were trying to crawl to safety, leaving a bloody trail in the mud behind them. The sight was a sobering one, as if the cadets needed to witness such a scene to take the fight seriously.

Then, after the cadets had passed the midpoint of the hill, a shell burst in their ranks without warning. Companies C and D bore the brunt of the explosion. Captain Govan Hill, commander of Company C, went down with a fractured skull, falling stiffly. His wound, bad as it was, looked even worse and gave rise to a cry among some of the cadets that Captain Hill had been killed.

"He ain't dead," shouted another cadet. "When a man is killed he don't fall like that. He crumples in a heap!"

The cadet's analysis of Captain Hill's fall proved prophetic. He would survive, despite the serious nature of his injury.

Private Charles Read was struck over the eye with a fragment of the same shell, which also bent the barrel of his gun at a strange angle.[3] The shell next removed Company C's James Merritt from the battle, his wound also serious.

Among the shell's other victims was John Wise, struck by a fragment just as he caught up with his friends. For Wise, the battle was over before it ever got started. His wound would turn out to be minor, but he would not fight today.

William Cabell, Company D's first sergeant, looked at Wise with pity as the luckless cadet fell. Then, following Ship's orders, he called out, "Close up, men!" The cadets continued onward.

Others among the corps forgot Ship's orders and stopped to help their fallen comrades. Immediately, the men of the 26th Virginia saw their opportunity to criticize once more.

"See, what did I tell yuh?" said one. "They ain't fighters!"

Ship quickly took charge and ordered, "Close up! Close up!"

The cadets immediately obeyed, much to the chagrin of the men of the 26th.

After several agonizing minutes, the cadets reached the safety of a fence at the bottom of the hill. Dropping into a ditch behind its rails, the cadets found the protection they had longed for on their march down the hill. As they looked around in wide-eyed wonder, they could see Wharton's men already throwing up a crude breastwork of rails, brush, and dirt, to provide a rally point if they would be forced back.

Ship quickly began to circulate through the line, inquiring if any were injured and trying to instill calm into the boys, now curiously giddy with the fear that typically accompanies the first time a soldier comes under fire.

"Y'all are doin' fine, boys!" he shouted, pounding the closest ones on the back in a gesture of encouragement. "Just stay calm, and keep it up!"

As the cadets lay in the ditch at the base of Shirley's Hill, gathering their wits and calming themselves, artillery shells continued to pass over them, thudding into the side of the hill. Thomas Jefferson remarked to Willis Harris, huddled next to him in the ditch, "Did you ever hear such a racket, Willis?"

Harris didn't even try to shout out an answer. He merely shook his head.

"Drop off yer blankets, knapsacks, and anything else y'all aren't gonna need to fight with," Ship exhorted the cadets. "Then, jest take a few minutes to relax and catch yer breath. We'll stay here fer a while until Wharton's men move out again."

The young soldiers did as they were instructed. They would not see their belongings again, as battlefield looters and human scavengers would swoop down and help themselves before the fighting even subsided.

---

[3] Read's twisted gun may be seen today at the VMI Museum.

With grim faces and drawn lips, the cadets huddled in the ditch, the rain pelting them once again. Cadet Sergeant Erskine Ross of Company A had fought before, as a member of what he fondly referred to as the Regulars. However, he had never been in a fight as loud as this one, and his face reflected the anxiety as much as anyone's.

After a brief rest of some thirty minutes, Breckinridge gave the orders to advance once more. Wharton's men quickly rose to their feet and knocked the fence railings down to facilitate passage. They raced across the road to an open grassy field and formed their line in preparation for marching up the long slope that would take them out of the comparative safety of the ravine and into the teeth of the firestorm. Just as they stepped out, an officer dashed down from the knoll in front of them, shouting that the Union skirmishers were scarcely 100 yards ahead. This information was all that some of the men needed to decide that they had seen enough for one day. All along Wharton's line soldiers could be seen slipping away, trying to wend their way back to the fence line and safety. Officers ran along the rear of the line and forced many of the skulkers back into formation at pistol point.

The cadets watched and waited. The fury of the fight continued as they concentrated on Wharton's advance. With the first line of battle slowly making its way up the slope in front of them, some of the fire was being drawn away from the cadets. None of them complained.

Then, it was their turn to advance. Evans raised his flag, almost immediately snagging the staff in the lower branches of a tree. As the cadets scrambled across the road, he wrestled with the staff, trying in vain to extricate the banner from the tree. Under different circumstances, the flag bearer's predicament would have drawn raucous laughter from the boys, but today, it wasn't even noticed. After much struggling, Evans was successful in freeing the flag from its entanglement and rushed after the cadets, who were already making their way up the slope.

By now the mud in the grassy field was ankle deep. Walking was becoming difficult, a trot nearly impossible. Fortunately, the only resistance the line of battle was meeting was coming on the left, away from the cadets. They continued their march in perfect formation.

The wounded and dead were appearing with greater frequency now, and it was often necessary for a cadet to step over the prone body of a fallen soldier. Those whose wounds were not so severe were able to cheer the young men of VMI as they passed. Some raised themselves up on one elbow and waved their hat as a salute.

The brief lull in the firing the cadets had experienced while lying in the ditch was now over. Minie balls screamed past their heads constantly, the boys cringing with each passing shot.

The cadets had now passed the original position of the Union line, and bodies clad in blue were mingled with those in butternut and gray.

Several of the cadets were surprised to note that the Union dead didn't look much different from those of the Confederacy. They were only dressed differently.

Suddenly, from the direction of Company C, a shot rang out. The proximity of the noise startled many of the youths. Until now, the cadets had been under orders to refrain from firing their weapons. The fact that they had done so while coming under direct fire was a tribute to their discipline.

"Who fired that shot?" demanded Ship as he looked at the cadets in Company C.

"I did, sir," seventeen-year-old John McGavock admitted sheepishly. "It wasn't my gun, though. It was a Yankee gun I just picked up, and it went off by accident."

"Well, be more careful," Ship shouted above the continuous roar. "And throw that thing away. There will be plenty of time after the fightin' to pick up spoils."

McGavock reluctantly did as he was told. The gun had appeared to be nearly new. Its shiny finish was what had caught his eye in the first place. It never crossed his mind that he had the honor of being the first cadet, except for the artillery, to fire a weapon at New Market, even if it was by accident. All he cared about was that he had just been given the order to throw away a better gun than he was carrying.

*   *   *

As the cadets were making their way slowly up the hill, their companions in the artillery were just as slowly pushing their way along the turnpike and into New Market proper. On the south edge of town Captain Minge directed the youths to set up their guns once more. As they unlimbered and prepared to fire, the boys' eyes drifted to the left of the pike, where they saw their first bodies. They were dressed in blue.

"Faster, boys, faster!" shouted Minge as the cadets quickly loaded, tamped, fired, and sponged. The inexperienced cadets may not have been as fast or efficient as their counterparts in McClanahan's Battery, but they more than made up for their lack of experience with enthusiasm. No battery worked harder than the one from the Virginia Military Institute.

General Breckinridge continually worked his way back and forth between the artillery and the infantry. Approaching the cadet artillery, he raised his sword and shouted encouragement.

"Give it to 'em, boys," he shouted. "Give it to 'em!"

The cadets did their best to comply.

After several minutes of firing, the artillery limbered up and moved their guns forward. The cadets followed with them. As they passed through the town, the smell of death blended with the smell of gunpowder. Bodies which had been lying in the streets from the skirmishing over the past two days were beginning to putrify and several of the cadets felt themselves becoming ill.

Setting up once again, this time on the northern outskirts of the town, the boys found themselves beside the cemetery they had first seen from the heights of Shirley's Hill. It was now deserted. Tombstones sat at odd angles, dislodged from their original positions by the shelling. Perhaps one of their shells had done some of this damage. There was no way of knowing.

Behind them, a fierce explosion took place when an enemy shell found its target, a caisson filled with ammunition. The cadets involuntarily flinched at the roar, turning to see what had happened. Pieces of wood and metal were thrown high into the air. The boys could only hope that nobody had been standing by the wagon when the shell hit.

The rain and heavy atmosphere were combining to keep the smoke from the artillery close to the ground. Targets could no longer be seen. The cadets, along with the rest of the artillery, were shooting in a general direction now, hoping they were doing some good.

And still it rained.

11

Shortly after the cadets had begun their ascent up the hill, Sigel had arrived on the scene. He had pulled his line back nearly a mile from its original position, hoping to gain an advantage through the increased elevation. He had placed six 12-pound smoothbores from Albert von Kleiser's 30th New York Battery next to the turnpike, with the 123rd Ohio Infantry on Kleiser's right, and the 18th Connecticut next to them. The two infantry regiments had stood side by side in the original position just west of New Market, and they had been two of the regiments that Breckinridge had seen from Shirley's Hill, moving into position. The third regiment, the 1st West Virginia Infantry, had pulled back to anchor the left flank of Sigel's second line, behind the Bushong Farm. The cavalry, under Major General Julius Stahel, took a position on the other side of the pike—Imboden's side.

The position of Sigel's first line of battle was almost as good as the one Breckinridge had chosen earlier in the day on Shirley's Hill. The Union right was guarded by a steep wooded slope which led down to the river. The left was also sloped and wooded, and was bounded by the pike. In the center, an open field would have to be crossed by any attacker. The Union line was further protected by a low stone wall behind which the Northerners were able to take cover while pouring their fire onto any advancing army.

The pulling back of the 18th Connecticut and the 123rd Ohio had left the town of New Market to Breckinridge, which he had promptly taken. While Breckinridge's troops were in the process of occupying New Market, Imboden and one of his aides had been sneaking through the small patch of woods between the town and Smith's Creek, hoping to find something, anything, which could be used to his advantage. He found far more than he had hoped for.

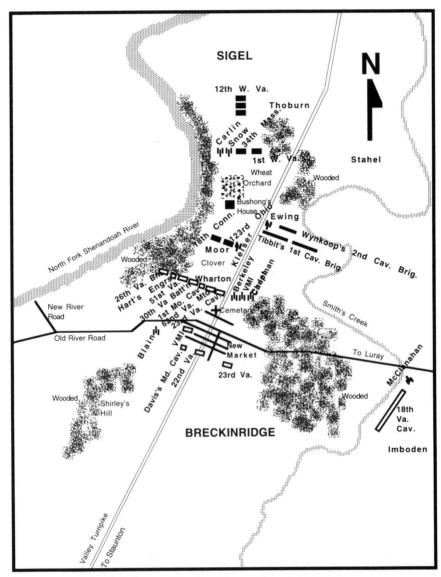

SIGEL

12th W. Va.

Thoburn

Carlin Snow 34th Mass.

1st W. Va.

Stahel

Wheat Orchard

Wooded

Bushong's House

8th Conn.

Ewing

123rd

Wynkoop's 2nd Cav. Brig.

Moor

Kleiser

Tibbit's 1st Cav. Brig.

Wooded

Clover

Berkeley

VMI

Chapman

26th Va. Bn.

Wharton

Hart's Engr.

51st Va.

30th Va. Batt'n

1st Mo. Cav.

62nd Va. Mtd.

23rd Va. Cav.

Cemetery

Smith's Creek

New River Road

Old River Road

Blain

VMI

New Market

To Luray

Davis's Md. Cav.

22nd Va.

23rd Va.

McClanahan

Wooded

Shirley's Hill

Wooded

18th Va. Cav.

BRECKINRIDGE

Imboden

North Fork Shenandoah River

Valley Turnpike

To Staunton

Relative positions of the armies at 2:00 P.M.

Map by Author

Coming to the end of the wood lot, the two had been able to see through the trees to the clearing beyond. A sea of blue coats met their eyes. There, they saw Stahel's cavalry massed in the open field just outside the woodline. A closer look revealed that a battery accompanied them.

Imboden and his aide knew they would have no choice but to deal with Stahel within a short time if Breckinridge continued his advancing pace. Better to do it now while the element of surprise could still be used to its fullest advantage. The two rushed back to McClanahan's Battery and the 18th Virginia Cavalry, waiting patiently on the south side of the Luray Road.

Imboden dispatched a messenger to Breckinridge, telling the commanding general that Imboden judged that he would be able to get onto the other side of Smith's Creek undetected, from where he would be in a position to strike the Union cavalry on its flank. Although this also meant that Breckinridge's right flank would remain unprotected for the entire time Imboden was engaged, the commanding general agreed.

"Tell General Imboden, as he knows this ground and I don't, that he should make any movement he thinks will be advantageous," he had told the messenger. "I will take all the responsibility and consequences!"

Imboden, upon receiving Breckinridge's approval, moved his troops to a slightly elevated position on the opposite side of Smith's Creek. The guns were quickly unlimbered and directed toward the Union cavalry, a scant one thousand yards away. Stahel's troops presented the kind of target that every artillerist dreamed of: a huge target in close order, with literally acres of unsuspecting enemy troops.

McClanahan's guns boomed, sending the Union cavalry into a state of confusion. Sensing the direction from which the artillery shelling was coming, the cavalry quickly retreated. This removed Stahel from Breckinridge's right flank, while offering the added benefit of opening Sigel's left flank for fire from McClanahan's guns.

Sigel had then responded by setting up his second line of battle at a point behind the Bushong Farm. From Breckinridge's perspective his alternate plan, that of becoming the attacker, was falling into place. As part of that plan, Imboden returned to his original mission of crossing the creek and advancing toward Mount Jackson to destroy the bridge and, along with it, Sigel's potential escape route. However, Imboden would soon discover that he would be unable to recross the rain-swollen stream, effectively taking his cavalry out of the battle.

*   *   *

With Union reinforcements arriving from Mount Jackson, the shelling now became even more intense. Officers were finding it difficult to make themselves heard over the constant and unceasing roar of the battle.

Still, however, Ship was able to keep the VMI cadets under control. They continued their march as if they were back at the Institute, performing on the parade ground for the people of Lexington. In fact, they would probably have been doing just that today if they had not been called by General Breckinridge to New Market. Their line, straight and precise, never wavered. The only concession they would give to the increased fire was to lower their heads, grip their guns a little tighter, and advance into the ever thickening smoke, not knowing what may be waiting for them on the other side.

The smell of sulfur became stifling, and the cadets found themselves coughing and choking as they advanced. It seemed as if the volume between the two mountain ranges was not large enough to contain all the smoke of the battle, yet somehow it did, and the cadets caught only an occasional glimpse of the enemy. As they advanced, they hoped the enemy was having as much difficulty seeing them.

Not infrequently a riderless horse streaked past the cadets in panic, the fate of its rider unknown, but obviously not good. The shriek and hiss of passing shells, combined with the thick, acrid smoke, made the scene almost surreal. The rain was no longer even noticed anymore, or were they simply getting used to it?

Cadet Charles Randolph, an eighteen-year-old private in Company C, was one of the cadets who had seen prior service in the Confederate army. At the age of sixteen he had fought in Company F of the 6th Virginia Cavalry. At the battle of Port Republic he had had the pleasure of meeting the great Stonewall Jackson, a fact that had placed him just a few notches below the gods in the eyes of his fellow cadets.

Not only had he met Stonewall, he had spoken with him. Jackson had dropped a glove while passing Randoph's position, a glove which Randolph had immediately retrieved. Jackson, taking the glove from Randolph, had looked into the youngster's eyes and asked him, "Are you a warrior, sir?"

Randolph, who had somehow summoned the ability to speak in the general's presence, had replied emphatically, "Yes, sir!"

Jackson had smiled and had taken Randolph on as his courier. Today, Randolph would be a warrior once again. The late general would have been proud of his young messenger.

*   *   *

"Bring those guns up here where they can kill somebody!" Breckinridge shouted at the artillery.

Faces begrimed with soot and powder, the artillerists strained to comply. Young Lewis Davis, who normally served in Company C, was not very familiar with artillery weapons, but did a serviceable job. It had been less than a month since he had celebrated his fifteenth birthday, and he was the youngest cadet at New Market. Aware of this, he had three goals. The first was a simple one: to avoid getting shot. The second was to be able to carry his share of the load in the battle. The third was not to cry if he became afraid. He was successful in all three.

Waving his sword, his horse prancing nervously in the unceasing clamor, Breckinridge had just returned to the artillery's position on the pike. He needed to know the positions of Sigel's artillery, as well as their strength. He had to draw their fire to achieve this. This was all part of the job for an artillerist, and they all accepted it stoically.

The big guns boomed, their clash causing the very insides of the artillerists to shake. The cadet gunners kept pace with the more experienced veterans. Nobody would ever be able to say that the artillerists from VMI were not doing their part.

Breckinridge also needed the barrage from the artillery to accomplish a second purpose. In the low hanging smoke, several of the regiments had become separated, and he needed some time to redress the lines. "I'll have them dress off the cadets' colors," he had said. "They're the only ones here who seem to know how to march in a straight line!"

Breckinridge was not sure what had happened to Imboden, but he knew his right flank was vulnerable. To protect it, he had decided on a bold maneuver. He would use the artillery to protect his flank. Going from battery to battery, he issued his new orders.

When he reached Captain Minge, the cadets strained to hear his instructions. The bedlam prevented it, so Minge relayed the information when Breckinridge moved on to Chapman's Battery.

"The general wants us to move up the pike with the infantry's advance," he shouted. "Berkeley's Battery will fire, then limber up and advance. Then we'll fire and do the same thing, and Chapman will repeat it while we're moving. We're all gonna jest leap frog along this road. The general says this will let us fire obliquely into the Union left without fear of hitting our own boys. As soon as we fire our next volley we'll move on up!"

The plan was ingenious, and would prove extremely effective. It had the effect of producing a nearly constant barrage from the Confederate artillery, and Breckinridge's flank would never be in any real danger.

*   *   *

Under heavy fire, the cadets advanced slowly. Breckinridge had instructed his officers to redress the lines, changing the plans in the process. Protected by a small swale, Breckinridge had decided to form his infantry into two lines to deceive Sigel. The two lines overlapped slightly in the center, but left Breckinridge with no reserves. Wharton's Brigade constituted the first line, while Echols's Brigade made up the second. Under Echols, the cadets were now on the second line, to the left of Edgar's

Battalion. Breckinridge had done this reluctantly, knowing this would expose the cadets to even more danger. However, it was a calculated risk.

The lines adjusted, the advance was resumed. The second line had been instructed by the general to dress off the VMI colors. The men of Edgar's Battalion had now had a good opportunity to observe the boys under fire, and were rapidly changing their opinions. These boys were not going to break and run, they had concluded, contrary to their earlier opinions. The veterans did not object to using the VMI flag as a reference point.

The pandemonium of the battle now presented another distraction the cadets had not anticipated, a distraction more disconcerting to some of them than any bullet. The screams of the wounded now penetrated through the noise, reaching the ears of the young soldiers and sending chills down their spines. They had known there were going to be wounded and dying men in a battle, of course, but nobody had ever told them that the dying may scream in pain.

Accompanied by writhing bodies, the screams were almost more than the boys could bear. Advancing faster made no difference. The screams sounded the same; they just came from different men. The cadets did their best to block out the cries of agony, but they were, for the most part, unsuccessful. Some would later remember the screams of agony nearly as much as they remembered the rain, the shells, and the other minute details of the battle.

Many of the veterans were now lying down when they shot. The cadets, however, still had not fired their weapons, and remained standing. This made them better targets, but they saw no point in lying down just to watch others shoot.

Out of the corner of his eye Charles Randolph could see his friends reacting to the minie balls whizzing past their heads. Randolph, Stonewall Jackson's former courier, yelled, "There's no use dodgin', boys! If a ball's gonna hit yuh, it's gonna hit yuh. Keep movin'!"

A few steps farther, Randolph fell, wounded by a ball he failed to dodge.

*   *   *

The pressure from Breckinridge's forces was becoming too great. The heavy Confederate fire was pushing the 18th Connecticut back, and they made a move to retreat to a small knoll some two hundred yards to their rear. This new position was in a small lane. It appeared to be part of a farm, with a small barn on their right, a house behind them, and two rows of fences.

The fire had been withering. Through the haze they had been able to catch occasional glimpses of the advancing Confederates, although they were still unable to see the extreme ends of the line, a fact which aided Breckinridge's deception.

Colonel August Moor, commander of Sigel's First Infantry Brigade, which included the 18th Connecticut, was concerned. The word "furious" may have also been applied to him at this point. He had just learned that five companies of the 28th and 116th Ohio Volunteers were still back at Mount Jackson, awaiting someone to tell them what to do. Moor, even though he needed every available man, needed help even more. He dispatched some staff officers to go to Mount Jackson, six miles from the battle scene, to find the two regiments from the Buckeye State and order them to get to New Market as quickly as they could. Even now it may be too late.

The 18th Connecticut settled in behind one of the fences, showing signs of confusion. They knew Sigel had set up a line of battle somewhere behind them, but just how far was anyone's guess. They could not take the chance of bolting for the safety of this line, so they prepared for the anticipated attack by kneeling behind what little protection the fence offered and began to fire again.

Inside the house behind the Union soldiers, Jacob and Sarah Bushong huddled in the cellar, Jacob holding Sarah in his arms. The bullets were now striking the clapboards of the house with regularity, a constant hammering that refused to stop. Jacob didn't voice his fear to Sarah of what would happen if one of the artillery shells should strike the house.

The sounds of the battle grew increasingly louder, indicating that someone was being pushed back. They were probably now close to the farm, if not already on it. By Jacob's reckoning, it had to be the Union that was losing ground. After all, they were the only soldiers he had seen near the farm. Right now, however, the continuing noise, unlike anything he had ever heard or ever hoped to hear again, brought fear to his heart. The terror-stricken livestock sharing his home added to the cacophony. Jacob knew the farm was being destroyed, but he didn't give that another thought. Personal safety, though; now, that was another matter.

                    *   *   *

Screaming their rebel yell, Wharton's line advanced. The second line, including the cadets, followed. A shift in the wind blew some of the smoke away, revealing that the ends of the cadet line had moved ahead of the center, resulting in what could best be described as an arc. Seeing this, Ship immediately gave the order, "Mark time!"

The cadets obeyed the order at once and the line was quickly dressed, much as they had practiced the maneuver dozens, if not hundreds, of times on the parade ground. Ahead, at the Bushong Farm, the men of the 18th Connecticut could not believe what they were seeing.

"I never seen anything like that in the middle of a battle," exclaimed one of the men, shaking his head in amazement.

Refusing to show the enemy any respect, even though he felt it in his heart, a second soldier remarked, "Aw, anybody could do that. We've drilled like that lots 'a times!"

"Never under fire, though!" the first man replied.

"Mebbe not, but we coulda, I'd bet," said his companion, refusing to admit that his friend was right.

"You can say we coulda," admitted the first man, "but we never did, and I hope we never do!"

Begrudgingly, the second man silently conceded. He wouldn't admit it to his friend, but he never had seen anything like it either.

Behind Wharton's men, their own line now redressed, the cadets pushed onward. On the left of Wharton's line a problem was developing. The cadets were not sure what was wrong, but those at the end of the line could see a few men of the 26th Virginia slipping out of line and moving to the right, between the two Confederate lines of battle. This time, however, they did not appear to be deserting.

What the cadets did not know, and were not in a position to see, was that a bend in the river was creating a pinch point. Squeezed by the river on their left and the 51st Virginia on their right, the 26th had no place to go. First one man at a time, then in twos and threes, finally company by company, the 26th was forced to temporarily halt and fall back in behind the 51st. Eventually, the entire battalion would be in the rear.

Meanwhile, Sigel had firmly established his second line of battle north of Jacob Bushong's wheat field. He anchored his right with the six three-inch rifles of Battery D, 1st West Virginia Artillery, commanded by Captain John Carlin. Next to Carlin, Captain Alonzo Snow's Battery B of the Maryland Light Artillery was set up. The 34th Massachusetts, staying in the position they had held from the time they had arrived on the field, was positioned on Snow's left, with the left flank anchored by the 1st West Virginia Infantry and Kleiser's Battery. Held in reserve behind the 34th Massachusetts was the 12th West Virginia Infantry, a regiment which had yet to enjoy the feeling of victory in battle.

Sigel felt reasonably comfortable with the position of his second line. Theoretically, it lay in the best defensive position on the field. Both rivers made large sweeping curves at this point, the north branch of the Shenandoah bending eastward, Smith's Creek curving westward. These coincidental bends narrowed the distance which had to be defended, allowing Sigel to concentrate his forces. His flanks protected by the two rivers, Sigel waited for the enemy to try to advance across the open uphill terrain immediately in front of him. For the enemy to win, he would have to drive this concentrated line, which was approximately a mile in length and anchored by eighteen guns on its right and four on its left. Yes, Sigel felt comfortable.

However, at the same time, the first line was feeling the pressure of the Confederate fire. In danger of being overrun, they finally broke for the rear. Officers screamed for the men to hold their positions, to no avail. Now in complete disarray, the men of the 18th Connecticut and the 123rd Ohio dashed for safety. Many were captured by the advancing Confederates, but some were killed or wounded by Sigel's second line, which thought that the shadowy forms rushing toward them through the smoke of battle were the enemy.

Realizing too late that the men who were running toward the second line were Union soldiers, the officers in the second line screamed for their men to refrain from firing. This brief lull, short as it was, brought a welcome respite to the cadets and their compatriots.

As Moor's panic-stricken line crashed through the 34th Massachusetts, the men in that line were totally disrupted. Several precious seconds were needed to restore some semblance of order.

Seeing what was taking place, and fearing that they may be overrun, Snow, Carlin, and Kleiser had their men double load their guns with grape and canister. The resulting fire decimated the 51st Virginia and the 30th Virginia Battalion. Huge holes appeared in the four companies on the 51st's right. Just before reaching the Bushong fence, they had to pull back. Undaunted, Wharton pushed the rest of his line forward.

Passing around the east side of the Bushong house, where the terrified Jacob and Sarah Bushong huddled in each other's arms in the cellar, the 62nd Virginia received the full force of the Union's fire. The color bearer fell, his flag quickly picked up by the soldier beside him, who also went down. In less than five minutes, five color bearers would be lost and the entire color company killed or wounded. Orders were prudently given to fall back. As they did, the cheers of the Union gunners echoed in the ears of the withdrawing Confederates.

*   *   *

The 51st and 62nd Virginia Infantries were decimated. Disaster was imminent. Many men of the 51st were running to the rear, their officers wildly swinging their swords to halt the retreat before it became epidemic. Several of the retreating men were forced back at the point of a pistol. The entire battle was in danger of being lost. Major Charles Semple, Breckinridge's assistant ordnance officer, saw the hole in the line appear as the grape and canister took their deadly toll. Semple had to get to Breckinridge.

Riding frantically, Semple found his general and quickly told him of the huge gap which had opened up and which was now in danger of being run through by the Union. Only the smoke, which had thus far prevented Sigel from seeing the breach, had kept this from taking place.

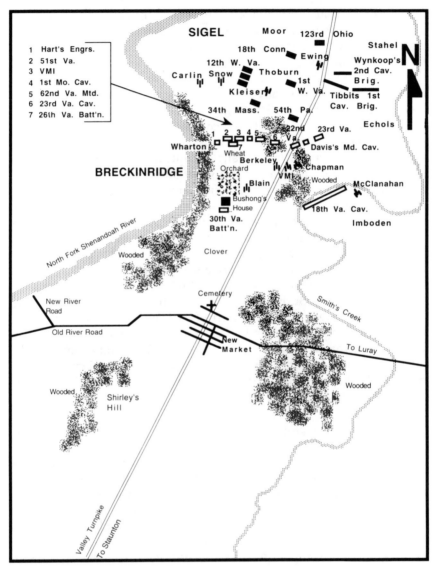

SIGEL

1 Hart's Engrs.
2 51st Va.
3 VMI
4 1st Mo. Cav.
5 62nd Va. Mtd.
6 23rd Va. Cav.
7 26th Va. Batt'n.

Moor
123rd Ohio
Stahel
18th Conn
Ewing
Wynkoop's
12th W. Va.
2nd Cav.
Carlin Snow
Thoburn
Brig.
Kleiser
1st
W. Va.
Tibbits 1st
Cav. Brig.

34th Mass.
54th Pa.
Echols

1 2 3 4 5 6 22nd Va. 23rd Va.
Wharton
Davis's Md. Cav.
Wheat
Berkeley
Chapman
Orchard
VMI
Wooded
McClanahan

BRECKINRIDGE

Blain
Bushong's
House
18th Va. Cav.
Imboden
30th Va.
Batt'n.

North Fork Shenandoah River

Wooded
Clover

New River
Road
Cemetery
Smith's Creek
Old River Road
New
Market
To Luray

Wooded
Shirley's
Hill
Wooded

Valley Turnpike
To Staunton

Relative positions of the armies at 3:00 P.M.

Map by Author

"As soon as Sigel spots that gap he is going to charge it immediately, and all will be lost, general!" Semple shouted, his mouth nearly beside the general's ear to make himself heard.

"Contract the lines!" Breckinridge shouted back.

"We can't, sir," Semple answered. "They are too pinned down by the heavy fire! General, why don't you put the cadets in line? They will fight as well as our other men."

"No, Charlie," Breckinridge resisted, "that will not do. They are only children and I cannot expose them to such a fire as they will receive on our center. Go back and tell Wharton and Echols they must contract the lines."

Semple could see that it was useless to protest. Breckinridge was adamant about not using the cadets.

Before he even reached the center of the line Semple could see that it was hopeless to try to contract the line and rejoin it. There was nobody in the center where the concentration of fire would be heaviest, and the two lines were now so close that it looked as if the Stars and Stripes would soon be a part of Breckinridge's line. He turned his horse and spurred it furiously, rushing back to Breckinridge as fast as his mount would take him.

"It is too late, General," Semple shouted, his voice taking on a ring of urgency. "The Federals are right on us. If the cadets are ordered up, we can close the gap in our center!"

"Will the boys stand?" Breckinridge asked, apprehensively.

"Yes, sir!" Semple answered with confidence. "They are of the best Virginia blood, and they will."

Breckinridge looked across the battlefield. He could barely make out the flowing white flag of the Virginia Military Institute, now riddled with bullet holes. He didn't want to use the cadets. He had never even been fully comfortable asking them to come along. Breckinridge, who had helped form national policy as vice president of the United States, was about to make a decision far more difficult than any he had ever been called upon to make while in Washington.

Breckinridge looked at the VMI flag in the distance, then back at Semple. He turned and fired a glance at the cadet artillery, seeing not boys, but four committed gun crews feverishly pouring fire onto the enemy. They looked no different than the other gunners.

Breckinridge's chest heaved with a deep sigh. With tears in his eyes, he looked back to Semple and said in a voice that was barely audible over the noise of the battle, "Put the boys in, and may God forgive me for the order."

Semple saluted and rushed back to the line. He was relieved to see that, although the gap was still there, it had not yet been filled by soldiers wearing blue uniforms. He found Ship and relayed Breckinridge's reluctant order.

Ship immediately had his young charges oblique into the gap. They responded without hesitation, and they found themselves standing on the first line, toe to toe with the enemy.

No longer tucked in behind Breckinridge's front line, the cadets were now a part of that line, and immediately came under even heavier fire. Still several hundred yards from the farm they could see through the smoke and haze, a shell struck in the midst of Company D. First Sergeant William Cabell and Privates Charles Crockett and Henry Jones, none out of his teens, were thrown into the air. Cabell landed in an awkward position, writhing in obvious agony as his lifeblood poured onto the soggy ground. With the cadets looking on in horror, his hands clawed at the ground, pulling up large clumps of grass. Crockett and Jones suffered less, their mangled bodies dead by the time they returned to the ground.

If the cadets were going to panic, this would have been the ideal time. Three of their companions had just met the most horrific of deaths directly in front of their eyes. Boys would have frozen in terror, but the cadets were now boys only in years. The past sixty minutes had seen them pass into adulthood, and they were now men. They glanced at their fallen friends, closed the gap, and moved on.

A scant fifty yards farther and another of their number would take his last earthly breath. William McDowell, who had turned seventeen just a few months earlier, fell with a bullet through his chest.

Cadet Captain Sam Shriver of Company C raised his sword high above his head, exhorting his company not to falter. As the cadets looked on in horror, Shriver's arm took on an awkward angle and his sword catapulted through the air as a minie ball passed cleanly through his elbow.

They had wanted a chance to take part in a fight. Now, they were in for the fight of their young lives, none of them knowing they stood on the threshold of history.

12

If anything, the battle was still in a crescendo of intensity. The cadets, although side by side with some of the Confederacy's best fighters, did not have to fear that they presented a weak spot in the line for the Union to exploit.

Private Pierre Woodlief of Company C, one of the baggage guards who had joined John Wise in his rush from the baggage wagons to the advancing cadet line on Shirley's Hill, went down. His close friend, sixteen-year-old George Lee, looked at his friend writhing in the mud, obviously in great pain.

"Captain Preston," Lee shouted, still looking at his closest friend. "May I please stop and tend to Pierre?"

Preston waved his only arm impatiently as a signal to Lee to keep up with the line. "Stay in rank!" Preston shouted. "We can't stop now!"

Lee looked back at his fallen friend as he advanced. He would almost have rather been shot, himself.

Not far from Lee, Company B's James Darden fell, bleeding profusely from a thigh wound. Almost immediately he forced himself back to his feet and struggled to keep up with his friends. Within a few steps he fell once more, this time with a severe arm wound.

Thomas Jefferson saw his friend Darden go down for the second time. Having heard Preston's orders, he had no intentions of stopping to help Darden. However, as he passed Darden's prone body, Jefferson could see the blood spurting from Darden's arm. Jefferson knew Darden would soon bleed to death if something wasn't done as quickly as possible. Dropping out of rank, he removed his canteen and tore at the strap. It refused to give. Finally, with a Hurculean effort, Jefferson ripped the strap from the canteen and swiftly tied it around Darden's helpless arm. Using it as a

tourniquet to stem the flow of blood, Jefferson instructed the injured cadet to keep the strap tight. "I'll be back as soon as I can to see how you
are," Jefferson shouted over his shoulder as he scurried to catch up with
his company. Jefferson's quick thinking would later be credited with saving Darden's life.

The cadets had now reached the Bushong House. Companies A and
B passed around the house on the right while Companies C and D went to
their left. The constant rapping of bullets against the side of the house
impressed the cadets. It was not unlike the sound made when a handful
of pebbles was tossed into a lake, only much louder and more prolonged.
Inside the house, huddled in the basement with their livestock, Jacob and
Sarah Bushong did not find the noise as fascinating.

Beyond the house and outbuildings the young soldiers could see an
orchard. Having been forced to separate to go around the house, they
were now somewhat disorganized. Ship would gather them together once
they reached the trees.

They were now closer to the enemy than they ever imagined they
would be. Despite the smoke, they now could make out the forms of the
Union soldiers just ahead. The United States flag was prominently displayed less than three hundred yards to their front.

Jacob Imboden, General Imboden's youngest brother, was hit by a
fragment of shell. Then, Private Preston Cocke had his gun shattered into
several pieces by another shell. The battle was gaining in intensity.

Ship turned to Frank Preston and gave him a hand signal, indicating
to the one-armed captain where he wanted him to position his company.
As branches crashed down around them, Ship thought to himself, "We've
just walked into the devil's living room!"

As the cadets passed from the last row of outbuildings into the orchard, they could see many of their number bleeding, but refusing to step
out of rank. The cadets had been taught that the first duty of a good soldier was to obey his orders. The order had been given to advance and it
had not yet been rescinded, so advance they would. Another blast from
the Union front and their line staggered, halting momentarily. Resolutely,
they pushed forward into the orchard.

As the cadets entered the orchard, they encountered a strange sight,
stranger than anything they could have imagined. Wounded Confederate
soldiers threaded their ways through the advancing ranks, trying to get to
the rear where the fire would be less concentrated. The withdrawal of the
wounded men in itself was not unusual, but the manner in which many
were retreating was. Several of the wounded who were still able to hold
their weapons had commandeered Federal prisoners to hoist some of the
more seriously wounded Confederates over their shoulders, and the
wounded men were now being transported to the rear on the reluctant
backs of their captives.

Just inside the orchard the cadets took shelter behind whatever protection they could find. Shot and shell tore splinters from the trees around the cadets, and branches and limbs fell on top of them. It seemed as if no human being would leave the orchard alive.

Private Franklin Gibson of Company B received the first of seven wounds he would receive that fateful day. Louis Wise was also hit, Gustavus Nalle quickly coming to his aid. Nalle had no choice but to ignore Wise's cries of pain as he half carried, half dragged his friend to a safer place behind one of the Bushong outbuildings.

Francis Smith of Company A was shot in the mouth, the ball shattering his jawbone and exiting through his neck. Almost at the same time another ball struck him in the shoulder, breaking his collarbone. Lucien Ricketts, still on horseback, quickly helped Smith onto his horse and proceeded toward New Market for treatment. "You're finished fighting for today, Francis," Ricketts informed his companion.

The advance was now slowed, and the ground was gained literally by inches. Pious Henry Wise began to swear vehemently at the top of his voice, to the complete surprise of the cadets who could hear him. Wise had never been known to utter a single foul word, and was considered by the cadets to be almost puritanical. He had always made it a practice to admonish the cadets against swearing. Now, however, he seemed to be making up for lost time.

As the cadets huddled in the orchard, James Preston, an eighteen-year-old private in Company B, reeled backwards, falling to the ground unconscious. Those who saw him fall were sure he had been killed. However, within minutes he had regained consciousness and, as he hurriedly examined his body for the wound that had knocked him off his feet, he came to realize that the ball had struck the Testament he had been carrying in his left breast pocket. Although the Testament was no longer readable, Preston's wound was minor and he was able to resume his place in the ranks.

Then Edward Smith of Company A was hit, followed quickly by Stanard and Jefferson. Two friends stopped and asked Jefferson if they could do anything to help. Refusing their offer, he painfully raised himself onto one elbow as he pointed forward. "That's the place for you," he shouted. "You can do me no good!"

Private Edmund Berkeley, who had already been wounded himself, found Stanard lying in a great deal of pain. His leg had been shattered by canister fire and he was bleeding badly. Berkeley struggled to fashion a tourniquet from an old towel. Applying it to Stanard's leg to stem the bleeding, he then proceeded painfully toward the rear for treatment.

A crisis was pending. The fire was becoming so heavy that it was no longer wise to move forward, yet it was just as imprudent to try to retreat. An unknown voice yelled loudly, "Fall back and rally on Edgar's battalion!"

The Bushong Farm as it appeared around 1880.
Courtesy of Hall of Valor Civil War Museum

Incensed, First Sergeant Andrew Pizzini cocked his gun. His eyes blazing, he shouted, "I'll personally shoot the first one of y'all that takes a step to the rear!"

The cadets, apparently more afraid of their irate companion than of the Federal fire, resumed their faltering push toward the enemy line.

*   *   *

Back at the turnpike Breckinridge saw that Stahel's cavalry was preparing to charge. He quickly directed McLaughlin to have Chapman's Battery, Berkeley's Battery, and Captain Minge's VMI Battery move up the pike to a low stone wall, where he had them set up. "Have them double load with canister!" he shouted to McLaughlin, who rapidly complied.

As Stahel's men made their advance, the artillery waited patiently. Coming over a small crest, the unsuspecting Union horsemen were met with a barrage which was devastating. Men and horses fell in mid-stride, reeling from the unexpected blast. Then, McClanahan's guns on the opposite side of Smith's Creek opened on them. The cavalry, not knowing which direction they could use for retreat, staggered and careened off one another in confusion.

As riderless horses ran aimlessly through the throng, one Union soldier daringly rode through the massed batteries at full gallop. Behind their lines he wheeled and rejoined his comrades. Despite the gravity of the situation, soldiers on both sides cheered at his bravery.

Perhaps inspired, or embarrassed, by this single horseman's daring ride, several Union officers enjoined their confused troops to retreat. Colonel John Wynkoop and Colonel William Tibbitts screamed as loudly as

The Bushong Farm as it appears today. This photo is taken from the approximate location of the shell explosion which killed Cabell, Crockett, and Jones, and wounded several others.

Photo by Author

they could, but the panic-stricken cavalry was not to be rallied. With some wounded so badly they were barely able to remain in the saddle, the battered Federal cavalry fled in disarray. They would no longer be a factor in this battle.

Sigel, seeing his cavalry routed, started for the pike to take command and try to stem the pandemonium. Several men of the 12th West Virginia, seeing their general appearing to flee the field, rose and followed. The enraged Sigel, unable to make himself heard or understood in the noise of the battle, was forced to return to his position. He would later complain sarcastically that he did not think a major general who commanded his own department should have to function as a watchman. Sigel, however, unwittingly had contributed to the confused state of the West Virginians. In the excitement of the fighting, he had unknowingly lapsed into his native tongue, shouting his orders in German and confounding all but his German-speaking subordinates.

On the other side of the line, the cadets continued to take heavy casualties. Frank Gibson, who had by now been wounded six times, was hit a seventh time, his leg shattered below the knee. This final wound mercifully took him out of the battle. He had already had two fingers shot off and been struck in the face, along with four lesser wounds. Yes, General Breckinridge, the cadets would fight, and they would fight well.

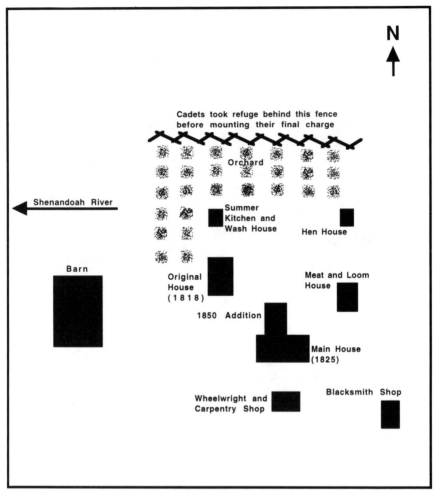

The above plan is believed to approximate the layout of the Bushong Farm at the time of the battle.

Courtesy of Hall of Valor Civil War Museum

Then, Commander Scott Ship was hit. Struck on the left shoulder by a nearly spent shell, he was knocked heavily to the ground. Stunned, he lay motionless in the mud. Captain Henry Wise, Old Chinook, immediately took command and ordered the cadets to advance to a rail fence at the northern border of the orchard. Several more cadets would fall in the short thirty yard run to the fence. One of the wounded was Private Edward Christian of Company B. Today was his sixteenth birthday. Shortly after Christian fell, Private James Goodwin of Company C, also was wounded. Goodwin was to turn nineteen the day after the battle. A third cadet, Private Alexander Stuart of Company D, had celebrated his eighteenth birthday the day before the battle. He would emerge unscathed.

Once at the fence, the cadets huddled as close to the ground as they could get. Captain Frank Preston lay on his only arm, determined that he would not lose a second limb. Peering ahead they could make out the lower portions of the Union gunners' legs and the wheels of their guns. Nothing else was visible through the thick smoke. The fence, about four feet high, and consisting of three small rails, offered little protection, but the young soldiers from Lexington were happy to find even that.

Unbelievably, the cadets had still not fired their weapons to this point. It had only been a short distance from where they had entered the front line of battle and, thus far, self-preservation had been their most urgent need. Now, Wise ordered them to fire.

Wise's order was met with a great deal of enthusiasm. The cadets, however, immediately learned that their wooden forestock channels had swollen badly from the constant rain of the past four days, and their ramrods could only be extracted with great difficulty. The rate of fire from the cadet corps was seriously hampered by this latest development, but the undaunted cadets did the best they could under the circumstances.

On the VMI left, Wharton's harried men were near retreat. They had been forced back several yards, leaving the cadets' left flank dangerously exposed. The Union guns took full advantage. Many cadets were undoubtedly saved over the next few minutes by the 26th Virginia, which sent a company of riflemen through the woods on the extreme left to lay down fire on Carlin and Snow.

*   *   *

It was now the middle of the afternoon. The battle had been raging for nearly four hours. Stahel had been routed and would no longer be a factor. Sigel would have to do something to take back the momentum or the day would belong to the Confederates. Although he had started the day with nearly a two to one advantage over Breckinridge, he now found himself outnumbered. He either failed to realize this or decided it didn't matter. He decided to launch a counterattack against the advancing Southerners.

Sigel directed the troops of the 34th Massachusetts, the 1st West Virginia, and the 54th Pennsylvania to make the attack. Colonel Joseph Thoburn rode along the lines shouting, "Prepare to charge! Prepare to charge!"

The Pennsylvanians had only recently arrived on the field and, nearly exhausted from their forced march, had deployed immediately into column to the left and rear of the West Virginians. Perhaps it was their bone-numbing fatigue, or maybe it was because of the ear-splitting noise of the battle; for whatever the reason, they never heard the order to join in the attack.

As the attack began, the 34th Massachusetts rose with fixed bayonets and advanced under a pelting salvo of bullets. The regimental mascot dogs ran on ahead of the regiment, as had always been their custom, only to be killed immediately. Behind the orchard fence the cadets fired as furiously as their fettered ramrods would permit, a fire which was added to by the artillery on the turnpike.

Colonel Jacob Campbell, commander of the 54th Pennsylvania, saw the 1st West Virginia rise and begin their attack. Although he had not received word of the plan, intuitively he ordered his men to fix their bayonets and follow the lead of the West Virginians. Sigel's men now had to pass through the same sheet of fire which they themselves had only a few minutes before been putting up before the Confederates. Both lines fought bravely, each determined not to be the first to give way. The two lines wavered but neither would retreat. The question now became who had the most resolve; who was most determined to hold his position.

The question was soon answered. Coming over a small crest, Jacob Campbell was distressed to see the 1st West Virginia already in retreat, even though the advance had proceeded less than one hundred yards. Then, Campbell's regiment came under heavy fire themselves from the 23rd Virginia. Without his realizing it, the 22nd and 23rd Virginia had both masterfully worked their way around Campbell's left flank. Now, with the 1st West Virginia falling back, he was also exposed to the fire of the 62nd Virginia and the VMI cadets on his right flank. He was in extreme danger of being surrounded! He quickly reacted, ordering his men to pull back while stopping every few feet to load and fire at their adversaries. Before the battle would be decided, the 54th Pennsylvania would take 254 casualties out of the 566 men they had engaged, the most of any unit in the fight. As Campbell pulled back, some stragglers of the 123rd Ohio joined them.

At about the same time Colonel George Wells of the 34th Massachusetts also saw the West Virginians retreating. Still unsure of what had happened, he immediately ordered a halt to the attack, but his men could not hear him over the pitch of the battle. The regiment continued to advance, suffering nearly 50 percent casualties. Desperately Wells ran to the front and grabbed his color bearer and turned him around. With Wells yelling, "Don't run! Keep your line!" his men were finally able to withdraw.

Reaching their starting point, Wells and his men dug in. On the left, Campbell's 54th Pennsylvania did the same. The 1st West Virginia, however, continued retreating, creating a huge gap between the two remaining infantry regiments. Both the 34th Massachusetts and the 54th Pennsylvania now stood alone, too far apart to help one another. With both flanks exposed, the two regiments bravely continued the fight.

*   *   *

Back in the Bushong orchard, cadet Private John Upshur struggled to get to the fence to join his comrades.

"Come on, Upshur," someone shouted, "there's no lagging in Company C today!"

But the cadet who shouted at the sixteen-year-old Upshur did not realize his comrade was not lagging intentionally. With his next step, Upshur's shattered right leg gave way, no longer able to support his weight. Epitomizing the determination that was to be the hallmark of the corps that day, Upshur painfully pushed himself forward with his good leg, leaving a trail of blood behind him to mark his agonizing route.

Less than two hundred yards now separated the cadets from the Union line. The 51st Virginia was reluctantly starting to give way on the cadets' left, while the 62nd Virginia was taking a battering on the right. Many of the beleaguered men of both regiments ran back through the ranks of the cadets, who were also drawing attention, positioned as they were on the immediate front of the 34th Massachusetts.

In addition, Sigel's eighteen guns poured a constant barrage of grape and canister into the corps and their fellow Confederates. The 34th Massachusetts and 54th Pennsylvania, both now entrenched at their original positions, continued their deadly fire. It seemed suicidal even to raise one's head. The next successful move in this deadly encounter would probably decide the outcome of the battle.

Colonel Edgar's 26th Virginia was inflicting heavy damage on the Union right, having advanced in comparative safety through the woods above the river. Woodson's company of Missourians, temporarily attached to the 62nd Virginia, bravely silenced another Union gun. Although this action took some of the pressure off the 62nd Virginia, Woodson would lose 60 of his 70 men in the effort. They had been close enough to the enemy to do their fighting with pistols.

Breckinridge realized the outcome of the battle now hinged on his next decision. There was no room for error. With little hesitancy, he ordered his line to make another advance.

Immediately, the color bearer for the 51st Virginia rose and rushed ahead of the line, only to be cut down by a storm of bullets. Another Virginian ran out and picked up the banner, only to meet the same fate. A captain in the 51st could be heard instructing his men, "Draw low and fire at their knees. Don't overshoot! Keep steady; we'll whip them."

Then the color bearer of the 26th Virginia rose and rushed forward, followed closely by the troops of that regiment. On the Union side, Colonel Wells of the 34th Massachusetts saw the flags of the two Virginia regiments moving forward and immediately knew what was coming. He feared the worst.

The fence at the north edge of the orchard, just past the Bushong House, which appears in the background. The cadets took refuge behind this fence just prior to their charge across the "Field of Lost Shoes."

Photo by Author

Seeing the rest of the Confederate line rise up, Henry Wise was determined that the cadets were not going to be left out. With yet another uncharacteristic oath, he shouted to his charges, "Get up from here and give it to the Yankees!" Responding immediately to their new leader's command, the corps rose as one, gave a shout, and forged forward.

Immediately in front of the cadets, the wheat field lay under two inches of water. This would provide no obstacle to the young soldiers, however, as they stormed through the water and ankle deep mud. Cadet after cadet had his shoes pulled off by the suction of the thick mud. Forever after, the cadets would refer to this wheat field as the "Field of Lost Shoes."

13

Back at the turnpike, the cadet artillerists saw color bearer Oliver Perry Evans raise the VMI flag and move forward out of the orchard. Taking a moment from their nearly continuous firing, they offered up a cheer, even though their comrades were unable to hear it. Quickly Minge directed them back to the business at hand, and they maintained their fire until the line had advanced too far to safely continue to do so without shooting into their own lines.

As they had done all day, the cadets maintained their order as they advanced across the "Field of Lost Shoes", despite the heavy firing from the Union line. For every cadet who fell, those on either side of the wounded youth closed the ranks and continued on, as they had been instructed to do when they first entered the fray. Even under heavy fire, orders were meant to be obeyed.

Even the heavens seemed anxious to get into the action, with the rain now falling as heavily as it had at any time during the day. The darkened skies lit up with the flash of lightning. The roar of any thunder that accompanied the flashes was lost in the noise of the battle.

Eager to make the charge across the open field, the cadets dashed forward through Jacob Bushong's knee high wheat, unmindful of the weather or the danger. Stopping only long enough to reload, they fired their weapons on the run.

Sigel, riding bravely back and forth behind the Union line, realized the danger he was now in. If he was to salvage the day he was going to have to give some more ground. He reluctantly ordered Carlin and Snow to pull their guns back. The gunners responded to the order immediately. In the frantic rush to get out of harm's way, one of Carlin's gunners fell, the wheel of the gun passing over him. Simultaneously, the cadets and the men of the 34th Massachusetts saw the attempt to remove the guns and interpreted the action identically: the Union gunners appeared to be abandoning the line!

As the guns were being limbered, those guns which still remained active continued their deadly work. Along the Confederate line the charging soldiers fell one after another. The onslaught just would not let up.

On the Union side, several of Wells' men saw the white flag with the seal of Virginia emblazoned on for the first time. The men were unsure of what regiment they were fighting. Some of them, unfamiliar with the cadets' uniforms as well as their flag, would later say they thought they were a French regiment. One thing they were sure of: whatever regiment it was, they were brave fighters! An admiring Union officer would later say, "I never really saw discipline until I saw those boys advance!"

The admiration for the cadets' performance was not restricted to their Union opponents. The same Confederate regulars who had mocked them on Shirley's Hill earlier in the day were now looking on them in awe. Wounded soldiers raised themselves up as they passed, cheering them on.

The rain was heavy, the bullets deadly, and the mud continued to suck the shoes from their feet. Some of the cadets stopped momentarily to retrieve their footwear, others continued toward their goal with no shoes. Through the fog and smoke they were now able to clearly see the men of Kleiser's Battery, trying to move their guns from the field.

As they watched, a shell which had come from the direction of the turnpike, perhaps from the cadet artillery, knocked the wheel off one of the guns. Its crew tried frantically to drag it to safety before the onrushing line arrived. Frank Preston, his one arm still intact, shouted, "They're going to run! They're trying to limber up!"

Henry Wise joined in the cry, almost beside himself now with the excitement of the charge. Waving his sword high over his head he screamed, "Take those guns! Take those guns!"

Back at the orchard, Scott Ship regained consciousness just in time to see the cadets in the midst of their charge. Proudly, he watched his boys proceed across the open field.

Seeing the charging cadets, the few men of the 1st West Virginia who still remained on the field now broke, leaving Kleiser's guns totally unprotected. Several cadets, sensing that the Union guns could now be taken, yelled "Shoot the horses! Shoot the horses!", knowing that this would prevent Kleiser from moving the guns.

With the cadets now nearly upon them, Kleiser's beleaguered gunners didn't even have the opportunity to spike their guns. They had waited too long, or perhaps the situation had come unraveled all too quickly. For whatever the reason, the guns could no longer be rendered unusable to their captors!

Kleiser, although only twenty-two years old himself, was experienced, with more than two years as an artillerist, but he had never been in a situation such as this. Most of his men were Germans, as was he, and the cadets could hear his frantic instructions being barked in a language strange to their ears.

Several of Kleiser's gun crew made one last desperate effort to get the guns off the field. Then, when it became apparent to them that they would not be able to resist any longer, they broke and left the field. The gun was now abandoned. The charging cadets, now within a few yards of the abandoned position, saw the last of the Federal gunners retreating without their cannon. And, although they were still receiving fire, it was finally lessening, and they instinctively knew that the outcome was now nearly decided. Covering the final twenty yards with a youthful yell, they swarmed over the unattended cannon. The gun now belonged to the cadets!

The prize was a beauty, a 12-pounder complete with its caisson. Evans climbed onto the caisson and proudly waved the VMI flag to the triumphant cheers of the cadets. For the moment, Evans and his comrades were oblivious to the continuing fire coming from the 54th Pennsylvania and 34th Massachusetts.

Other cadets, perhaps more practical, urged Evans to get down from his perch. When he had done so, several latched onto the wheels and turned the captured gun in the direction of the 34th Massachusetts, astutely taking immediate advantage of the ground they had just gained. Those on the right of the VMI line turned their attention to the unprotected right flank of the 54th Pennsylvania. Several of the cadets took prisoners.

Seeing the performance of the cadets, Major Peter J. Otey of the 30th Virginia would comment admiringly, "I never saw anything like it!"

General Breckinridge himself would later remark, "Those boys fought better than the oldest soldiers we had!"

The 34th Massachusetts stood up to the concentrated fire as long as they could. By now, ten of their officers had fallen, including their lieutenant colonel, William Lincoln. They were losing their support on the right as Carlin and Snow moved their guns.

Behind them the 12th West Virginia had already begun their retreat and would be of no help. Under a furious assault from Wharton and Echols, their position became untenable and they finally were forced to give way. They refused to break and run, however, and only reluctantly retreated, facing the Confederates and firing the entire way.

On their left, the men of Jacob Campbell's 54th Pennsylvania were also begrudgingly giving ground. Joined by more of the men from the 123rd Ohio who had not yet fallen back, they likewise refused to break

The position of the Union right, with the Bushong Farm in the background. The Bushong Barn appears just above the cannon muzzle, with the house at the extreme left, fronted by the orchard. The open ground between the farm and the cannon is part of the Field of Lost Shoes.

Photo by Author

and run. Walking backward and firing as they retreated, the Pennsylvanians successfully delayed the advancing Confederates long enough for Sigel to regain some order. The retreat, although not a model of efficiency, became more organized.

*   *   *

Giddy with the smell of victory, the cadets hovered around their captured trophy for several minutes. As they congratulated themselves, sixteen-year-old Charles Faulkner of Company B approached with 23 Union prisoners. One of the cadets shouted, "What did you do, Charlie? Surround them?"

Faulkner simply grinned and proceeded to the rear to turn over his prize to an officer who was already supervising the rounding up of the Union captives.

Wise, after allowing the cadets to enjoy the fruits of their effort for a few minutes, then called out, "Let's form up! This battle isn't over yet!"

Obediently the cadets resumed formation and began the pursuit of the now rapidly retreating Federal army, which was only firing at their pursuers occasionally now. The Confederates, on the other hand, poured volley after volley into the retreating Northerners. In the distance the cadets

Approximate location of Kleiser's battery, captured by the cadets.

Photo by Author

saw a Union battery careening wildly toward the bottom of the slope. As they watched, it struck a small stump and turned over. Several of the cadets cheered mockingly.

"Mark time," Wise commanded, "half-wheel to the right!"

Advancing down the backside of Bushong's Hill, they had difficulty containing themselves. They had tasted battle. They were now blooded. And they had won!

* * *

The grizzled sergeant in the 62nd Virginia examined the Federal pistol he had just picked up as he advanced down the hill. "Y' know," he said to his friend marching on his right, "I jest realized it was a year ago today that we laid Ole Stonewall to rest. Reckon this battle woulda made him real happy."

The second man, more interested in stemming the flow of blood from his wounded hand than in looking at his friend's war souvenir, merely grunted. The shell fragment had hit something else first and was nearly spent by the time it had struck him, but his hand, which had given him no pain during the heat of the battle, was now beginning to throb badly.

The sergeant, paying no attention to his friend's injured hand, went on. "I ain't never been what yuh might call a religious man, but I ain't sure Stonewall didn't have somethin' to do with this here battle today, what with this rain and all. This is his Valley, don't ferget. Almost seems like he wanted to do whatever he could up there, jest so's he could say he had a hand in this."

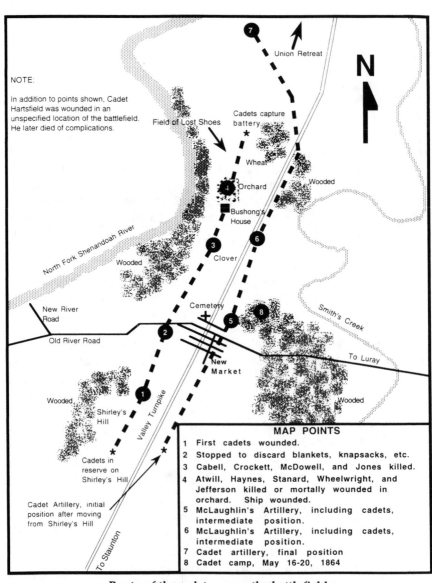

NOTE:

In addition to points shown, Cadet Hartsfield was wounded in an unspecified location of the battlefield. He later died of complications.

Union Retreat

N

Field of Lost Shoes

Cadets capture battery
*

Wheat

Orchard
4

Wooded

Bushong's House

North Fork Shenandoah River

3
Clover

6

New River Road

Cemetery

Wooded

5
8

Smith's Creek

Old River Road

To Luray

New Market

Wooded

2

Wooded

1

Shirley's Hill

Valley Turnpike

*
Cadets in reserve on Shirley's Hill

*

Cadet Artillery, initial position after moving from Shirley's Hill

To Staunton

MAP POINTS

1 First cadets wounded.
2 Stopped to discard blankets, knapsacks, etc.
3 Cabell, Crockett, McDowell, and Jones killed.
4 Atwill, Haynes, Stanard, Wheelwright, and Jefferson killed or mortally wounded in orchard. Ship wounded.
5 McLaughlin's Artillery, including cadets, intermediate position.
6 McLaughlin's Artillery, including cadets, intermediate position.
7 Cadet artillery, final position
8 Cadet camp, May 16-20, 1864

Route of the cadets across the battlefield
Total route slightly more than two miles

Map by Author

His wounded friend looked to his left at the cadets, now marching once again in perfect formation as they joined in the chase of Sigel's army. "Y'all can't ferget them boys over yonder, neither. They's his, too," he said, wrapping a grimy rag around his wound.

The sergeant watched the cadets for a moment, nodding his head in admiration. "He taught 'em to fight real good," he said softly, "and that's a fact!"

*　　　　　*　　　　　*

"Do you think it's finally over?" Sarah Bushong asked tentatively as she huddled with her husband, Jacob, in the darkened cellar of her house.

The constant clatter of bullets against the sides of the house, which they had been hearing for the past several hours, finally seemed to be letting up. A flash of lightning momentarily brightened the cellar, which had become nearly pitch dark in the gloom of the late afternoon storm.

"Seems like mebbe they're movin' on toward Mount Jackson," Jacob offered. "I think I'll go up and take me a look, jest to see if I can find out what's goin' on."

"Please be careful, Jacob," said Sarah.

Jacob ignored her admonition. After four hours of shelling, if there was one thing he didn't need right now it was Sarah telling him to be careful. As if he was going to rush right up the stairs and challenge any Union soldiers who may be straggling past!

Cautiously he made his way to the first floor. Although gunfire could still be heard in the distance, it sounded as if it was moving away from the farm. He slowly proceeded to the parlor and peered through the window. What he saw almost made him sick. Men lay in every conceivable position, all over his yard. One man directly outside the window lay with his right arm still extended above his head, his ramrod clutched in his already stiffening fingers. He apparently had been shot just as he was reloading, the ball killing him so quickly that his hand never had the time it needed to relax its grip.

The slaughter had not been limited to humans, either. Several horses, some dead, some still living, littered the ground. Most of those still living showed evidence that they would soon be joining those who were dead. One struggled unsuccessfully to rise, its shattered hind quarters unable to move.

As sad as the sight was, Jacob turned his gaze to the men, some of whom were moving slowly but painfully. Others would move no more. In the gathering darkness he could see that many were dressed in the blue uniforms of the hated Yankees, while others wore gray or butternut. Strangely, Jacob felt the same pity for the Northerners as he did for the boys from the South. Many of them would see their homes no more.

Interior of Jackson Memorial Hall at VMI. At the front of the chapel is B. West Clinedinst's famous mural of the cadet charge.

Courtesy of VMI Museum

Jacob slowly surveyed his property as well as he could from the window. Most of his fence was gone, either knocked over or shot into small pieces. Several of his trees now looked like snags extending heavenward, the branches torn off by artillery shells. The hen house had been nearly destroyed and was now leaning so badly that it looked like a light breeze would cause it to topple into an unrecognizable heap of wood. The meat and loom house, while still standing, had a number of large holes in the side visible from his vantage point. He could not see the rest of the farm, but he had a fairly good idea of what he would see if he could.

The damage even extended into the interior of the house. Stray shells had splintered large chunks from the walls, and much of the furniture showed the signs of having been struck several times. His gun, the one over the mantle that he had planned to use against the Yankees himself if he had to, would fire no more, its stock having been shattered and the barrel bent awkwardly. Strangely, it still hung over the fireplace, just as it had when he had placed it there. "It sure didn't look like that when I set it up there, though," he mused.

The movement of a badly wounded soldier crawling slowly toward the house caught his eye. It was just a young boy. And what kind of uniform was that? Jacob had never seen a soldier dressed like that before, and he wasn't even sure which side he had fought on. One thing that Jacob knew without a doubt, though, the boy needed help.

The charge of the cadets at New Market, as depicted by B. West Clinedinst (VMI 1880) in the Jackson Memorial Hall at VMI.

Courtesy of VMI Museum

"Sarah," he shouted, "you'd best be comin' up here. I'm gonna need some help here!"

Not waiting for his wife to come up from the cellar, Jacob rushed outside, stumbling over a prone body which apparently had tried to take shelter on his porch as his final effort. The man, a Union soldier, had not quite reached his destination.

Turning the corner of the house Jacob spied the boy once more, still crawling slowly, turned slightly onto his left side. His right hand clutched at his belly, and Jacob could see the gaping wound even in the gathering darkness. Somewhere behind him, another wounded man moaned in pain.

Just as Jacob reached the wounded youth, Sarah rounded the corner of the house. Her eyes darted left and right as she ran to Jacob's side, unable to take in all the carnage at one glance.

"How badly is he hurt?" she asked.

"Pretty bad, it appears," answered Jacob. "Let's try to get him inside out of this rain."

With Jacob taking the boy under the arms and Sarah grasping his legs at the knees, the two laboriously struggled to get him into the house. Several times the boy screamed out in pain, despite the Bushong's efforts to handle him gently. Once inside, they placed him gently on the floor. Sarah, not yet having seen the destruction in her house, looked for the lantern which was normally on the table. Pieces of the base were there, but little else.

"Fetch some candles, Jacob," she ordered, "and hurry!"

Surprised at his wife's tone, Jacob stood transfixed.

Looking up at him, she said once more, sternly, "Don't jest stand there, old man! This boy could die if we don't do somethin', and I can't do nothin 'till I see what's wrong with 'im!"

Sarah's biting voice, in sharp contrast to her normal soft speech, startled Jacob Bushong into action. Rushing into the next room he rummaged around until he found a candle. Outside, he could see what looked like a wagon wheel, leaning at an odd angle and still burning. He ran outside and lit the candle from the small flame that still flickered on the wheel. Returning inside, he dripped some wax onto the table and stuck the candle into it before it hardened. There would be no time to find a proper candle holder!

Already Sarah had torn the boy's coat open and was examining his wound. Tearing a large piece from her skirt she gently dabbed at the bloody opening, the boy flinching at her touch.

"I'm gonna need some water," she said. "Could you get me a bucket?"

Wordlessly, Jacob dashed back outside to the well. Filling the bucket, he turned to run back into the house when he saw the two shadowy figures dragging an injured companion between them. His feet left two furrows in the mud as his friends hauled his limp body toward Jacob's porch.

"Can y'all help us, mister?" the taller of the two inquired. "Our friend's hurt real bad here."

"Bring him on inside," Jacob directed. "We'll do what we can."

As the evening progressed, more soldiers would be brought into the Bushong home, now a makeshift hospital. The Bushongs would try to treat them all, making no distinction between uniforms. They did not know it, but many of their neighbors were being far less charitable, refusing to even allow wounded enemy soldiers into their homes.

*   *   *

Colonel George Patton of the 22nd Virginia and his counterpart from the 62nd Virginia, Colonel George H. Smith, walked casually down the small hill as their troops continued the pursuit of Sigel's army. The two were cousins, as well as good friends, and they discussed their respective parts of the now finished battle as they walked.

Hearing a horse behind them, they turned simultaneously just as General Breckinridge approached.

"Congratulations, General," Patton exclaimed.

"Thank you, gentlemen," Breckinridge responded. "Your men performed admirably today. We can all be proud of what we did."

The two colonels agreed. Breckinridge dismounted and offered the use of his horse. "I shouldn't be riding when you who did the fighting are walking. Why don't you ride for a while and I'll walk."

"Oh, no sir," both said incredulously. "That just wouldn't be right."

"Well, then," said the general, "we'll all walk!"

Leading his horse, the three discussed the battle and what Sigel may try to do when he got to Mount Jackson and found the bridge burned.

"We may still have some more fighting to do before the day is out," said Breckinridge.

Patton chuckled. "I'd like to be there to see Sigel's face when he finds out John was burnin' the bridge while the fightin' was goin' on."

The three laughed together. The two colonels complimented Breckinridge on his plan to send General Imboden to the bridge. Cutting off Sigel's only retreat route was ingenius.

After some lighthearted banter, Breckinridge turned serious. "I just remembered something," he said. "I must go and see those young boys."

Mounting his horse, he bade farewell to Smith and Patton and rode in the direction of the cadets.

With the Union army now in full retreat, the cadets had been receiving no resistance as they proceeded down the hill behind the Bushong Farm. So, as they marched they gathered souvenirs, material which had been discarded by the Yankees in their haste to fall back. Guns, clothing, knapsacks, canteens; there was plenty for everyone! Soon the boys were having difficulty carrying all their booty. Moses Ezekiel dropped some of his mementos and had to backtrack to pick them up.

Seeing the familiar figure of the general approaching, Samuel Adams of Company C became alarmed. There were only two cadets younger than the fifteen-year-old Adams, and he wasn't sure what to expect. Breckinridge was upon them now, so there would be no possibility of discarding the collected relics without being seen. Adams was sure the general was about to give them a good tongue lashing for gathering their trophies.

To the young private's immense relief, Breckinridge had no such thought in mind. Instead he said, as the cadets stood respectfully at attention, their souvenirs at their feet, "Young men, I have to thank you for the result of today's actions. I am proud of you. More than I can express. You have done more than your share for the day, and I can ask you to do no more. You may fall out and rest here. The remainder of the army can take care of Mr. Sigel."

The exhausted cadets fell out of rank, dropping onto the ground for some much needed rest.

Riding away, Breckinridge slowed his horse long enough to say, "Well done, Virginians! Well done!"

14

At the turnpike the cadet artillery crews limbered their guns and, with the rest of the artillery, began the pursuit of the Union army. They were still receiving occasional fire from the Federals and it was necessary to remain alert at all times. There would be time to relax later, and, for now, chasing General Sigel had a high priority.

The 34th Massachusetts and 54th Pennsylvania had joined forces and were now retiring slowly and in an orderly fashion, in contrast to the rest of the Union forces. These two regiments were still to be reckoned with, as they stopped often to fire another volley at the Confederate forces following closely behind. Their combined effort was buying much needed time for Sigel's forces, disorganized as they were, to gain valuable ground.

The mood among the artillery crews, however, was lighthearted and the air was filled with a great deal of good-natured banter, despite the dismal weather. The source of much of this banter was a member of Chapman's Battery, a tall, thin man who could not have weighed much more than one hundred pounds. From the onset of the battle he had kept up a constant chatter until the guns reached the town. At that point the noise became so great that he could not have been heard even if he had been talking, which, many of the cadets suspected, he probably was. If he had stopped talking during the battle, he was making up for lost time now, as his mouth had not stopped since the artillery had limbered up. His friends referred to him as "Sponge," a nickname which had no apparent meaning. Some of the cadets had asked him how he had acquired the appellation, and his friends had immediately laughed uproariously.

"Y'all gonna tell 'em, Sponge?" a sergeant asked.

Sponge answered the sergeant with an oath, which precipitated more laughter.

"Well, then," replied the sergeant, "I reckon I'll have to."

For the first time since the battle had ceased, Sponge chose to remain quiet.

"Take a good look at 'im," instructed the sergeant to those who had asked. "Y'all ever see a human bein' that skinny? I mean, I'll grant y'all this much, there ain't none of us here eatin' enough to get fat, but Sponge is skinnier than anyone I ever seen. Even before the war he was skinny."

Sponge was now grinning good-naturedly, but still not saying anything.

The sergeant continued. "Well, the first day this battery was organized we all took one look at ole Sponge here, and we all agreed that he weren't no thicker than one of them sponges we swab out the gun barrel with, after we fire a volley. Matter 'a fact, first thing we told 'im was not to stand beside the sponge 'cause somebody might jest grab him and try to use 'im. And that ain't all bad, though. We figger we're one of the luckiest gun crews in General Lee's army, 'cause if we ever lose our real sponge, we'll jest dip his head in a bucket and run him down the barrel. Fact is, we've talked about doin' jest that very thing some day when we're drillin', jest to make sure he fits. My own personal opinion is that he ain't quite big enough to douse the sparks on the sides 'a the barrel, but that there's jest me doin' the talkin'."

The rest of the crew laughed again, seemingly oblivious to the unruly retreat scene that was unfolding several hundred yards ahead of them.

Another man joined in the conversation. "Ain't no other crew in the Confederacy, or prob'ly the Union either, fer that matter, that has a spare sponge that walks alongside the gun," he said. "We don't even have to carry 'im!"

Sponge picked up a splinter of wood from the road and tossed it playfully at his latest tormentor, much to the delight of his fellow artillerists.

Before the conversation could continue, a voice shouted, "Watch yerself! They's fixin' to fire at us again."

The rear guard of Sigel's army, the Pennsylvanians and their counterparts from Massachusetts, had turned and were again aiming their weapons at the artillery. The cadets, along with the men of the other artillery crews, either took refuge behind their guns or flattened themselves onto the ground. The minie balls hummed like bees as they passed harmlessly by.

One of Berkeley's gunners climbed onto his caisson and waved his hat in a wide arc at the Union soldiers as he mocked them.

"Y'all missed us agin!" he shouted at the hapless Federal soldiers. "Old Abe sure ain't gittin' his money's worth outta this box of minies!"

A Union soldier could be heard shouting something back, but the words were unintelligible.

"Mebbe he's agreein' with yuh, Caleb," said Sponge, as he stood up once more. "Why don't we show 'im how to shoot?"

Sponge's crew enthusiastically endorsed the suggestion and quickly threw themselves into setting up their gun. The cadets, as well as the other batteries, waited patiently for them to finish their task. Many "helpful" comments were offered to the crew as they labored, to the amusement of the rest who were watching. It was becoming more like a picnic than a pursuit following a brutal battle. Within minutes the crew had unlimbered, sighted, loaded, and sent a shell in the direction of the blue-coated soldiers, who quickly scattered to whatever protection they could find. Not having taken the time to properly sight the gun, the shot fell short of its mark, and because of the four-day rain it burrowed into the mud instead of bounding along the ground. The gunners enjoyed the effect their action had taken on the Union soldiers. The crew laughed and slapped one another on the back as they prepared to resume the march after the enemy.

As the guns rumbled down the turnpike a frustrated cadet, John Webb, said to no one in particular, "I wish those Yankees would just stop and set up. I want to get a few more shots at those boys before we quit."

Francis Lee, who normally served in Company D with Webb, and who now was walking side by side with Webb as part of the cadet artillery, agreed. "Those fellas shootin' right now are the only ones that seem to have any fight left in 'em. Look at all those others runnin' on ahead. We'll never catch up with them!"

"Ain't nothin' faster than a Yankee on retreat, son," said Sponge. "'Specially when they's a minie ball chasin' after 'im."

Murmurs of agreement arose from Sponge's crew.

"Them boys'll be stoppin' soon," offered one of the gunners. "They'll be gettin' to that bridge 'fore long, and when they find out it's burnt they'll settle in and fight again. Leastways, fer a while, 'till they see they ain't gonna be able to git away. Then they're gonna have to surrender."

Webb and Lee said nothing, but both had the same thoughts. Although they were near exhaustion, it had been a great day, and they would both like to fire just a few more shots at the enemy.

*　　　　　*　　　　　*

On the rear slope of Bushong's Hill, several of the cadets were nearly beside themselves as they searched for friends and roommates who were unaccounted for. With the cries of the wounded now having replaced the sounds of gunfire in the background, nearly every cadet seemed to be searching for someone.

"Has anyone seen William?" Robert Cabell asked frantically. "Did you see my brother anywhere?" He received no positive response. The sixteen year old dashed from group to group, occasionally grabbing a cadet by the arm and spinning him around to see his face, passing along to the next group when he realized the cadet he had turned was not his brother. "William!" he shouted. "Where are you?"

Robert Cabell was in Company B, and he had not seen his older brother William, who was at the other end of the line in Company D, since they had formed on Shirley's Hill earlier in the morning.

"Captain Wise," he shouted, spying Henry Wise walking toward him. "Have y'all seen William anywhere?"

"No, I haven't," replied Wise. "Have you seen Louis anywhere?" Wise, as was Cabell, was looking for his own brother.

"No, sir," replied Cabell. "Do yuh think we can break ranks and go back across the field and look?"

"I don't reckon that would hurt any," agreed Wise. "General Breckinridge already said we were done for the day."

The two started back up the slope toward the crest of Bushong's Hill, heading toward the position of the gun which they had captured. Others, seeing them starting back up the hill, joined in the search for other missing cadets.

Reaching Kleiser's captured gun they asked the cadets who had remained with the trophy if they had seen any of their missing friends. The answer was negative, and the searching cadets began to retrace their steps across the "Field of Lost Shoes." Over the path of the charge, wounded soldiers lay shivering in the rain. Normally the cadets would have stopped to render assistance, but right now they had a more important mission. They had to find their missing comrades and relatives.

"Over here's one of 'em," came a shout. Then, "It's Walter Jones! I'll help him. He doesn't seem to be hurt too bad!"

Several cadets rushed to Jones, who could not be seen as he lay in the wheat. The others pressed on, checking each prone body unless they could see at a glance that it wasn't a cadet. The task was a grisly one.

"Here's Charlie Smith!" a cadet shouted, almost tripping over the eighteen year old. "Someone help me! He's hurt real bad!" Three cadets immediately ran to the side of the stricken Smith, who had been badly wounded by an exploding shell.

As the gruesome parade wended its way back through the wheat field toward the orchard, cadet after cadet dropped out to assist a wounded comrade. It wasn't long before the field was dotted with kneeling young men, cradling injured friends in their laps. Wise and Cabell had been unsuccessful in locating their brothers, however.

Reaching the orchard, Wise spied Ship in a seated position, his back leaning against a tree. Rushing to his side, Wise reached for his canteen to give his wounded commander some water. Ship waved him off. "How'd the boys do?" Ship inquired in a painful tone.

"They did real good, sir," Wise answered with a grin. "Even took a gun!"

A faint smile came to Ship's face. "I knew they'd do good," he said in a low voice. "I told the general they would. I told him."

"Yes, sir," Wise replied, hoping he didn't sound too impatient. He wanted to continue the search for Louis. "Is there anything I can do for you, sir?"

"I'll be fine," said Ship. "Y'all take care of the boys, first. Are any of them hurt bad?"

'We don't know yet, sir," answered Wise. "We're still tryin' to find some of them. I'm lookin' for my brother Louis, myself."

"Well," said Ship, "y'all go ahead and look for him. I'll be fine right here. I hope he is not hurt."

"Thank you, sir," replied Wise. Then, after one last check to make sure that Ship was comfortable, Wise resumed his search. As he looked for Louis, others worked their way past him into the orchard.

As Wise meandered through the orchard in the dwindling light, he was amazed at how many cadets had fallen in such a small area without his seeing them fall. Momentary self doubts about his leadership skills surfaced as he berated himself for not paying closer attention to the cadets who had come under his charge after Ship had been wounded. Then, he realized that nobody could have known how many had been wounded, including Commander Ship himself. The fire in the orchard had been horrendous. At times it would have been suicidal simply to raise one's head to see who was crouched next to him. He had done as much as anyone could have been expected to do, including taking over quickly and decisively when Ship had been wounded.

As he wrestled with his thoughts, he was interrupted by the urgent cries of cadet Nalle. "Captain Wise! Over here. I have Louis over here."

Wise rushed to Nalle, who was waving his arms frantically to get his attention. "He's over here behind this shed, sir!" Nalle repeated. "He's hurt, and he's in a lot of pain. You'd better come!"

Wise ran to the shed which Nalle had pointed out, thinking as he ran that he would never be able to explain to his mother how he had left his brother to die on the battlefield. Rounding the corner of the shed he spied Louis huddled at the far end. He wasn't moving.

"Louis! Are you all right?" Wise shouted in a near panic.

The younger Wise opened his eyes at the familiar sound of his brother's voice. "It hurts real bad, Henry," he gasped, unable to speak without a great deal of pain.

"Just stay still, Louis," Henry directed. "You're gonna be fine. Just don't move."

Henry gently and tenderly removed Louis's jacket and examined his body carefully. Louis had two small wounds, neither of which appeared to be life threatening. Henry breathed a sigh of relief. "It doesn't look too bad, Louis," he said. "I know it hurts, but after you've had some time to heal up, you're gonna be as good as new."

Louis managed a weak smile. He knew he was going to recover, now that Henry was here. He had always looked up to his older brother, and if Henry said the wounds weren't serious, Louis believed him. He was going to live!

*   *   *

When Wise had stopped to tend to Ship, Robert Cabell had continued on his way. It wasn't that he wasn't interested in Ship's condition, but he knew there was little he would be able to do for Ship that wasn't being done already, and it was important to him that he locate his brother. Only two years separated the two, and they had always been close. Robert had to find him and help him if he was wounded.

"William!" he cried out. "William Cabell! Where are you?"

It took Robert several minutes to look at all the wounded cadets in the orchard. Although he wanted to help them, he had to find William, and there were more than enough willing hands to render assistance to the wounded.

There lay his friend, Edward Christian. Over there was Willis Harris, Jack Stanard's roommate. He didn't know Harris very well, but he seemed like a nice boy. Rolling over another prone body, he recognized Luther Haynes, who was in Company C with Robert. Haynes looked as if he had suffered a serious wound, but Robert could not take the time to check on him. He found Samuel Phillips, Charles Walker, and Reuben Akers, one after another. Then David Pierce and Jesse Dickinson. None seemed to be wounded badly, and after a few quick words with each he resumed his frantic search. None had seen William.

Reaching the south end of the orchard, Robert scanned the yard around the Bushong house quickly. There were many wounded there, but he saw none wearing the familiar uniform of the Institute. Passing the house he noticed a throng of wounded men sitting and lying on the front porch, apparently waiting to be taken inside. William was not among them, and in his distraught state it never occurred to Robert to look inside the house.

Now the lane. Robert remembered crossing this small road. It was here that the firing had first intensified. Had he seen William here during the battle? Robert wracked his brain trying to remember the last time he had seen his brother, but he could not say with any degree of certainty where it may have been.

Could he have passed William as he searched? Surely he wouldn't be this far back. For a brief moment Robert considered turning and going back to the orchard. "I think I saw him there during the fight," Robert told himself. "No. I couldn't have. The fire was so intense there that I just huddled behind that fence. I couldn't have seen him. I don't even know who that was beside me."

"It's starting to get dark. If I don't find him soon I may not find him until tomorrow. If he's hurt bad that may be too late. I have to find him now!"

The tormented cries of the wounded and dying echoed in Robert's ears as he worked his way back across the field of clover in front of the small farm. At least here the bodies were more visible than they were back in the wheat field. And there weren't quite as many to be checked. "If William is here he shouldn't be hard to find," he thought.

"Can you spare me some water, son?" said a weak voice as he stepped over yet another body. Robert was startled by the plea which came from directly beneath his feet. Taking his canteen out he realized that it was almost empty. Still, he gave it to the wounded man, hardly taking the time to remove its cork.

Over there! A body wearing the unmistakable uniform of a cadet! Robert rushed to the side of the motionless figure, gently rolling it over. Disappointed, he recognized the face of another boy from his company, William McDowell. Except for the fact that his jacket was torn open, exposing a splotch of red on his chest, McDowell almost looked to be sleeping. As Robert looked on his friend with pity, he realized that, he would wake no more.

Cadets Alexander Stuart and Edward Tutwiler, both from Company D, joined Robert as he stood looking at McDowell's body. The three talked about their deceased friend for a minute or two, then Robert asked if they had seen William. Neither had.

Robert then excused himself to resume his search, while Tutwiler and Stuart placed McDowell's body on an old oilcloth to remove him from the battlefield. Robert had never been that close to a dead person before, and the experience left him shaken.

A scant fifty yards beyond McDowell's body he saw three prone figures, all cadets. None was moving as he approached. "William?" he called tentatively. There was no response.

Reaching the first body he immediately recognized Charles Crockett. From Company D, Crockett had only been at the Institute for a few months, and Robert had not had the opportunity to get to know him very well. His body badly twisted, Robert knew without looking closely that he was dead.

Robert then reached the second body and knew at once that he had finally located his brother, William. Sobbing uncontrollably, he threw himself onto his brother's lifeless form. Never again would the two frolic in the stream behind their home.

*   *   *

John Wise gingerly crawled over the fence at the northern edge of the Bushong orchard. His wound was hurting more with every step, even though he knew it wasn't very serious. Someone had told him to go toward New Market, where he would find a hospital. Wise hoped he came across one before that.

"You need some help, John?" a familiar voice queried.

It was Moses Ezekiel.

"Yeah," answered Wise. "I got hit and it's startin' to hurt pretty bad."

"There's a farmhouse over yonder where they've been takin' some of the wounded," said Ezekiel. "Maybe they'll be able to help y'all over there."

"Thanks," Wise replied, starting in the direction Ezekiel had pointed.

"Y'all need me to go along with you?" Ezekiel asked, his voice sincere with concern.

"No," said Wise, "I think I can make it. Maybe y'all can help some of the others that are hurt worse."

Wise worked his way toward the farmhouse. It wan't hard to find. There was a steady stream of wounded men going in the same direction. He just followed them.

Reaching the house, Wise pushed his way inside. Moans and cries emanated from most of the men in there.

Almost immediately he saw a familiar form. He was lying on his back, his eyes staring lifelessly at the ceiling. Jack Stanard!

Wise knelt beside the still warm body of his friend. Stanard's leg was mangled. It looked like he may have bled to death. He took Stanard's lifeless hand in his and held it gently as a tear formed and ran down his cheek. "Why did I say we should catch up with the others?" Wise sobbed, recalling that he had persuaded Stanard to abandon the baggage wagon and join in the fray. "If only I had stayed back with the wagon, Jack would still be alive. Why? Why?"

He felt a gentle hand on his shoulder. Looking up, he saw a bearded face. The man was wearing a blue jacket. He was a Yankee.

"Come on, son," the man said softly. "We can't help him now. Was he a friend of yours?"

Wise nodded, unable to speak through the sobs.

"He was a brave young man," the Yankee was saying. "I understand from some of our boys that all of you were. Schoolboys, I heard." The last sentence was more of a question than a statement. Wise nodded again.

The man, a surgeon, led him outside. "He only died a few minutes ago. I tried to help him, but there were just so many wounded. I couldn't spend much time with him. I hope you understand."

Wise looked at the doctor. He seemed like a good man.

"I have to get back inside," the doctor said. "There are still many others to take care of, and more coming in by the minute. Go back to your regiment. Tell them your friend did not suffer. He was unconscious when I first got to him and he never cried out. He's in a better place now."

"Thank you, sir," Wise was able to say. Then the flood of tears came again. Jack was gone, and it didn't have to be. If only Wise had been content to stay with the wagon, Jack would have stayed, too. And he'd still be alive. Then he remembered the last night of the march, and Jack's premonition of his impending death. It had come true. Maybe there was nothing Wise could have done, after all.

*   *   *

Ezekiel watched John Wise walk toward the farmhouse. Ezekiel considered running after his friend and walking with him, just to make sure he was not hurt badly, but then talked himself out of it. His wounds didn't seem to be holding him back much, and he didn't appear to be having any trouble walking.

"You hurt, Moses?" someone asked.

Ezekiel turned to see Benjamin Colonna. "No, Duck," Ezekiel replied, using Colonna's more familiar nickname. Nobody ever called him Benjamin. "I'm fine. How about you?"

Colonna smiled. "All the parts seem to be where they're supposed to be, so I guess I'm all right," he said.

Colonna stepped aside to allow two stretcher bearers to pass.

"You room with Thomas Jefferson, don't you?" Colonna asked.

"Yes, I do," answered Ezekiel. "Why do you ask?"

"I just saw some of the boys carrying him into that hut over there," Colonna answered. "I was just about to walk over and check on him. Do you want to join me?"

"Certainly," Ezekiel responded. "Did it look like he was hurt bad?"

"Couldn't tell for sure," said Colonna, as the two started for the hut. "I saw him layin' in the orchard after he was hit and he was still movin', if that means anything. He was yellin' somethin' and pointin' toward the Yankees."

"Ouch!" Ezekiel exclaimed as he struck his foot against a hidden rock. Instinctively he grabbed his foot.

Colonna looked at Ezekiel's foot, then commented, "You lose your shoes in that wheat field, too?"

"Yeah," answered Ezekiel. "I couldn't keep 'em on. That mud just pulled them right off."

"Mine stayed on, for some reason," said Colonna. "But I saw a lot of the boys without shoes, so the mud must have got a lot of 'em."

The two had now reached the small hut. Stepping onto the porch they saw that it, too, had been ravaged by the battle. A large hole in the front wall replaced what had once been the door, and they had to step over the post that had, before the shelling began, held up the corner of the porch roof. Stepping inside, they took several seconds to allow their eyes to adjust to the darkness. Jefferson lay on his back, his face a strange ashen color even in the poor light.

When Ezekiel called his name Jefferson's eyes fluttered open momentarily and appeared to be trying to focus on the sound of his voice. Then they closed again.

"We can't just leave him here," said Ezekiel. "You stay with him while I go into town and try to find a wagon. We'll move him into one of the hospitals."

Ezekiel stepped back outside into the ever present rainfall and began his shoeless hike into town.

15

The chase of Sigel's army had gone nearly three miles. Sigel had scaled Rude's Hill, a small promontory just north of Bushong's Hill, where he had set up his batteries on the crest. Now, he was shelling the pursuing Confederates. The battle was on again, although not nearly as heated. Not yet, at least.

Breckinridge had halted in a small grove of trees on the right of the Valley Turnpike. The cadets, with the rest of McLaughlin's artillery, were unlimbering and preparing to return the fire of the Union gunners.

As the Confederate guns roared back to life and began to shell their Union counterparts, Imboden arrived and immediately made for Breckinridge. Breckinridge, muddy from the waist down, was on foot.

"I couldn't fire the bridge, sir!" Imboden said.

A surprised Breckinridge could not believe what he was hearing. Everything had been going so well, and now this. He thought he had Sigel trapped. Now, Sigel had an escape route that would take him clear into Maryland, if he chose to go that far.

"What happened?" asked Breckinridge. He had not been aware of any engagements that would have delayed Imboden.

"We couldn't get back across Smith's Creek, sir," was the reply. "We stayed on the east side of the creek and our guns set up every so often to lay some fire onto Sigel's flank. We had no opposition. Everything was perfect. Then, when we tried to cross the stream the water was too high. We almost lost several horses. After several tries we decided to come straight to the bridge and cross that way, then fire the bridge behind us. Only trouble is, Sigel's cavalry was already there."

"Well, I guess it doesn't matter," said a disappointed Breckinridge. "We'll still get him. We had to halt anyway. Every one of our cartridge boxes are empty, and the troops have been marchin' without any ammunition for the last hour. We had to stop to replenish. I sent for the ordnance wagons while we were still chasing Sigel. I didn't want to stop when we had him on the run. When he stopped I figured he must have reached the bridge and saw that it was gone."

Breckinridge took off his hat and shook it to get rid of the accumulated rain water. "The wagons are here now and the men are refilling their boxes," he went on. "As soon as everyone is ready we'll just have to go after him again."

Imboden and Breckinridge flinched involuntarily as a Union shell struck nearby. As the clods of earth and mud settled, Imboden said, "If you'll excuse me for saying this, sir, shouldn't you be taking cover somewhere that isn't quite as open as these little trees?"

Breckinridge looked around and laughed. "This is the first place I've been today that isn't ankle deep in mud," he said, "And I'm not about to leave. I think I'd rather face Sigel's guns than wade through one more inch of mud."

"We have seen our share today, sir. I'll agree to that," said Imboden.

"How is your brother?" asked Breckinridge.

Imboden's brother Jacob, a VMI cadet, had been wounded in the battle.

"He'll be fine, sir," answered Imboden. "I just left him. He'll be a little sore for a while, but he's pretty tough for a little guy."

"I'm glad to hear that," Breckinridge said. "Those boys from VMI did quite a job today. Your brother can be proud of the part he played."

"I'll be sure to tell him, sir," Imboden replied. "He'll be happy to hear that you said that."

"I meant every word, too," said Breckinridge. "Those boys are fighters!"

Before Imboden could respond an aide arrived and said, "Ammunition's all restocked, sir. Everyone's ready to go."

Breckinridge turned to his staff. "Order the line forward!" he said.

As the orders went out, Breckinridge gave Imboden his instructions. "Oblique your cavalry to the left, General," he said. "Have McLaughlin's guns go as fast as they can down the pike. Wharton and Echols can have their men move toward Rude's Hill."

Sigel, viewing the forward movement of Breckinridge's line, immediately pulled his own line back. He took them over the top of Rude's Hall and down into the flat on the other side, which was known as Meem's Bottom.

Breckinridge's army continued their relentless pursuit. Under Lieutenant Carter Berkeley, the artillery charged down the hard road like a cavalry unit. The cadets were required to rush to keep up.

The artillery reached the crest of Rude's Hill just as Sigel's army crossed the bridge which was to have been burned by Imboden. Within minutes the artillery was firing at Sigel again, but in the gathering darkness it was difficult to determine what effect, if any, the shelling was having.

"We'll halt here, for now," said Breckinridge. "If Sigel wants to start things up again in the morning, we'll be ready. I strongly suspect that he's had enough, though."

As the Confederates set up their camp, a soft orange glow appeared in the valley below Rude's Hill. Soon it was bright enough to see what the source of the glow was.

"The Yanks are burning the bridge, General!" one of Breckinridge's aides called back from his vantage point at the crest of the hill.

Breckinridge rushed to the top of the hill and looked at the fire below him.

"Should we go down and try to put it out while we can still save the bridge, sir?" the aide inquired.

Breckinridge stroked his chin thoughtfully. "No," he finally said, "let it burn. We'll just let Mr. Sigel figure out how to get back up the Valley without a bridge!"

*   *   *

Back in town the cadets were amazed to find they were being treated as heroes.

As they marched into town on the turnpike they were surprised to see veteran soldiers lining the road on both sides, cheering and waving. Some of the cadets recognized faces who had mocked them earlier in the day. Detractors no longer, they shouted and cheered as loud as anyone. Louis Wise, still hurting from his wounds but able to march, would later say, "It was the proudest moment of my life."

The young cadets, resisting the urge to say "I told you so" to the throng of veterans. They marched as they had been taught: professionally and as representatives of the Virginia Military Institute.

Nothing was too good for the boys from VMI. They were the center of attention in New Market. Private citizens, hearing that the cadets' blankets and haversacks had been stolen while they were fighting, insisted that they eat and sleep in their homes. Veteran soldiers slapped them on the back and acted as if they had been friends for years. Only a sullen group of Union prisoners failed to recognize the cadets as heroes.

Wet and hungry, the cadets had gained the respect and admiration of everyone in town. They had borne their hardships without complaint. And why not? They were VMI cadets!

*   *   *

The day after the battle dawned warm and dreary, although the rain had finally stopped. The wounded had been brought into private homes for treatment, and every cadet had been accounted for. Sadly, that accounting revealed that five of their number had been killed. Several others were wounded badly and could easily increase that number. The joy the cadets felt at having played a major part in the victory was tempered by the sobering realization that the victory had not been without its price.

Some of the cadets went from house to house, searching for wounded friends. Others set about to the somber task of helping build coffins. Some of their comrades would not be returning to Lexington with the rest of the corps.

Dr. Robert Madison, the surgeon, and Dr. George Ross, the assistant surgeon, both of whom had accompanied the corps on its march from Lexington, had their work planned for them. More than fifty cadets had been wounded, several of them very seriously. It would take all the skills they could muster to save some of these boys. The two would labor throughout the day and long into the night, not even stopping to eat, nursing the wounded cadets.

A camp was set up at the edge of a small wood lot, just north of town. Those cadets who had served in the artillery rejoined the corps at the camp. Stories were swapped and tall tales were spun. The cadets agreed to a man that this part of soldiering wasn't too bad. And the adoration wasn't too hard to take, either!

The part that they would have preferred to do without came in the afternoon, when they assembled at the cemetery of St. Matthew's Church. The last time the cadets had seen this cemetery had been from the crest of Shirley's Hill, as they had watched the Union gunners of Alonzo Snow setting up to shoot at them.

Cadets William Henry Cabell, William Hugh McDowell, Jacqueline Beverly Stanard, Charles Gay Crockett, and Henry Jenner Jones had been killed in the battle. Their remains had been placed in the hand made caskets and transported to St. Matthew's Cemetery, and the cadets now were gathered to say goodbye. A brief ceremony was conducted, following which the five coffins were gently lowered into the graves.

Where the cadets had been brave soldiers the previous day, today they were grieving friends. This, too, was a part of soldiering.

*   *   *

Sigel's performance at the Battle of New Market destroyed the little bit of confidence Grant may have still had in him. Grant believed that Sigel had lost a battle which should have easily been won. In Grant's mind, it was apparent that something would have to be done. Just four days after the battle, at the urging of Major General H. W. Halleck, Grant decided to replace Sigel with General David Hunter. Grant's frustration with the German general was so strong that he intimated to Halleck that he didn't care who replaced Sigel. He just wanted him replaced.[4]

Meanwhile, the cadets were ordered on May 17, two days after the battle, to report to General Imboden. It was Breckinridge's wish that the cadets be relieved of their duties so they could return to the Institute. However, Imboden still felt that he needed their services. He thought that the cadets could be of use in Richmond, guarding the city. This, according to Imboden, would allow badly needed veterans to go to the front with Lee, who was still engaged with his nemesis, Grant.

Imboden's argument was accepted, and the cadets proceeded to Staunton, being greeted as heroes every step of the way. They arrived in Staunton on May 21, but their stay there was short. They left the next day by railroad for the Confederate capitol. At Richmond they were given another hero's welcome, and Governor William Smith himself presented the corps with a new flag to replace their bullet-riddled banner. President Jefferson Davis offered his personal congratulations, and the Confederate Congress passed an official resolution thanking them for their performance.

While in Richmond they set up camp at Camp Lee, where they remained for nearly a week, moving on May 28 to Carter's Farm. They remained there until June 6, when they received their orders to return to Lexington, arriving back at the Institute on June 9. It had been an eventful month since they had last seen the towers of the barracks. Their envious classmates who had been selected to remain behind were there to greet their return.

Their stay at VMI was short lived, as word was received the very next day that Union forces were approaching Lexington. On June 11, the rumor was substantiated, as General Hunter's forces were seen in the hills north of the town. The cadets could hear artillery and sharpshooter fire all day, but they were not involved in any of the shooting, themselves. By midafternoon, with the Confederate army under pressure from Hunter, the cadets left the Institute. They had not even had the opportunity to get settled back in. Within hours, Federal forces occupied the grounds of VMI.

Leaving the grounds of VMI once more, the cadets marched to the mouth of the North Anna River, where they set up camp once again. They spent the next four days on guard duty near Balcony Falls.

On Sunday, June 11, the enemy was reported advancing, and the cadets broke camp and fell back an additional two miles, taking a defensive position at a mountain pass. However, the Union forces did not appear, and eventually the cadets were ordered to report to Lynchburg.

Arriving in Lynchburg on June 15, the cadets took a position on the north side of the river, remaining there until June 24, at which time they

---

[4] Grant's message to Halleck concerning replacing Sigel may be read in its entirety in Appendix D.

were ordered back to Lexington. They returned to the Institute on June 25, where they were greeted by a scene of total devastation.

While Hunter had been in Lexington he had torched VMI. Little remained. He had also planned to burn the adjoining Washington College but he was persuaded by his protesting officers that enough was enough. With Washington College spared, the cadets set up temporary quarters in those buildings.

Superintendent Smith, recognizing the hardships the cadets had endured since their departure in early May, and realizing that the Institute was in no condition to hold classes, made the decision to reward the young men with a furlough. On June 27 he assembled the cadets and told them how well they had performed, and that he was proud of them. He then granted all the cadets furloughs until September, at which time they were to report to the Almshouse in Richmond, where classes would be held.

With this furlough, the most exciting chapter in the history of the Virginia Military Institute came to a close. The boys had done all that had been asked of them, and more. They had spilled their blood on the field of battle. They had buried several of their friends. They had captured a cannon, an accomplishment unachievable for many regiments who fought the entire war.

Yes, General Breckinridge. The boys will fight.

EPILOGUE

The Battle of New Market was over. It was now a part of history. Compared to other battles in the Valley, such as Opequon and Cedar Creek, this battle was relatively inconsequential. However, on its own terms, the Battle of New Market had considerable significance.

It was significant because this battle saved the Valley for a few more weeks. Those crucial few weeks provided time for the harvesting of the important spring wheat crop so badly needed by General Robert E. Lee's army.

It was significant because Grant was pushing Lee very hard, to the point where Lee probably would not have been able to withstand an assault from the direction of the Valley, an assault which would have been possible had Sigel's march been successful. With Sigel out of the way, Breckinridge was able to bring his two brigades to assist Lee at the critical Battle of Cold Harbor.

It was significant because Lee had nobody to spare to defend Lynchburg, from where crucial supplies were shipped to the Army of Northern Virginia. This supply line would have easily been compromised by Sigel if he had been successful at New Market. Accomplishing this, Sigel would have been relatively free to strike Lee's flank, seriously impairing Lee's ability to defend Richmond. Breckinridge's victory over Sigel at New Market prevented this, however, and a month later Lee was able to send troops to Lynchburg. These troops proved crucial in the repulse of an attack by General David Hunter, Sigel's successor.

Yes, it was significant for all these reasons. But perhaps it was most significant because of the involvement of the cadets. Never before, and never since, has a school been called upon to send its entire student body into battle. This, in itself, makes the Battle of New Market unique among the 326 conflicts in the Shenandoah Valley throughout the Civil War.

139

General Imboden, in assessing the importance of the Battle of New Market, would go so far as to say that New Market represented the most important secondary battle of the entire war. Its success for the Confederacy was crucial, and it was achieved, in large part, by the performance of the cadets.

Imboden himself drew praise from Sigel, who said he had a great deal of respect for Imboden's timely and skillful maneuvers throughout the battle. Sigel credited Imboden's battery with inflicting severe damage on his left flank.

Sigel, reluctant to accept blame for the defeat, sent reports back that he had been badly outnumbered. Other early reports[5] by Sigel left considerable doubt as to who was the winner. Sigel's erroneous and misleading reports led to the following New York *Tribune* headline of May 18, 1864: SIGEL WHIPS THE REBELS AT NEW MARKET.

After the battle Sigel withdrew down the Valley. Major General Henry W. Halleck, never a supporter of Sigel to begin with, cabled Grant that ". . . Sigel is already in full retreat on Strasburg. If you expect anything from him you will be mistaken. He will do nothing but run. He never did anything else." Four days later, Sigel was relieved of his command. His successor, General David Hunter, requested that Sigel stay in the Department of West Virginia and take over the Reserve Division, which was made up of the troops at Harpers Ferry and those along the Baltimore and Ohio Railroad. Sigel initially complied with Hunter's request, but less than a year later he resigned his commission.

Following the battle Breckinridge was hailed as the new hero of the Valley, and the inevitable comparisons with Stonewall Jackson quickly followed. The Richmond *Daily Dispatch* called him a "worthy successor of Jackson." The rival Richmond *Enquirer* added a similar endorsement a day later. In February 1865, Breckinridge was appointed Secretary of War by President Jefferson Davis. Following the defeat of the Confederacy he came under indictment for treason, and he spent the next three years in self-imposed exile in England and Cuba, where he was beyond the reaches of U.S. Marshals. He was able to return to the United States in 1869 under a general amnesty. He died at the age of 54 in 1875, spending the last few years of his life opposing the activities of the Ku Klux Klan in Kentucky.

In the town of New Market, the townspeople steadfastly refused to allow the Federal dead to be buried in the local cemetery. The Confederates buried them as best they could in shallow graves outside town. Over the next few weeks, early summer rains washed the dirt away and exposed the bodies, sending a sickening stench through the town.

The people of New Market also exhibited great reluctance to even provide medical treatment for the wounded Union soldiers, and chastised those among them who did. As an illustration of the feelings the people of

---

[5] See Appendix D for these reports.

New Market had for the enemy, many of the dead and wounded Union soldiers were robbed as they lay on the battlefield.

Scott Ship recovered from his wounds at New Market, changed his name to Shipp in 1883, and succeeded General Smith as superintendent of VMI in 1890. He also served on the Board of Visitors at West Point, and as the president of the Board of Visitors at the United States Naval Academy.

Superintendent Smith arrived in New Market a few days after the battle to take the wounded cadets who could travel back to the Institute. Those who were more seriously wounded stayed in New Market until they could be moved.

Family plot of Scott Ship, who commanded the cadets at New Market. Ship's marker, reflecting his name change to Shipp in 1883, is on the left. He is buried at Jackson Memorial Cemetery in Lexington, not far from the grave of Stonewall Jackson.

Photo by Author

The respect that the cadets found so lacking during their march to New Market was present everywhere the cadets went in the days and weeks following the battle. Cheered by veterans and private citizens alike, they were praised and adored throughout the South. Breckinridge, who would always have difficulty discussing his decision to use the cadets in the battle, forever referred to them affectionately as "my cadets."

This newly found respect extended to those who fought against them, as well. A member of the 54th Pennsylvania Infantry was so impressed by the performance of the cadets at New Market that he later sent two of his own sons to the Institute. Henry A. DuPont, Captain of Battery B of the 5th United States Artillery, which didn't reach the field until the retreat was well under way, became a United States senator after the war. In that capacity he sponsored legislation to provide federal funds to reimburse the Virginia Military Institute for the costs associated with rebuilding the barracks which had been burned by Hunter.

The cadets' capture of the Union gun has not been without controversy. There are those who would pass off the achievement as superfluous, saying that Kleiser's abandonment of the piece made it a simple matter of moving into and occupying the vacated position. These individuals maintain that the cadets have been given far more credit than they deserve, simply because they were in the right place at the right time. The evidence, however, does not support this argument.

Others, perhaps caught up in the drama of the episode, prefer to think of the capture of the gun as having come about only after a prolonged and fierce hand-to-hand combat. This theory, likewise, is probably not so.

The truth, no doubt, lies between the two extremes. Was the gun abandoned? It appears that it was, but the question must be asked: Why was it abandoned? Given the choice, Kleiser would have taken the gun with him when he left the field. The obvious answer is that it was abandoned because the cadets were dangerously close, and that it was becoming apparent to those firing the gun that the position was no longer tenable.

Thus, while the hand-to-hand combat theory is unlikely, so too is the idea that the gun was there simply for the taking. It is unfair, and historically inaccurate, to minimize the role the cadets played in the capture of the weapon. The fact that the gun was no longer attended by Kleiser's crew at the time the cadets made the capture should, in no way, diminish the actions which immediately preceded the seizure. Had the cadets not been literally thrown into the breach, the gun may not have been captured by anyone, and the battle would probably have had a different outcome.

Heroes all, the cadets are deserving of the accolades which they have been receiving for more than a century.

In addition to being good soldiers, the cadets would excel as individuals throughout their lives, as well. Some went on to become statesmen, physicians, inventors, authors, and engineers. Several founded the Alpha Tau Omega national fraternity. One, Erskine Mayo Ross, founded Glendale, California. Another, George Edward Raum, became a well-known Egyptologist, and was credited with helping discover the Sphinx.

In 1894, Harry A. Wise (Chinook) took on the responsibility of gathering information on the battle from each of the cadets, as they recalled their own part. By then a graduate student at Johns Hopkins University, Wise eventually rose to professor of European history at the University of Michigan. The material, once it was collected, was turned over to E. Raymond Taylor, who used it to assemble an authoritative history of the battle.

Of the four boys who went to Carrington Taylor's home in Staunton while en route to New Market, John Wise and Louis Wise were wounded, and Jack Stanard was killed. Only Taylor himself emerged from the battle unscathed.

Jack Stanard, although killed in the battle, lived on in name. His brother Robert, who also served in the Confederate army, survived the war, married, and had a son. The son was named Beverly, Jack Stanard's middle name.

Over the next several weeks, five more cadets would succumb to the effects of their wounds, bringing to ten the number of cadets who were killed at New Market. The names of Samuel Francis Atwill, Luther Cary Haynes, Alva Curtis Hartsfield, Joseph Christopher Wheelwright, and Thomas Garland Jefferson were added to the Roll of Honor, joining their five classmates who had died on the field.

Jefferson had been transported to the home of Lydie Clinedinst in New Market, where he was lovingly cared for by color bearer Oliver Perry Evans and Jefferson's friend and roommate Moses Ezekiel for two pain-filled days. On May 17, shortly after Ezekiel read from the New Testament to his friend, Jefferson became delirious. A short time later, he died.

As for Ezekiel, he did become the famous artist he aspired to be, despite graduating at the bottom of his class at

Sir Moses Ezekiel, one of the New Market cadets. Ezekiel became a world famous sculptor. Several of his works, including the famous monument in honor of the cadets, Virginia Mourning Her Dead, can be found at VMI.

Courtesy of Hall of Valor Civil War Museum

The New Market Battle Monument, Virginia Mourning Her Dead, on the
VMI campus. This sculpture, honoring the cadets, was crafted by Sir Moses
Ezekiel, one of those who fought at New Market. The six headstones behind
the monument mark the final resting places of six of the cadets killed in the
battle. The wreath in front of the monument, as well as the flowers at each
grave, is placed as part of VMI's New Market Day ceremony on the anniversary
of the battle.

Photo by Author

VMI. He received countless awards and honors from around the world.
His Confederate monument stands in Arlington National Cemetery. One
of Ezekiel's best known works is a monument to his comrades who fought
with him that fateful day in May 1864. Entitled "Virginia Mourning Her
Dead," it stands on the grounds of the Virginia Military Institute.

Ironically, when Hunter destroyed the buildings at VMI in June 1864,
he also destroyed many of the files. As a result, no records were left to
show which cadets had stayed behind and which cadets had gone into
battle. The decision was made to consider all cadets at the Institute at the
time of the battle as being "New Market Cadets." Thus, the names of all
are recorded on Ezekiel's monument.

Two years after the battle, the five cadets buried in St. Matthew's
Cemetery in New Market were exhumed. A detail of cadets went to New
Market and escorted the five bodies back to the Institute for reburial. Of

The graves of Cadets Atwill, Crockett, Jefferson, Jones, McDowell, and Wheelwright. The plaque behind the monument was placed in memory of Cadets Cabell, Hartsfield, Haynes, and Stanard, who are buried elsewhere.

Photo by Author

the ten cadets who died in the battle, six are buried under Ezekiel's monument at VMI. Cadets Atwill, Crockett, Jefferson, Jones, McDowell, and Wheelwright rest there. A plaque dedicated to the other four cadets, Cabell, Hartsfield, Haynes, and Stanard has been placed behind the monument.

Each year, on May 15, New Market Day is celebrated at the Virginia Military Institute before large crowds. This tradition honors the New Market Cadets in an impressive and stirring ceremony.

The entire corps of cadets assembles on the parade ground, marching to the sound of muffled drums. Spectators in attendance remain respectfully quiet, although there is no official directive to do so.

When the corps has assembled, the names of the ten cadets who were killed at the Battle of New Market are solemnly read as a roll call. As each name is called, a cadet specially chosen for the honor of representing that individual, steps forward. With a sharp salute, he reports crisply, "Died! On the field of honor, sir!"

After the last name is called, an honor guard consisting of six cadets kneels gently at each of the six headstones marking the graves of Cadets Atwill, Crockett, Jefferson, Jones, McDowell, and Wheelwright. A bouquet of flowers is placed at each headstone. A wreath is then placed at the base of the monument Virginia Mourning Her Dead.

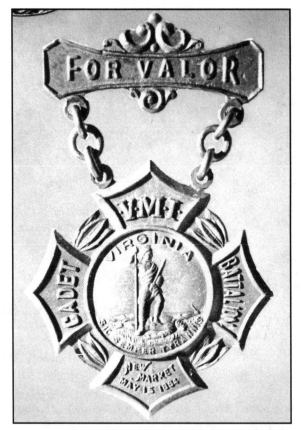

The New Market Cross of Honor awarded in 1904 to each of the New Market Cadets by the VMI Alumni Association.

Courtesy of Hall of Valor Civil War Museum

Following the placing of the wreath a 21-gun salute is fired by seven cadets to honor their fallen compatriots. This is followed by the playing of taps. Women in the assemblage dab gently at their eyes. Men, many of whom have served in combat themselves, gulp and swallow with difficulty, trying to force the lump from their throats. Others in the crowd simply allow the tears to flow, unashamed, accompanied by the occasional muffled sob from somewhere deep in the crowd. On this day, North and South no longer matter. We are all one again.

On this day the corps has reserved one last tribute to the 1864 Cadets. As the last notes of taps drift away, the corps passes in review. With the band playing, the corps marches smartly to the end of the parade ground and turns onto Letcher Avenue. Marching with fixed bayonets, they pass the Science Building, Mallory Hall, then the Preston Library. In front of the next building, Nichols Engineering Hall, stands the battle monument and the graves of the six New Market Cadets. As each company approaches the monument the command "Eyes Right!" is given. The company guidon is sharply dipped and each cadet's head snaps crisply to the right in respect, a position that is held until the entire company has passed the monument.

With the passing of the final company, the solemnity is broken. Many drift toward the monument, some to pay their own respects, others simply out of curiosity. Once again the crowd smiles and laughs. Reunions between families and cadets ensue. But for a short period of time on this May 15, and for every May 15 to come, the hearts of those in attendance are transported back to a rainy day in 1864 when 257 young boys became men, and solidified their place in history in the process.

In 1904 the VMI Alumni Association presented each New Market Cadet with a bronze Cross of Honor. If the cadet had passed away by that time, the medal was presented to his nearest kin. The association wanted to assure that each cadet or family of a cadet had received the proper recognition.

Today, the Shenandoah Valley is peaceful once again. An interstate highway bisects the battlefield at New Market. Thousand of cars pass through the area every day, most of their occupants having no idea what took place on this hallowed site. That is unfortunate, for the memories of the brave men on both sides who fought here deserve better.

But some eighty miles to the south, those memories are still alive. The New Market Cadets still live on in the minds of those who walk the halls of the Virginia Military Institute, and who is to say the New Market Cadets do not still walk those halls as well?

Appendix A

Casualties

In the Blink of an Eye

Four hours. Two hundred forty minutes. Compared to the life span of the average human being it is but a miniscule portion. A blink of an eye. But in that blink of an eye on May 15, 1864, the Corps of Cadets from the Virginia Military Institute marched into immortality.

In the blink of an eye, 257 boys stepped onto a battlefield, emerging as men on the other side.

In the blink of an eye, 10 of their companions and classmates fell, never to rise again. Many others received wounds, some so devastating that they suffered the pain for the rest of their lives. All wore their scars as badges of honor, forever proud of their roles in history.

In the blink of an eye, the cadets of VMI were transformed from boy soldiers to heroes, performing as a group in a manner never seen before or since.

In the blink of an eye, they became legends.

In the blink of an eye 257 youths were robbed of their innocence in a way that no one ever should be. They came under fire, and passed the test.

In the blink of an eye, 10 brave young men paid the ultimate price. They carried common names: Atwill, Cabell, Crockett, Hartsfield, Haynes, Jefferson, Jones, McDowell, Stanard, Wheelwright . . . but what they did was far from commonplace.

Who among us knows what these 10 young heroes may have become had they been given the chance to live? If the achievements of their classmates can be used as a barometer, they would have been successful. There may have been a great physician in the group. Or a judge, or a banker. Maybe there would have been a governor among them. Or perhaps a future president of the United States.

We'll never know, because they were plucked from us just as they approached the threshhold of manhood. They never had the chance to reach their potential. They were gone too soon. In the blink of an eye.

Died on the Field of Honor

Information on the cadets who became casualties at the Battle of New Market is adapted from "The V. M. I. New Market Cadets" by William Couper.

Atwill, Samuel Francis - Corporal, Company A

Age 18. He received a calf wound in the orchard. Although a bad wound, it was not considered life threatening, and he was promoted to cadet sergeant about six weeks after the battle. He contracted lockjaw, however, as a result of his wound, and died what was described as an excruciating death on July 20, 1864 in Staunton. His body was returned to VMI two years after the battle where it was reinterred beneath the New Market Battle Monument.

Cabell, William Henry - First Sergeant, Company D

Age 18. He was killed instantly by the explosion of a shell before he reached the Bushong Farm. His body was found by his younger brother, Robert, a member of Company B, who had gone back over the battlefield to search for him. He was temporarily buried at New Market, then reburied at Hollywood Cemetery in Richmond, next to his mother's ashes. While a cadet, he had ranked first in his class of 24. He also had an older brother serving in the volunteer army. Ironically, William became a VMI cadet at the urging of his father, who thought that, at William's young age, it presented a better alternative than going off to war.

Crockett, Charles Gay - Private, Company D

Age 17. Killed instantly by the explosion of a shell, believed to be the same one killing Cabell and Jones. He had only been a cadet about four months when he was killed at New Market. He was buried under the New Market Battle Monument at VMI.

Hartsfield, Alva Curtis - Private, Company B

Age 19. Wounded at an unknown location on the battlefield. He went with the rest of the corps to Richmond after the battle. There he was placed in a hospital for treatment of measles, which he had contracted while in camp, either at New Market or en route to New Market. Successful in getting a furlough while recuperating, he attempted to walk to his home to North Carolina. He collapsed in Petersburg, Virginia and was taken to a hospital, where he died on June 26, 1864. Because of his wound, and because he contracted measles while at New Market, his death was attributed to the effects of the battle and he was counted as one of those killed or mortally wounded in the battle. He had attended the University of North Carolina before transferring to VMI. He is buried in Petersburg.

Haynes, Luther Cary - Private, Company B
Age 19. He had just returned from a furlough because of a "family affliction" when the corps was called to New Market. He was wounded in the Orchard and died around June 15, 1864 in Richmond. He was believed to have only been wounded and was carried on the rolls as such until his sister informed authorities in 1904 that he had died from his wounds. In 1910 it was agreed that his name should be included with those who died as a result of the battle. He is buried at his home, "Sunny Side", in Essex County, Virginia.

Jefferson, Thomas Garland - Private, Company B
Age 17. He was wounded in the orchard and died three days later in the home of a Mrs. Clinedinst. He was attended by Cadets Moses Ezekiel and Oliver Evans, the corps color bearer. Jefferson is credited with saving the life of Cadet James Darden earlier in the battle when he improvised a bandage from his canteen strap and stemmed the flow of blood from the severed arteries in Darden's badly wounded arm. Jefferson is buried under the New Market Battle Monument at VMI.

Jones, Henry Jenner - Private, Company D
Age 17. Killed by the same exploding shell which killed Crockett and Cabell. Jones had only been a cadet for about 10 months at the time of his death. He was buried by his fellow cadets in New Market. About three years later his body was returned to Lexington and buried under the New Market Battle Monument.

McDowell, William Hugh - Private, Company B
Age 17. Killed in the field before Bushong's Farm. Slightly built, he was shot through the chest. He was from North Carolina, and he was considering accepting a position on General James Conner's staff when the corps was ordered to New Market. McDowell was temporarily interred at New Market, then removed and reburied under the New Market Battle Monument at VMI.

Stanard, Jacqueline Beverly - Private, Company B
Age 19. He was mortally wounded in the orchard, and died a few hours later. He had been in a relatively safe area of the battlefield, assigned to attend the baggage wagon, but elected to join his friends in the battle despite his premonition that he would be killed. He had been confirmed in the church just a week before the battle. Stanard had resigned as a cadet in

January 1864 but was restored by the Board of Visitors eight days later. Buried temporarily at New Market, his body was reburied at Orange, Virginia.

Wheelwright, Joseph Christopher - Private, Company C
Age 17. Believed to have been mortally wounded in the orchard. He was taken off the battlefield by several of his comrades after the battle. He was moved to the home of a Dr. Newman in Harrisonburg, where he died on June 2 despite the efforts of Dr. Newman and his family. Temporarily interred, he was ultimately moved back to Lexington for burial under the New Market Battle Monument on the campus of VMI.

Cadets Wounded at New Market

Official records of the battle indicate that 47 cadets received wounds at New Market. However, it is believed that there were at least four additional wounds not reported. The following is thought to include all who received wounds, reported and unreported.

Akers, Reuben Cornelius, Private, Company D, Age 19
Berkeley, Edmund, Jr., Private, Company D, Age 17
Bransford, John Francis, Private, Company B, Age 17
Buster, William Dennis, Private, Company A, Age 19
Christian, Edward Dunscomb, Private, Company B, Age 16
Cocke, Preston, Private, Company D, Age 18
Corling, Charles Thompson, Private, Company A, Age 21
Darden, James David, Private, Company B, Age 19*
Dickinson, Jesse Irvine, Private, Company D, Age 16
Dillard, William, Jr., Private, Company D, Age 17*
Garnett, Griffin Taylor, Private, Company D, Age 17
Garrow, Harris Walker, 3rd Sergeant, Company B, Age 17
Gibson, Franklin Graham, Private, Company B, Age 19*
Goodwin, James Hugh, Private, Company C, Age 19
Harris, Willis Overton, Private, Company B, Age 17
Harrison, Carter Henry, Private, Company A, Age 18
Hill, Archibald Govan, Captain, Company C, Age 25
Howard, John Clarke, Private, Company A, Age 18
Imboden, Jacob Peck, Private, Company D, Age 17
Johnson, Porter, Private, Company B, Age 18
Jones, Walter Smith, Private, Company C, Age 17
Macon, George Kennon, 2nd Corporal, Company A, Age 18
Marshall, Martin, Private, Company D, Age 17
Mead, Henry Johns, Private, Company A, Age 19
Merritt, James Love, Private, Company C, Age 18

Moorman, Edwin Steptoe, Private, Company D, Age 18
Pendleton, Robert Aldridge, Private, Company A, Age 16
Phillips, Samuel Travers, Private, Company B, Age 17
Pierce, David Stuart, Private, Company D, Age 17
Pizzini, Andrew, Jr., 1st Sergeant, Company B, Age 17
Preston, James Grainard, Private, Company B, Age 18
Randolph, Charles Carter, Private, Company C, Age 18
Read, Charles Henry, Jr., Private, Company C, Age 18
Ship, Scott, Commander of Cadet Corps, Age 24
Shriver, Samuel Sprigg, 4th Captain, Company C, Age 21*
Smith, Charles Henry, Private, Company C, Age 18
Smith, Edward Harvie, Jr., Private, Company A, Age 18
Smith, Francis Lee, Private, Company A, Age 18*
Spiller, George, Private, Company A, Age 18
Stuart, John Andrew, 1st Sergeant, Company C, Age 20
Triplett, John Richards, 4th Corporal, Company D, Age 19
Upshur, John Nottingham, Private, Company C, Age 16
Walker, Charles Duy, Private, Company C, Age 15
Walker, Charles Pinkney, Private, Company B, Age 17
Watson, William Pryor, Private, Company A, Age 17
White, Thomas Wilson, Private, Company A, Age 17
Whitehead, Henry Colgate, Private, Company B, Age 18
Wise, John Sergeant, 3rd Corporal, Company D, Age 17
Wise, Louis C. , 2nd Sergeant, Company C, Age 19*
Woodlief, Pierre W., Jr., Private, Company B, Age 18
Wyatt, John Wesley, Battalion Quartermaster, Age 24

* Indicates wounded more than once. All of these received two wounds except Gibson, who was wounded seven times in this battle.

TOTAL CASUALTIES

As with any battle, the actual numbers of casualties at New Market are open to dispute. This is particularly true for those on the Confederate side of the ledger. However, best estimates of total casualties are as follows:

Union
    Actively engaged: 6,275

Killed or mortally wounded	96
Wounded	520
Missing	225
Total Casualties	841

% Casualties (vs. actively engaged) - 13.4%

Confederate

Actively engaged: 4,087

Killed or mortally wounded	50
Wounded	480
Missing	10
Total Casualties	540

% Casualties (vs. actively engaged) - 13.2%

Appendix B
The New Market Cadets

Staff Officers

Name	Age	Rank
Gilham, William	Unknown	Colonel, Acting Superintendent
Ship, Scott	24	Commander of Cadets, professor, wounded
Madison, Robert Lewis	36	Surgeon, not a cadet, Robert E. Lee's physician
Ross, George	25	Assistant Surgeon, not a cadet
Wyatt, John Wesley	24	Battalion Quartermaster, slightly wounded
Whitwell, John Croyle	36	Asst. Quartermaster & Commissary, not a cadet
Woodbridge, Jonathan Edwards	20	Sergeant Major
Davenport, Gideon Allen	18	Battalion Quartermaster Sergeant
Weston, Cary	19	Cadet Adjutant
Crocken, James Henry	43	Musician (Fife), not a cadet
Marks, Jacob	42	Musician (Drummer), not a cadet
Staples, Richard	Unknown	Musician (Drummer), not a cadet

Company A Officers

Name	Age	Rank
Wise, Henry Alexander	21	Captain
Hardy, William Charles	21	1st Lieutenant
Morson, William Alexander	21	2nd Lieutenant
Ross, Erskine Mayo	17	1st Sergeant
Duncan, William Tandy	20	3rd Sergeant
Douglass, James Travilla	19	4th Sergeant
Royster, Lawrence	23	1st Corporal
Macon, George Kennon	18	2nd Corporal, wounded in arm
Brockenbrough, Robert Lewis	17	3rd Corporal
Atwill, Samuel Francis	18	4th Corporal, killed

Company A Privates

Name	Age	Comments
Adams, Roger Atkinson	18	
Allen, Donald	16	
Anderson, Charles Jeffries	15	
Ashley, Chester Grafton	16	
Bagnall, John Seldon	20	
Binford, Reuben Joseph	16	
Bowen, Henry Clay	18	
Buster, William Dennis	19	
Butler, William Hazlewood	18	Wounded, died of typhoid while still a cadet

Company A Privates (continued)

Name	Age	Comments
Cocke, Philip St. George	20	
Corling, Charles Thompson	21	Wounded
Cousins, Robert Henry	16	
Davis, John Alexander	17	
Garrett, Henry Winder	19	
Goodykoontz, Alfred Eli	19	Detailed to stay with equipment during battle
Harrison, Carter Henry	18	Wounded by shell fragment
Hiden, Philip Barbour	19	
Hill, James Maurice	18	
Howard, John Clarke	18	Wounded in hand
Hubard, William James	19	
James, Fleming Wills	17	
Lewis, William Lynn	19	
Mallory, Edmund Skinner	17	Had been cadet only 10 weeks at time of battle
McVeigh, Newton	17	
Mead, Henry Jones	19	Wounded in thigh
Mohler, David Guin	17	
Page, Francis Walker	18	
Payne, Alexander Spotswood	18	
Pendleton, Robert Aldridge	16	Wounded in head
Raum, George Edward	17	
Skaggs, Sanford Bernard	18	
Smith, Edward Harvie	18	Wounded

Company A Privates (continued)

Name	Age	Comments
Smith, Francis Lee	18	Wounded twice, in jaw and shoulder
Spiller, George	18	Slight wound of head
Spiller, William Hickman	17	
Watson, William Pryor	17	Wounded in right arm
White, Thomas Wilson	17	Badly wounded when right leg was shattered.
White, William Henry	17	
Wimbish, Lewis Williams	16	Had been cadet only six weeks at time of battle
Wingfield, Samuel Griffin	17	
Wood, Henry Thomas	19	
Wood, Philip Southall	15	
Wood, William Morison	18	
Woodruff, Zachary Taylor	16	

Company B Officers

Name	Age	Rank
Preston, Frank	22	1st Captain and professor, not a cadet
Shafer, Carlton	20	2nd Captain
Gretter, George Washington	18	1st Lieutenant
Pizzini, Andrew, Jr.	17	1st Sergeant, wounded by saber
Evans, Oliver Perry	21	2nd Sergeant, color bearer in battle
Garrow, Harris Walker	17	3rd Sergeant, wounded

Company B Officers (continued)

Name	Age	Rank
Patton, William Macfarland	18	4th Sergeant
Hayes, Thomas Gordon	20	1st Corporal
Jarratt, John Braxton	20	2nd Corporal
Barton, Bolling Walker	17	4th Corporal

Company B Privates

Name	Age	Comments
Bayard, Nicholas James	18	
Bowen, William Brownley	17	
Bransford, John Francis	17	Wounded in foot
Cabell, Robert Gamble	16	Brother of William (killed); Robert found body.
Carmichael, William Smith	18	
Christian, Edward Dunscomb	16	Wounded, celebrated birthday the day of battle
Clarkson, John Henshaw	17	Detailed to look after dead and wounded
Cocke, John L.	16	
Cocke, William Ruffin Coleman	17	
Crank, John Thomas		
Darden, James David	19	Wounded twice, in left thigh and left arm
Dillard, John Lea	16	Had been cadet only 12 days at time of battle
Faulkner, Charles James	16	
Garrett, Van Franklin	17	

Company B Privates (continued)

Name	Age	Comments
Gibson, Franklin Graham	19	Wounded seven times at New Market
Grasty, William Clark	16	
Happer, Richard Walton Baugh	17	
Harris, Willis Overton	17	Wounded
Hartsfield, Alva Curtis	19	Killed
Haynes, Luther Cary	19	Mortally wounded
Hundley, Charles Buckler	17	Had been cadet only 10 weeks at time of battle
Jefferson, Thomas Garland	17	Mortally wounded
Johnson, Porter	18	Wounded
Kemp, Wyndham	19	
Lee, George Taylor	16	
Leftwich, Alexander Hamilton	16	
Lewis, Norborne Clack	17	
Mason, Simon Blount	16	
McCorkle, James William	23	
McDowell, William Hugh	17	Killed
Patton, John Ross	17	
Penn, James Gabriel	18	
Perry, William Edward S.	17	
Phillips, Samuel Travers	17	Wounded
Powell, John James Audubon	17	
Preston, James Brainerd	18	Slightly wounded
Preston, Thomas Wilson	17	

Company B Privates (continued)

Name	Age	Comments
Redwood, Washington Franklin	18	
Richeson, Jesse Douglas	18	
Roane, John	15	Second youngest cadet in battle
Stacker, Clay	17	
Stanard, Jacqueline Beverly	17	Mortally wounded
Tardy, Alonzo Hunt	16	
Taylor, John Eugene	17	
Tunstall, Richard Baylor	15	
Walker, Charles Pinkney	17	Wounded slightly in left side
Washington, Lloyd	17	
Wesson, Charles Macon	16	
Wharton, John Edward	19	
White, John Sproul	18	
Wilson, Richard Grey	17	
Woodlief, Pierre W., Jr.	18	Wounded

Company C Officers

Name	Age	Rank
Hill, Archibald Govan	25	1st Captain, skull fractured by shell
Shriver, Samuel Sprigg	21	2nd Captain, wounded twice in same elbow
Boggess, Albert	25	2nd Lieutenant, professor, not a cadet
Stuart, John Andrew	20	1st Sergeant, wounded in right leg

Company C Officers (continued)

Name	Age	Rank
Wise, Louis C.	19	2nd Sergeant, wounded twice
Redd, Alexander Fletcher	18	3rd Sergeant
Dinwiddie, Hardaway Hunt	19	1st Corporal, "on the colors" in battle
Wood, Julian Edward	20	2nd Corporal, in color guard at battle
James, John Garland	19	3rd Corporal, in color guard at battle
Ridley, Robert	19	4th Corporal

Company C Privates

Name	Age	Comments
Adams, Samuel Burton	15	Third youngest cadet at battle
Barraud, Daniel Cary	17	AKA Wilson, D.C.B.
Blundon, Robert Montague	18	
Booth, Samuel William	20	
Buffington, Edw. (Carter) Stanard	16	
Chalmers, William Murray	18	
Crawford, William Beamish	19	
Dunn, John Robert	17	
Ezekiel, Moses Jacob	19	Sculptor of "Virginia Mourning Her Dead"
Fry, Hugh Walker	17	
Fulton, Charles Montraville	16	Transferred to Univ. of Virginia, where he died
Goode, Hilary Langston	17	
Goodwin, James Hugh	19	Wounded, celebrated birthday the day after the battle

Company C Privates (continued)

Name	Age	Comments
Harrison, William Lambert	18	
Jones, Walter Smith	17	Wounded
Langhorne, Maurice Daniel	16	
Maury, Reuben	16	
McGavock, John Williamson	17	
Merritt, James Love	18	Seriously wounded by shell
Minor, James Hunter	16	
Mitchell, Stephen Trigg	18	
Morson, Arthur Alexander	17	
Morson, James Bruce	16	
Noland, Nelson Berkeley	17	
Page, Philip Nelson	17	
Pendleton, William Wood	18	
Price, Ferdinand Bowman	17	
Randolph, Charles Carter	18	Wounded
Read, Charles Henry, Jr.	18	Wounded over right eye
Ricketts, Lucien Cincinnatus	16	
Roller, Peter Wilson	16	
Rose, George McNeil	17	
Rutherford, Thomas Meldrum	15	
Shields, John Hardy	17	
Slaughter, William Lane	16	
Smith, Charles Henry	18	Wounded by shell

Company C Privates (continued)

Name	Age	Comments
Taylor, Blair Dabney	16	
Taylor, Carrington	18	
Thompson, Knox	16	
Turner, Charles William	17	Had been cadet only one month at time of battle
Upshur, John Nottingham	16	Wounded seriously in leg, never returned to VMI
Walker, Charles Duy	15	Severely wounded
Walker, Robert Emmett	17	
Walton, N. Tieman	19	
Wheelwright, Joseph Christopher	17	Mortally wounded

Company D Officers

Name	Age	Rank
Robinson, Thomas Beverly	28	1st Captain, professor, not a cadet
Colonna, Benjamin Azariah	20	2nd Captain, mapped battlefield after war
Hanna, John Francis	20	1st Lieutenant
Marshall, Alfred	18	2nd Corporal
Wise, John Sergeant	17	3rd Corporal, slightly wounded
Triplett, John Richards	19	4th Corporal, wounded
Cabell, William Henry	18	1st Sergeant, killed
Nelson, William	19	2nd Sergeant
Echols, Joseph Rowland	20	3rd Sergeant
Etheridge, Christopher Melville	19	4th Sergeant

Company D Privates

Name	Age	Comments
Akers, Reuben Cornelius	19	Wounded in right arm
Alexander, William Kirkwood	18	
Arbuckle, Andrew Alexander	16	
Barney, William Henry	19	
Baylor, James Bowen	15	
Beattie, William Fountain	18	
Berkeley, Edmund, Jr.	17	Wounded in head by shell
Brown, James Andrew	17	
Clark, Gaylord Blair	18	
Clendinen, Thomas Rufus	17	Had been cadet only nine days, had previously been POW
Cocke, (John) Preston	18	Wounded
Coleman, John James	19	
Corbin, James Parke, Jr.	16	
Crenshaw, Samuel David	19	Deafened and demented by battle noise
Crews, Beverly Sydnor	17	
Crockett, Charles Gay	17	Killed
Crockett, Henry Stuart	17	
Dickinson, Jesse Irvin	16	Wounded in leg
Dillard, William, Jr.	17	Wounded twice, in head and right leg
Eubank, Willis Melton	16	
Garnett, Griffin Taylor	17	Wounded
Gray, John Bowie	17	
Hamlin, Edward Lumpkin	19	
Hanna, John Spraggins	18	

Company D Privates (continued)

Name	Age	Comments
Harvie, James Blair	17	
Harvie, James Seddon	17	
Horsley, John	19	
Imboden, Jacob Peck	17	Wounded, brother of General Imboden
Jones, Henry Jenner	17	Killed by explosion of shell
Kennedy, William H.	20	Suicide victim 13 years after battle
Kirk, William Myers	18	
Knight, Emmett Carter	16	
Letcher, Samuel Houston	16	Last cadet on extreme left of line
Locke, Robert Nelson	17	
Lowry, Thomas Samuel	18	
Lumsden, William James	18	
Marks, Charles Harrison	17	
Marshall, Martin	17	Wounded, part of knee shot away. Originally thought to have been killed.
McClung, Thomas William	17	
Moorman, Edwin Steptoe	18	Wounded in arm by grapeshot
Nalle, Gustavus Brown Wallace	18	
Peirce, David Stuart	17	Wounded
Phelps, Thomas Key	16	Had been cadet only six weeks at time of battle
Radford, William Norvell	18	
Reid, John Jett	17	
Reveley, George Francis	20	
Sowers, John Franklin	18	

Company D Privates (continued)

Name	Age	Comments
Stuart, Alexander Hugh Holmes	18	Celebrated birthday the day before the battle
Tunstall, John Liggat	18	
Tutwiler, Edward Magruder	17	
Venable, William Latham	17	
Ward, George William, Jr.	16	
Wellford, Charles Edward	20	
Witt, James Etchison	18	

Artillery Officers

Name	Age	Rank
Minge, Collier Harrison	19	Captain, highest ranking cadet
Claybrook, Frederick William	19	2nd Lieutenant, Co. D, in charge of 3″ rifled gun
Welch, Levi	21	2nd Lieutenant, Co. B, in charge of 3″ rifled gun
Glazebrook, Otis Allan	18	1st Corporal, Co. D, 1 in class, gunner on 3″ gun
Henry, Patrick	17	3rd Corporal, Co. B, gunner on 3″ gun

Artillery Privates

Name	Age	Comments
Bennett, William George	17	From Company B
Chrichton, John Ashton	18	From Company C

Artillery Privates (continued)

Name	Age	Comments
Davis, Andrew Jackson	20	From Company C
Davis, Lewis Stuart	15	From Company C, youngest cadet in battle
Hayes, William Chilton	19	From Company A
Larrick, James Septimus	25	From Company A, oldest cadet in battle
Lee, Francis Tompkins	18	From Company D
Morgan, Patrick	19	From Company A
Overton, Archibald Walter	18	From Company C
Seaborn, George Andrew	18	From Company A
Shriver, Thomas Herbert	18	From Company C
Smith, William Taylor	20	From Company C
Tate, Charles Beverly	17	From Company C
Taylor, William Chamberlyn	19	From Company C
Temple, Peter Chevallie	20	From Company A
Thomson, Augustus Pembroke	17	From Company A
Webb, John Samuel	18	From Company D
Whitehead, Henry Colgate	18	From Company B, wounded in left collar bone

Cadets Who Did Not Participate in Battle

Name	Age	Rank/Company
Blankman, John Sergeant	15	Private, Company C, left behind on guard duty
Carmichael, John	16	Private, Company A, left behind on guard duty
Cullen, Simon	18	Private, Company C, left behind on guard duty

Cadets Who Did Not Participate in Battle (continued)

Name	Age	Rank/Company
Davis, Thomas Dixon	21	1st Lieutenant, Company C, on furlough
Early, John Cabell	16	Private, Company C, ill, left behind on guard duty
Hankins, Mark O.	17	Private, Company B, left behind on guard duty
Hawkes, Arthur Wells	16	Private, Company B, left behind on guard duty
Hupp, Robert Craig	18	Private, Company B, on sick leave
Johnson, Francis Smith	16	Private, Company D, left behind on guard duty
Jones, Thomas Williamson	17	Private, Company B, left behind on guard duty
King, Dent Poston (aka Henry Dent)	18	Private, Company D, left behind on guard duty
Lamb, Wilson Kerr	16	Private, Company C, left behind on guard duty
Lee, Robert Fleming	15	Private, Company C, left behind on guard duty
Martin, Thomas Staples	16	Private, Company C, sick in hospital
Martin, William Bruce	17	4th Sergeant, Company C, ill, left behind on guard duty
Shaw, William Brenton	20	2nd Sergeant, Company A, ill, regular color bearer
Tabb, John	17	Private, Company B, ill with typhoid pneumonia
Tackett, John Ford	17	Private, Company B, left behind on guard duty*
Tomes, Francis Iselin	17	Private, Company C, left behind on guard duty
Toms, Anderson Clay	16	Private, Company C, left behind on guard duty
Turner, Etheldred Lundy	17	Private, Company B, became ill enroute
Veitch, Wilberforce	17	Private, Company B, left behind on guard duty
Wood, Hunter	18	5th Sergeant, Company A, on suspension
Wood, Martin Birney	19	Private, Company D, left behind on guard duty**
Yarbrough, William Tilton	18	Private, Company B, left behind on guard duty

* Arrived at VMI the day the cadets departed. He was assigned to guard duty until the cadets returned.
** Unable to march due to leg wound suffered at Antietam.

Appendix C
Participating Regiments

FEDERAL ARMY
MAJOR GENERAL FRANZ SIGEL

First Infantry Division - Sullivan, Gen. Jeremiah

First Brigade - Moor, Col. August
   18th Connecticut - Peale, Maj. Henry
   28th Ohio - Becker, Lt. Col. Godfred
   116th Ohio - Washburn, Col. James
   123rd Ohio - Kellogg, Maj. Horace

Second Brigade - Thoburn, Col. Joseph
   1st West Virginia - Weddle, Lt. Col. Jacob
   12th West Virginia - Curtis, Col. William
   34th Massachusetts - Wells, Col. George
   54th Pennsylvania - Campbell, Col. Jacob

First Cavalry Division - Stahel, Gen. Julius

First Brigade - Tibbitts, Col. William
   1st New York (Veterans) - Taylor, Col. Robert
   1st New York (Lincoln) - Adams, Col. Alonzo (not engaged)
   1st Maryland Home - Daniel, Maj. J. Townsend
   21st New York - Otis, Maj. Charles
   14th Pennsylvania - Duncan, Capt. Ashbell

Second Brigade - Wynkoop, Gen. John
   15th New York - Roessler, Lt. Col. Henry
   20th Pennsylvania - Douglas, Lt. Col. Robert
   22nd Pennsylvania - McNulty, Capt. Caleb

Artillery

    Battery B, Maryland Light - Snow, Capt. Alonzo

    30th Battery, New York - von Kleiser, Capt. Albert

    Battery D, 1st West Virginia - Carlin, Capt. John

    Battery G, 1st West Virginia - Ewing, Capt. Chatham

    Battery B, 5th U.S. - du Pont, Capt. Henry (not engaged until retreat)

CONFEDERATE ARMY

MAJOR GENERAL JOHN BRECKINRIDGE

Infantry Division

    First Brigade - Echols, Brig. Gen. John

        22nd Virginia - Patton, Col. George

        23rd Virginia Battalion - Derrick, Col. Clarence

        26th Virginia Battalion - Edgar, Col. George

    Second Brigade - Wharton, Brig. Gen. Gabriel

        30th Virginia Battalion - Clark, Lt. Col. J. Lyle

        51st Virginia - Wolfe, Col. John

        62nd Virginia Mounted - Smith, Col. George

        Company A, 1st Missouri Cavalry - Woodson, Capt. Charles

    Attached Commands

        Hart's Engineer Company - Hart, Capt. William

        Augusta-Rockingham Reserves - Harman, Col. William (not engaged)

        Davis's Company, Maryland Cavalry - Davis, Col. T. Sturgis

        23rd Virginia Cavalry - White, Lt. Col. Robert

        VMI Cadets - Ship, Col. Scott

Cavalry, Valley District - Imboden, Brig. Gen. John

        18th Virginia - Imboden, Col. George

        23rd Virginia - White, Col. Robert (Dismounted)

        2nd Maryland Battalion - Gilmor, Maj. Harry

        McNeil's Company, Partisans - McNeil, Capt. John

        43rd Battalion - Mosby, Col. John

Artillery

        Chapman's Battery - Chapman, Capt. George

        Jackson's Battery - Blain, Lt. Randolph

        McClanahan's Battery - McClanahan, Capt. John

        VMI Cadets - Minge, Capt. Collier

Appendix D
Letters and Documents Pertaining to the Battle of New Market

In the following letter, General Robert E. Lee expresses his appreciation to the cadets of VMI for offering their services, but that he thinks it is better for the corps to remain at VMI for the present:

HQ, Army No. Va.
25th April 1864
Major Genl Wm. H. Richardson
A.G. of Virginia, Richmond

General—

Your letter of the 22d inst. enclosing that of General Francis H. Smith in which he proposes to tender the services of the Corps of Cadets at the Virginia Military Institute for the approaching campaign is received.

I desire to express my appreciation of the patriotic spirit that actuates Genl. Smith in making this proposal, and my gratification at finding that it meets with your concurrence. I do not think however that it would be best at this time for the Corps to be called to this Army. It is now in a situation to render valuable aid in defending our western frontier which may be menaced simultaneously with the general advance of the enemy in the east. It will thus prevent the necessity of detaching troops from this army. I think it would be advisable for Genl. Smith to hold the command in readiness to cooperate with Genl. Breckinridge & Genl Imboden in case of necessity, & to notify those officers of the fact. Should it at any time become necessary or expedient to have the services of the cadets with this army, it is very gratifying to me to know that they are so freely placed at my disposal.

Very Resp. Yr. Obt. Servt.

signed/R.E. Lee Genl.

VMI Superintendent Francis Smith reports the readiness of the Corps of Cadets to Major General John Breckinridge, requesting orders from Breckinridge:

May 2, 1864
HQ, VMI
Maj. Gen. John C. Breckinridge
Comd. Dept. of Western Va. Dublin Depot

General

I have the honor to enclose herewith a letter from General R. E. Lee, Commanding Army of N. Virginia, addressed to the Adjutant General of Virginia—also—a copy of instructions from the Governor of Virginia communicated by the Adjutant General defining my duty as Superintendent of the Virginia Military Institute.

Under these instructions and suggestions, I now respectfully report to you, for such orders as the emergencies of the approaching campaign may call forth. The Corps of Cadets numbers an aggregate of 280, of whom 250 may be relied upon for active duty, leaving 30 as a necessary guard to the Institution and as disabled. The command is organized as a battalion of infantry of four companies, and is usually accompanied by a section of Artillery. It is fully equipped, except in horses, and these are impressed in case of need. We have abundance of ammunition, tents, knapsacks, shovels & picks, and will be prepared to march at a moment's notice.

Brig. Gen. Imboden is about constructing telegraphic communication between the Institute and Staunton. This he hopes to have in operation by the middle of May. In the mean time he will communicate with us by signals. Any intelligence from Dublin Depot had better be forwarded to Gen. Imboden at Staunton, with instructions to be immediately transmitted to me.
I remain, General,

very respt. yr. obt. servant
signed/Francis H. Smith

Breckinridge's letter to Smith thanking him and giving him some general directions:

Hq, Department of W. Va.,
Dublin Depot, May 4, 1864

General—

I have just received your letter of the 2d instant, concerning one from General Lee to the Adjutant General of Virginia, also a copy of the instructions to you from the Governor.

I am gratified to learn that a battalion of cadets 250 strong, with a section of artillery, will be ready to move on a moment's notice. This force will be very effective in assisting to repel or capture destructive raiding parties.

The limits of my department have not been defined in the east, and I have been unable to adopt many precautions east of Monroe and Greenbrier. I have, however, thrown up a work at the railroad bridge over the Cow Pasture, another at the bridge over Jackson River, and a line of rifle pits at Island Ford. Col. Wm. L. Jackson is covering the approaches to these points, and to Rockbridge, from that general direction. It may be necessary for you to move in that quarter, or to protect the iron furnaces in Botetourt or in Buchanan. I will try to send the earliest intelligence through General Imboden, as you suggest, or if it should be beyond reach of telegraph, by special couriers.

General Imboden will, of course, apprise you of my movements in direction of Millboro, Staunton, etc. Fully appreciating your patriotic feelings, and those of the young gentlemen you command.

I am, General,

Your obedient servant
signed/John C. Breckinridge.

Dispatch from Breckinridge to Smith requesting that the Corps be sent to assist him:

Staunton, Va., May 10, 1864
Maj. Gen. F. H. Smith, Supt. VMI

Sigel is moving up the Valley—was at Strasburg last night. I cannot tell you whether this is his destination. I would be glad to have your assistance at once with the cadets and the section of artillery. Bring all the forage and rations you can. Have the reserves of Rockbridge ready, and let them send at once for arms and ammunition, if they cannot be supplied at Lexington.

Yours respectfully,
John C. Breckinridge, Major General

Smith informs Breckinridge that the Corps is ready to move. He spells out their strength and their weaponry:

May 11, 1864, 6 a.m. Maj. Gen. J. C. Breckinridge, CSA.
General

Your dispatch of yesterday by courier was recd. by me at 9 P.M. I immediately gave orders to Lt. Col. Ship, Commandant of Cadets, to have his battalion in readiness to move this morning at 7 o.c. They are now forming, & will reach Bell's 16 miles today & be in Staunton tomorrow.

I have issued to them rations for 2 days, & will send with them 500 lbs. of bacon & as much beef as I can find transportation for. I have 64 barrels of flour near Staunton. I send 100 bushels of corn for forage.

The cadets are armed with Austrian Rifles & take 40 rounds of ammunition. The section of Artillery will consist of 3 in. iron rifles & the ammunition chests of the limbers & caissons will be filled. I have 10 or 12 6 lb. brass pieces here, mounted, and 1 12 lb howitzer, if any should be needed.

Horses have been impressed for the Artillery & transportation, but the horses are slow in coming in. The artillery have orders to reach the Infantry Battalion tonight.

I have ordered the four companies of reserves to rendezvous here & will arm & equip them, and hold them in readiness to move at a moment's notice. No commanding officer has been appt. to this Battalion. I will [illegible] the Commd. of the Post of Lexington to supply rations should they be called out.

Your dispatch finds me very unwell, but I shall hope to be with you tomorrow. Lt. Col. Ship has orders to report to you on reaching Staunton. If the reserve companies are required to move to Staunton, I will have them in readiness to move tomorrow & shall get transportation for 6000 lbs bacon from the commissary of C.S. here.

signed/Francis H. Smith.

Smith informs General Richardson that the Cadets are en route to Staunton:

May 12, 1864
Maj. Gen. W. H. Richardson, A.G.

My dear Sir
On Tuesday night at 9 o. clock I recd. a dispatch from Maj. Gen. Breckinridge, by courier, that an advance up the valley was threatened by Sigel, & directing me to move the cadets with a section of Artillery to Staunton where he was. The order was accordingly given, & they left at 7 A.M. yesterday, expecting to reach Staunton today.

I am detained by a severe hoarse cold, but expect to join by day after tomorrow. It appears the movement of Sigel is a mere demonstration by way of diversion. I was also ordered to have the reserves in readiness & I am today making arrangements to issue their arms & ammunition.

signed/F. H. Smith

The following letter is the last letter ever written by Cadet Jaqueline (Jack) Stanard. It was written in Staunton while he was enroute to the Battle of New Market, where Stanard was killed at the age of 19. The original letter, written in pencil on both sides of 4¹/₂" x 9¹/₂" lined paper, is in the VMI Archives. To conserve paper, Stanard's last few lines are crosswritten vertically. The letter as reproduced here includes Stanard's spelling and grammatical errors, just as they were written.

Staunton May the 12th 1864

My darling Mother
   No doubt a letter written from this place will take you greatly by surprise. Well to releive your anxiety I will tell you before going further and keep you from uneasiness. On Tuesday night an order came from Gen. Breckinridge calling us immediately to Staunton. In obedience to his orders we fixed up and left on Wednesday morning at half past 8, marched 18 miles by half past two, when we camped. The roads were very good but were quite dusty and then it was very warm. This morning we left camp under quite different circumstances, it having rained during the night and has continued to do so all day, the roads were perfect loblolly all the way and we had to wade through like hogs. We came 18 miles from 5 to 12 however and are tonight encamped one mile out of town. I have run the blockade and come in to take tea with Cary Taylor, and that I might write this letter. Am I not good? I have a strong notion of staying in until 2 tonight with him so as to dry of[f], for I have been like a wet mouse all day [-] so disagreeable in camp. We will
{Page 2}
leave in the morning early and expect to have to march to Harrisonburg (down the Valley) a distance of 26 miles. The Yankees are reported coming up the

Valley with a force of 9000 strong. Our corps will run Gen. B[reckinridge] up to 5000 may be more. I hope we may be able to lick them out. I have suffered more with my feet this march (so far) than I ever did on all the others together. I hope to get me a more comfortable pair of shoes when this will be remedied. I got my trunk the evening before I left all safe. It was in the nick of time and my biscuit and ham for my rations. If you want to write to me direct you[r] letter to me at this place Care of Edmond M. Taylor, Staunton, he will send them to me. I expect we will be down out this time for some weeks. I told you that you had better let me join Lee at once [,] this could be the way but you must not make yourself uneasy about me. I will take care of myself. One of my messmates from this place is going to fill my haversack with something better than we draw so I won't suffer for some days at any rate, although I hope not [crosswriting begins] at all. Well, darling Mother I have written enough I suppose to relieve your mind as to our destination so I must stop and go in the parlor. Some young ladies there. You will have a hard time trying to make this out I shan't undertake it. Saw <Fedic?> T. this evening. Give my love to all acqu[aintan]ce & friends. Hope Bob come out all right and all the Berry Hill friends & visitors. I shall write when ever I have an opportunity. An now dear Mother that I may be spared to see you all again, and that you may continue in good health will be the nightly prayer of

Your darling boy
Bev

Breckinridge's first report of the battle, made that same evening:

NEW MARKET, May 15, 1864 - 7 p.m.

This morning, two miles above New Market, my command met the enemy, under General Sigel, advancing up the Valley, and defeated him with heavy loss. The action has just closed at Shenandoah River. Enemy fled across North Fork of the Shenandoah, burning the bridge behind him.

JNO. C. BRECKINRIDGE
Major-General

General S. Cooper
Adjutant and Inspector General

Sigel's first report of the battle. Note his inflated estimate of the Confederate forces:

HEADQUARTERS DEPARTMENT OF WEST VIRGINIA,
May 15, 1864 - 8 p.m.

A severe battle was fought to-day at New Market between our forces and those of Echols and Imboden, under Breckinridge. Our troops were overpowered by superior numbers. I, therefore, withdrew them gradually from the battlefield, and recrossed the Shenandoah at about 7 p.m. Under the circumstances prevailing I find it necessary to retire to Cedar Creek. The batle was fought on our side by 5,500 in all against 8,000 to 9,000 of the enemy. We lost about 600 in killed and wounded, and 50 prisoners.

F. SIGEL
Major-General

ADJUTANT GENERAL U. S. ARMY

Sigel's follow-up report made the day following the battle:

HEADQUARTERS DEPARTMENT OF WEST VIRGINIA,
Near Strasburg, May 16, 1864

After the battle of yesterday I retired gradually to Strasburg and Cedar Creek, bringing all my trains and all the wounded that could be transported from the battlefield with me. In consequence of the long line and trains which had to be guarded I could not bring more than six regiments into the fight, besides the artillery and the cavalry. The enemy have about 7,000 infantry, besides the other arms. Our losses are about 600 killed and wounded, and 50 prisoners. Five pieces of artillery had to be left on the field after being disabled or the horses shot. The retrograde movement to Strasburg was effected in perfect order, without any loss of material or men. The troops are in very good spirits, and will fight another battle if the enemy should advance against us. I will forward the full report, with list of casualties, by letter.

FRANZ SIGEL
Major-General

ADJUTANT-GENERAL U. S. ARMY

General Robert E. Lee congratulates Breckinridge on his victory and gives him additional orders:

SPOTSYLVANIA COURT-HOUSE, May 16, 1864
(Via Guiney's Station.)

General J. C. BRECKINRIDGE:

I offer you the thanks of this army for your victory over General Sigel. Press them down the Valley, and, if practibable, follow him into Maryland.

R. E. LEE
General

Smith gives Richardson a preliminary report on the Corps' involvement in the battle:

May 17, 1864
HQ, VMI
Maj. Gen. William H. Richardson A.G.

General—

Your telegraphic dispatch of the 16th and the letter of Gov. Smith of the15th were duly received by this evening's mail.

The suspension of the mails has delayed your rec. of my letter of the 12th informing you that acting under the instructions of Gen. R. E. Lee, the Corps of Cadets had been called out by Maj. Gen. Breckinridge to assist him in meeting a threatened advance of the enemy up the valley under Gen. Sigel.

A dispatch from Gen. Breckinridge asking for the cadets to be immediately marched to Staunton was recd. by courier at 9 p.m. on the 10th. At 7 a.m. on the 11th the battalion of cadets, in four infantry companies, and a section of artillery, marched under the command of Lt. Col. Ship with two days rations. They reached Staunton on the 12th and immediately advanced with the command of Gen. Breckinridge to meet the enemy. My health confining me here, Col. Gilham went as Acting Supt.

I have now the honor to report that I have just recd. an official dispatch from Col. Gilham, dated New Market May 16, in which he states "that all the cadets were engaged, and bore a most important and conspicious part in the battle of the previous day." and my account testifies to the great gallantry and splendid conduct of the cadets.

I regret to report many casualties.

Five cadets were killed viz. Cadet W. H. Cabell, C. Crockett, H. Jones, McDowell, and Stanard.

Wounded—Lt. Col. Ship, slightly and on duty & Comd. of Cadets Lt. A. Govan Hill, Asst. Professor & Comd. Company Cadets White, T., Dillard of Amherst, Gibson F., Randolph, Macon, Dickinson (slightly), Upshur, Darden, Woodlief, Smith F., Smith E., Walker, Haynes, Garnett, Goodwin (slightly), Peirce (slightly), Jefferson, Marshall, M., Atwill, Moorman, Merritt, Shriver S., Garrow, Read C.H., Pendleton R., Wise J. (slightly), Triplett, Wise L. (slightly), Berkeley, Christian, Stuart, J.A., Wheelwright, Mead (slightly), Bransford, Spiller, G., Johnson, P., Harris (slightly).

Besides sending Col. Gilham & Col. Ross to aid in providing every necessary comfort for the cadets, I ordered Surgeon Madison, Asst. Surgeon

Ross, Hospital Steward Kohle, the Hospital attendant with four servants, an ambulance & full medical supplies to accompany the command. On Saturday, in anticipation of a fight I sent a wagon with supplies of coffee, sugar, tea, and other comforts.

I have succeeded in getting a private conveyance to go down tomorrow, altho still very unwell, and shall take clothing & other supplies to meet the necessities of the wounded.

Lt. Hill is severely wounded in the head.

The present duty of the cadets may modify your suggestion & that of the Sec. of War and Governor, in reference to the orders sending the cadets to Richmond. Under the circumstances, I shall be constrained to refer your dispatch to Gen. Breckinridge, and in the meantime respectfully request you to make known the position of the cadets to the Governor & Sec. of War. Your dispatch to Staunton will reach me there.
I remain, General,

very Respt.

signed/Francis H. Smith.

Dispatch to General Kelley from Sigel, briefly reporting on the battle:

HARPER'S FERRY, May 17, 1864
General Kelley:
   SIR: Information from General Sigel just received. He fought Breckinridge on the 15th near New Market, and fell back to Strasburg. Our loss in killed and wounded about 600, with 5 pieces of artillery. Enemy's loss reported to be 1,000. Lieutenant-Colonel Lincoln, Thirty-fourth Massachusetts, wounded. The enemy's forces were Echols' and Imboden's, commanded by Breckinridge. Our loss in prisoners 50.
   Respectfully,
LAWRENCE,
Operator

Sigel requests additional help from General Kelley. He also engages in further political damage control, reiterating that Breckinridge greatly outnumbered him in the battle:

MARTINSBURG, MAY 17, 1864
Brigadier General KELLEY:
   After two days' skirmishing, a severe battle was fought at New Market between our forces and those of Echols and Imboden, under Breckinridge. I had to withdraw our troops from the battlefield toward evening, and

recrossed the Shenandoah. I will go back to my position behind Cedar Creek and accept another battle, if necessary. The troops are in very good spirits, but greatly outnumbered, as Breckinridge has evidently thrown his principal forces against me. I will, however, do my best and depend on your assistance. I wish that you send me immediately the Fourth Virginia Infantry, and the Second Maryland Infantry, as there is no serious danger for Cumberland and New Creek, or other places west, as long as I can maintain my position here. Please inform General Crook by any means, and direct him to operate against Staunton, and to destroy if possible the railroad between Staunton and Jackson River Depot.

F. SIGEL

Major-General

Battle report of Col. Jacob M. Campbell of the 54th Pennsylvania Infantry:

HDQRS. FIFTY-FOURTH REGT. PENNSYLVANIA VOLS.,

Camp near Cedar Creek, Va., May 18, 1864

COLONEL: I have the honor to submit the following report of the part taken by the Fifty-fourth Regiment Pennsylvania Volunteers in the recent engagement near New Market on the 15th instant:

The regiment having marched in the morning from Woodstock, had just gone into camp at Mount Jackson, when I received orders to march rapidly toward New Market. Forming hastily, we at once marched as directed, and in obedience to renewed orders to that effect hastened our steps, and without halting or rest arrived much fatigued on the field. According to your orders we at once deployed into column by division to the left and rear of the Twelfth West Virginia, which regiment shortly afterward moved toward the right, unmasking us, and about the same time my regiment was deployed and took position on the left of the First West Virginia and on the extreme left of the line of battle. We remained in this position, partly shielded from the fire of the enemy by the crest of a hill in front, until, observing the regiment on my right making a charge in the absence of orders, presuming it proper to imitate their example, I ordered the Fifty-fourth also to charge, which was done with alacrity and spirit. Advancing beyond the crest of the hill, a rapid, vigorous, and, as I believe, effective fire was for some time kept up on the enemy, and every effort made by them to advance on the front occupied by my regiment was firmly and resolutely resisted and proved abortive, although we sustained a galling and destructive fire, in which many of my men were killed and wounded. The enemy, however, pressed forward his right, which extended some distance beyond our left, and was rapidly flanking me in that direction despite the most determined resistance, when my attention was called to the fact that the regiment on my right (owing to the overwhelming numbers brought against it) had given way, and the enemy was advancing at almost right angle with my line and extending beyond the rear and right of my regiment. A few minutes only would be required to completely surround my regiment, and in the absence of any appearance of advancing support I was reluctantly compelled to order my command to retire. This was done in as good order as the circumstances would allow, two stands being made by a portion of the command before passing beyond musket-range, and the whole of it final rallying and forming at a point indicated by the colonel commanding brigade.

Lieut. Col. John P. Linton was wounded, but remained upon the field rallying and encouraging the men until the final close of the action, rendering most valuable and efficient service.

Captain Graham, of Company E, was killed* early in the engagement, and Second Lieutenant Anderson, of the same company, fell afterward, leaving the company in command of the second sergeant, the first sergeant being also severely wounded.

Captain Geisinger, of Company H, fell mortally wounded, and about the same time Lieutenant Killpatrick, of the same company, was seriously injured and brought off the field.

Lieutenant Colburn, of Company B, fell just as the command commenced to fall back. He was brought to a house in the rear of our line, but finally fell into the hands of the enemy in a dying condition.

Capt. William R. Bonacker fell mortally wounded,* I believe, as we were in the act of falling back, gallantly encouraging his men. His conduct throughout the whole engagement was most cheering and encouraging to his men, and his loss is deeply to be regretted. Indeed, the conduct of officers and men throughout was all that I could ask or desire, and entitles them to the highest praise.

The number of officers and men of my regiment in the engagement was 566. Our loss is 5 commissioned officers killed or mortally wounded, and 2 wounded and brought off the field. Of the noncommissioned officers and privates, 27 are known to be killed, and 42 wounded, all of whom fell into the enemy's hands. We brought off the field 98 of our wounded. This number does not include some 30 who were so slightly wounded as not to be thought necessary to report.

The enclosed report of casualties will show the rank, name, and company of all the killed and seriously wounded, amounting in the aggregate to 174.

I have the honor to be, very respectfully, your obedient servant,

JACOB M. CAMPBELL,
Colonel Fifty-fourth Regt. Pennsylvania Volunteers.

---

*This was an error. Graham survived and was mustered out March 12, 1865, and Bonacker on October 10, 1864.

J. H. Morrison informs J. L. Jones of the death of his brother, Cadet Henry J. Jones, in the Battle of New Market. He also informs him of the burial site:

HQ , V.M. Institute
May 18th, 1864
J.L. Jones
Charlotte, NC
Sir—

I am directed by the Supt to inform you, that acting under the suggestions and instructions of General R.E. Lee and the Governor of Virginia, the Corps of Cadets was made subject to the orders of General Breckinridge to cooperate with him if at any time a threatened advance of the enemy might either endanger us here, or the safety of Gen Lee's army.

On the 9th inst a dispatch was received from General Breckenridge informing the Supt that Genl. Sigel was advancing up the valley and urging the immediate junction of the cadets with his command at Staunton. This order was promptly obeyed, and resulted in a general victory over the enemy on the 15th inst near New Market in which the cadets bore an important and conspicuous part.

I regret to inform you that your brother [Henry Jenner Jones, VMI Class of 1867] was killed. Five cadets were killed and thirty-seven wounded. Your brother's remains were interred, together with the others, in the cemetery at New Market on the evening of the 16th inst. His grave is so marked that there will be no difficulty in distinguishing it if at any time you should desire to have his remains removed.

Providence has so ordained it that these young men should be sent off in early youth—they fell nobly fighting in a just cause, in which all Southern youths are willing to pour out [their] heart's blood. I am sir,
Very respectfully,

yr obt servt
J.H. Morrison, A.A. V.M.I.

Halleck requests Grant's answer regarding relieving Sigel of his command:

WASHINGTON, May 18, 1864 - 4 p. m.

Lieutenant-General Grant,
       Near Spotsylvania, Va.:

The Secretary of War directs me to say that the President will appoint General Hunter to command the Department of West Virginia, if you desire it. Please answer as early as possible.
                 H. W. Halleck
                 Major-General and Chief of Staff

Grant agrees to relieve Sigel of his command. Note Grant's obvious frustration with Sigel's performance:

NEAR SPOTSYLVANIA COURT-HOUSE

May 19, 1864-10:30 a.m. (Received 5 p.m.)
Major-General HALLECK:
Washington, D.C.:
By all means I would say appoint General Hunter, or anyone else, to the command of West Virginia.

U. S. Grant
Lieutenant-General

General Order assigning Hunter to the command of the Department of West Virginia:

GENERAL ORDERS,   WAR DEPT., ADJ. GENERAL'S OFFICE
No. 200   Washington, May 19, 1864

By direction of the President, Maj. Gen. D. Hunter, U. S. Volunteers, is assigned to the command of the Department of West Virginia.
By order of the Secretary of War:

E. D. TOWNSEND,
Assistant Adjutant-General

Sigel's report of the battle to the Assistant Adjutant-General, Captain Wager:

HEADQUARTERS DEPARTMENT OF WEST VIRGINIA
Cedar Creek, May 19, 1864 (Received 11 p. m.)
Captain Wager,
Assistant Adjutant-General:
Your dispatch dated May 17, 10 p.m. has been received. I reported to the Adjutant-General , from Mount Jackson and Strasburg on the 15th and 16th instant, that we had met Breckinridge on the 15th at New Market, and fought him the whole day with about 5,500 men against about 8,000 to 9,000 men. After a loss of 800 killed and wounded, I withdrew my force slowly to Mount Jackson. The enemy sustained heavy losses. I deemed it prudent to withdraw behind Cedar Creek, in which position I am at present, with my advance between Strasburg and Woodstock. The enemy has made no advance; his main force is at Mount Jackson and New Market and his cavalry at Woodstock. I will watch his movements, follow him closely if he withdraws, and resist him if he advances. I have ordered the last two regiments from the interior of the department to join me, and have directed General Crook, through General Kelley, to operate from Lewisburg in the direction of Staunton.

F. Sigel
Major-General

Sigel acknowledges his dismissal:

GENERAL ORDERS   HDQRS. DEPT. OF WEST VIRGINIA
No. 27   Cedar Creek, Va. May 21, 1864

By an order of the President of the United States, I am relieved from the command of this department. Major-General Hunter, U. S. Volunteers, is my successor. In leaving the troops under my immediate command I feel it my duty to give my most sincere thanks to the officers and men who have assisted me so faithfully during the last campaign. Having no other wishes and aspirations but to serve and to promote the great cause, which we are bound to defend, I hope that final success may crown the indefatigable zeal and good will of this army.

SIGEL
Major-General

Hunter announces his assumption of command:

GENERAL ORDERS   HDQRS. DEPT. OF WEST VIRGINIA
No. 28   Martinsburg, W. Va. May 21, 1864

Agreeable to the orders of the President of the United States, the undersigned assumes command of the Department of West Virginia. All reports and returns will be made to the headquarters of the department, as at present directed; and all communications for the commanding general of the department will be promptly forwarded to him in the field. In addition to the present department staff, Lieut. Col. Charles G. Halpine is announced as assistant adjutant-general, and Maj. Samuel W. Stockton as aide-de-camp. And these officers will be respected and obeyed accordingly.

HUNTER
Major-General, Commanding

J. T. L. Preston informs R. I. McDowell of the death of his son, Cadet William H. McDowell, at the Battle of New Market:

Virginia Mil. Institute
May 25th, 1864
Mr. R.I. McDowell
Mount Mourne, Iredell Co. N.C.

Sir—
You have doubtless received before this the mournful intelligence that your [noble] son has been added to the long list of the gallant dead who

have fallen in defending their country against the invasion of a ruthless foe. The newspapers have furnished you with accounts of the victory gained by Gen. Breckinridge over Sigel near New Market, and every notice of the fight bears unequivocal testimony to the value of the aid rendered by the Corps of Cadets and the [illegible] valour that they displayed in the action. You have also received, I suppose, an official letter from the Adjutant informing you of the sad event.

I can add nothing more except the statement that the fatal ball passed entirely through his body, entering a little to the [illegible] of the breastbone and coming out on the left of the spine, passing probably through the heart, so that it may be concluded that his death was instantaneous.

This I received from Col. Gilham who examined the body before its interment. I have not been able to see anyone who was near him when he fell, as the cadets have not returned to the Institute, [having been] ordered to Richmond.

The Quartermaster will endeavor to preserve any mementos or any property of the cadets who have fallen, but cannot at present while the Corps is absent identify what belongs to each. The letter which you gave me for him [3 words illegible] and which weighed as a heavy burden on my heart after I heard before I reached home, that the words of affection it contained could never reach the eyes closed in death forever—together with a second one received from the office for him, I have directed to be kept subject to your order not choosing to subject them to the risk of the mail in the present uncertainty of transmission.

I offer no words of condolence. I know how to sympathize with you for my noblest son fell slain in battle not two months after he left the Institute—and I know by experience that the only comfort for so great a sorrow must come from a source higher than any on earth.

Yrs truly

J.T.L. Preston

Excerpt from the Superintendent's Annual Report, July 1864, concerning the Battle of New Market (Page 33 of the original document).

*   *   *

Battle of New Market
On the night of the 10th May a dispatch was received from Major General J.C. Breckinridge, by special courier, calling upon me for cooperation on the

part of the corps of cadets, in his effort to repel the advance of General Sigel. Orders were immediately given to Lieutenant Colonel S. Ship, commandant of cadets, to proceed without delay, with a battalion of infantry of four companies, and a section of artillery, and to report to General Breckinridge at Staunton. Having previously communicated to General Breckinridge the letter of General R. E. Lee, addressed to the adjutant general of Virginia, and the instructions of the governor, as conveyed in general orders of date September 5, 1863, I signified to him my readiness to give to him such support as my authority under these instructions would warrant. The corps of cadets was accordingly placed at the disposal of General Breckinridge, subject to the limitations thus expressed. As soon as the cadets reached Staunton, the command of General Breckinridge immediately moved down the Valley to meet the enemy. A sanguinary battle took place on the 15th May, near New Market, resulting in a signal victory by the confederate forces, the capture of a battery of artillery, many small arms, horses and prisoners. The enemy were pursued to Mount Jackson, where the further pursuit was arrested by their burning the bridge behind them.

In this sanguinary battle the cadets were engaged; and the casualties reported (six killed and forty-two wounded) show the prominent part borne by them in this struggle. I have been informed by Gen. Breckinridge that it was not his intention to put the cadets into the battle, unless absolutely required. He considered the necessity for using them urgent; and had they not been freely used, the result of the battle, in his judgment, might have been different. He assured me that the officers and cadets had borne themselves with conspicuous gallantry; and it was a source of great satisfaction to him to bear testimony to their patient endurance of severe hardships, under a forced march in a storm of rain, and the fine discipline exhibited by them through the whole expedition.

The report of Lieut. Col. Ship will present in detail the events of this memorable battle with the names of those who participated in it, with the list of killed and wounded.

Having been prevented by illness from accompanying the cadets on this expedition, Col. Gilham was requested to go as acting superintendent, that he might provide for the general wants and comfort of the cadets, and discharge such duties as would properly devolve upon the superintendent. He was enabled to provide for the wounded, and to have proper arrangments made for the burial of the killed.

Having joined the corps in Staunton, I there received the orders of the adjutant general directing me to move the cadets to Richmond to aid in the defence of the capital. Having reported to the governor and secretary of war, in obedience to orders, the cadets were assigned to the command of Maj. Gen. Ransom, and were encamped about two miles from the city limits.

The report then moves into a discussion of other matters.

Report of Lt. Col. Scott Ship on the Battle of New Market and its aftermath:

Headquarters Corps of Cadets, July 4, 1864.

General:

In obedience to General Orders No. 21, Headquarters Virginia Military Institute, June 27, 1864, I have the honor to submit the following report of the Corps of Cadets, under my command, in the field, from May 11th to June 25th, inclusive.

In obedience to orders from Major General Breckinridge, communicated through you, at 7 a.m. on the morning of May 11th, the Corps of Cadets, consisting of a battalion of four companies of infantry and a section of 3-inch rifled guns, took up the line of march for Staunton. The march to Staunton was accomplished in two days. I preceded the column on the second day some hours for the purpose of reporting to General Breckinridge, and was ordered by him to put the Cadets in camp one mile south of Staunton.

On the morning of the 13th, I received orders to march at daylight on the road to Harrisonburg, taking position in the column in the rear of Echols's Brigade. We marched eighteen miles and encamped, moved at daylight on the 14th, marched sixteen miles and encamped.

At 1 o'clock on the night of the 14th received orders to prepare to march immediately, without beat of drums and as noiselessly as possible. We moved from camp at 1:30 o'clock, taking position in the general column in rear of Echols's Brigade, being followed by the column of artillery under the command of Major McLaughlin. Having accomplished a distance of six miles, and approached the position of the enemy, as indicated by occasional skirmishing with his pickets in front, a halt was called, and we remained on the side of the road two or three hours in the midst of a heavy fall of rain. The General having determined to receive the attack of the enemy, made his dispositions for battle, posting the Corps in reserve. He informed me that he did not wish to put the cadets in if he could avoid it, but that should occasion require it he would use them very freely. He was also pleased to express his confidence in them, and I am happy to believe that his expectations were not disappointed, for when the tug of battle came they bore themselves gallantly and well.

The enemy not making the attack as was anticipated, and not advancing as rapidly as was desired, the line was deployed into column and the advance resumed. Here I was informed by one of General Breckinridge's aides, that my battalion, together with the battalion of Colonel G. M. Edgar, would constitute the reserve, and was instructed to keep the section of artillery with the column, and to take position, after the deployments should have been made, two hundred and fifty or three hundred yards in the rear of the front line of battle, and to maintain that distance. Having begun a flank movement to the left, about two miles south of New Market, the nature of the ground was such as to render it impossible that the artillery should continue with the infantry column. I ordered Lieutenant Minge to join the general artillery column on the main road and to report to Major McLaughlin. After that I did not see the section of artillery until near the close of the engagement. Major McLaughlin, under whose command they served, was pleased to speak of the section in such complimentary terms that I was satisfied then that they had done their duty.

Continuing the advance on the ground to the left of the main road, and south of New Market, at 12:30 p.m. we came under fire of the enemy's batteries. Having advanced a quarter of a mile under the fire, we were halted, and the column was deployed, the march up to this time having been by flank in column. The ground in front was open, with skirts of woods on the left. Here General Breckinridge sent for me, and gave me in person my instructions. The General's plans seem to have undergone some modification. Instead of one line, with a reserve, he formed his infantry in two, artillery in rear and to the right, the cavalry deployed and guarding the right flank, left flank resting on a stream. Wharton's Brigade of infantry constituted the first line, Echol's brigade the second. The battalion of Cadets, brigaded with Echols, was the last battalion but one from the left of the second line, Edgar's battalion being on the left. The lines having been adjusted, the order to advance was passed. Wharton's line advanced, Echols followed at two hundred and fifty paces in the rear. As Wharton's line ascended a knoll it came in full view of the enemy's batteries, which opened a heavy fire, but not having gotten the range, did but little damage. By the time the second line reached the same ground, the Yankee gunners had gotten the exact range and their fire begun to tell on our line with fearful accuracy. It was here that Captain Hill and others fell. Great gaps were made through the ranks, but the Cadet, true to his discipline, would close in to the center to fill the interval, and push steadily forward. The alignment of the battalion under this terrible fire, which strewed the ground with killed and wounded for more than a mile on open ground, would have been creditable even on a field-day.

The advance was thus continued, until, having passed Bushong's house, a mile or more beyond New Market, and still to the left of the main road, the enemy's batteries, at two hundred and fifty or three hundred yards, opened upon us with canister and case shot, and their long lines of infantry were put into action at the same time. The fire was withering. It seemed impossible that any living creature could escape, and here we sustained our heaviest loss, a great many being wounded and numbers knocked down, stunned, and temporarily disabled. I was here disabled for a time, and the command devolved upon Company A. He gallantly pressed onward. We had before this gotten into the front line. Our line took a position behind a line of fence. A brisk fusillade ensued, a shout, a rush, and the day was won. The enemy fled in confusion, leaving killed, wounded, artillery and prisoners in our hands. Our men pursued in hot haste, until it became necessary to halt, draw ammunition, and reestablish the lines for the purpose of driving them from their last position on Rude's Hill, which they held with cavalry and artillery, to cover the passage of the river, about a mile in their rear. Our troops charged and took the position without loss. The enemy withdrew, crossed the river, and burnt the bridge.

The engagement closed at 6:30 p.m. The Cadets did their duty, as the long list of casualties will attest. Numerous instances of gallantry might be mentioned, but I have thought it better to refrain from specifying individual cases, for fear of making invidious distinctions, or from want of information withholding praise where it might have been justly merited. It had rained almost incessantly during the battle, and at its termination the Cadets were well-nigh exhausted. Wet, hungry, and many of them shoeless—for they had lost their shoes and socks in the deep mud through which it was necessary to march—they bore their hardships with the uncomplaining resignation which characterizes the true soldier.

The 16th and 17th were devoted to caring for the wounded and the burial of the dead.

On the 17th I received an order from General Breckinridge to report to General Imboden, with the request on the part of General Breckinridge, that the Corps be relieved from further duty and be ordered back to the Institute. The circumstances of General Imboden's situation were such as to render our detention for a time necessary. We were finally ordered by him to proceed to Staunton, without delay, for the purpose of proceeding by rail to Richmond, in obedience to a call from the Secretary of War. Returning, the Corps marched into Staunton on the 21st, took the cars on the 22d, reached Richmond on the 23d, were stationed at Camp Lee until the 28th, were then ordered to report to Major General Ransom, ordered by him to encamp on the intermediate line. On the 28th left Camp Lee, took up camp on Carter's farm, on intermediate line, midway between Brook and Meadow Bridge roads, continued in this camp until June 6th. On the 6th received orders to return to Lexington; reached Lexington the 9th; Yankees approached on the 10th, drove us out on the 11th; we fell back, taking the Lynchhurg road, marched to mouth of the North River, and went into camp. Next day (Sunday, the 12th) remained in camp until 1 p.m., scouts reported enemy advancing, fell back two miles and took a position at a strong pass in the mountains to await the enemy. No enemy came. We were then ordered to Lynchburg, went there; ordered to report to General Vaughan; ordered back to Lexington; reached Lexington on the 25th; Corps furloughed on June 17th.

I am, General, very respectfully, your obedient servant
Scott Ship, Lieutenant Colonel and Commandant.

Message from U. S. Grant to Halleck. Near the end of the message (highlighted portion) Grant expresses his lack of confidence in Sigel and suggests he be relieved of all duties:

City Point, Va., July 7, 1864
(Received 9 p.m.)

Major General Halleck, Chief of Staff:
The number of dismounted cavalry sent from here reaches nearly 3,000 men; the whole force sent about 9,000. Will it not answer your purposes to retain the artillery you were preparing to send here to distribute among the 100-days' men, instead of sending back a regiment of heavy artillery? It breaks up a brigade to send one of these large regiments now. The dismounted cavalry took with them such arms and accouterments as they had, but they were not completely armed. Won't Couch do well to command until Hunter reaches? **All of General Sigel's operations from the beginning of the war have been so unsuccessful that I think it advisable to relieve him from all duty, at least until present troubles are over. I do not feel certain at any time that he will not after abandoning stores, artillery, and trains, make a successful retreat to some safe place.**

U. S. Grant
Lieutenant-General

Bibliography

Barrett, J. G. and R. K. Turner, Jr. *Letters of a New Market Cadet, Beverly Stanard.* Chapel Hill: University of North Carolina Press, 1961.

Board of Visitors, *Report of the Board of Visitors of the Virginia Military Institute.* Lexington, Virginia, July 1864.

Boatner, Mark Mayo. *The Civil War Dictionary.* New York: David McKay & Co., Inc., 1959.

Breckinridge, John C. Letter to Francis H. Smith, May 4, 1864 (VMI Archives).

Breckinridge, John C. Dispatch to Francis H. Smith, May 10, 1864 (VMI Archives).

Bruce, D. H. "The Battle of New Market, Virginia." *Southern Historical Society Papers,* vol. 25, 1907.

Couper, Colonel William. *One Hundred Years at VMI.* Richmond, 1939.

Couper, Colonel William. *The V.M.I. New Market Cadets.* Charlottesville, Virginia: The Michie Company, 1933.

Crim, E. C. "Tender Memories of the VMI Cadets." *Confederate Veteran,* vol. 34, June 1926.

Davis, William C. *The Battle of New Market.* Baton Rouge and London: Louisiana State University Press, 1975.

Davis, William C. *The Day at New Market.* Harrisburg, Pa.: Historical Times, Inc., 1971.

Fitz-Simmons, Charles. *Sigel's Fight at New Market.* Chicago: MOLLUS - ILLINOIS, date unknown.

Garrison, Webb. *A Treasury of Civil War Tales.* Nashville: Rutledge Hill Press, 1988.

Gatch, Thomas B. "Recollections of New Market." *Confederate Veteran,* vol. 34, June 1926.

Gatewood, Andrew C. L. Letter to parents, April 16, 1864 (Andrew C. Gatewood Papers, VMI Archives, MS#068).

Hotchkiss, Jedediah. *Map of the Shenandoah Valley*, 1862.

Howard, John C. "Recollections of New Market." *Confederate Veteran*, vol. 34, February 1926.

Imboden, Brigadier General John D., Confederate States of America. "The Battle of New Market, Virginia, May 15, 1864." New York: *Battles and Leaders of the Civil War*. Vol. 4. R. U. Johnson and C. C. Buel, editors, 1887.

Jackson, Mississippi, *Clarion Ledger*, December 1907.

Johnston, Colonel J. Stoddard. "Sketches of Operations of General John C. Breckinridge." *Southern Historical Society Papers*, vol. 7, June 1879.

Lee, Robert E. Letter to Major General William H. Richardson, April 25, 1864 (VMI Archives).

Lexington, Virginia, *Gazette*, May 25, 1864.

Morrison, J. H. Letter to J. L. Jones, May 18, 1864 (VMI Archives).

Morton, Howard. "The New Market Charge." *Southern Historical Society Papers*, vol. 24, 1896.

New York *Times*, May 18, 1864.

New York *Tribune*, May 18, 27, 1864.

Official Records of the Union and Confederate Armies in the War of the Rebellion, ser. 1, vol. 32, pt. 3.

Official Records of the Union and Confederate Armies in the War of the Rebellion, ser. 1, vol. 33.

Official Records of the Union and Confederate Armies in the War of the Rebellion, ser. 1, vol. 34.

Official Records of the Union and Confederate Armies in the War of the Rebellion, ser. 1, vol. 37, pt 1.

Official Records of the Union and Confederate Armies in the War of the Rebellion, ser. 1, vol. 40, pt 3.

Official Records of the Union and Confederate Armies in the War of the Rebellion, ser. 1, vol. 51, pt 2.

Parsons, J. W. "Capture of Battery at New Market." *Confederate Veteran*, vol. 17, March 1909.

Pond, George E. *The Shenandoah Valley in 1864*. New York: Charles Scribner's Sons, 1901.

Potts, J. N. "Who Fired the First Gun at New Market?" *Confederate Veteran*, vol. 17, September 1909.

Preston, J. T. L. Letter to Mr. R. I. McDowell, May 25, 1864 (VMI Archives).

Richmond *Dispatch*, May 19, 1864.

Richmond *Enquirer*, May 20, 1864.

Richmond *Times - Dispatch*, April 24, 1898; October 8, 15, 1905; January 19, 1908, June 23, 1912.

Shank, S. T. "A Gunner at New Market, Va." *Confederate Veteran*, vol. 26, May 1918.

Ship, Lieutenant Colonel Scott. Official Report, *Battle of New Market and Aftermath*, 1864 (VMI Archives).

Sigel, Major General Franz, United States Volunteers. "Sigel in the Shenandoah Valley in 1864." New York: *Battles and Leaders of the Civil War*. Vol. 4. R. U. Johnson and C. C. Buel, editors, 1887.

Smith, Francis H. *History of the Virginia Military Institute*. Lynchburg, Virginia: J. P. Bell Co., 1912.

Smith, Francis H. Letter to Major General John C. Breckinridge, May 2, 1864 (VMI Archives).

Smith, Francis H. Letter to Major General John C. Breckinridge, May 11, 1864 (VMI Archives).

Smith, Francis H. Letter to Major General W. H. Richardson, Adjutant General, May 12, 1864 (VMI Archives).

Smith, Francis H. Letter to Major General W. H. Richardson, Adjutant General, May 17, 1864 (VMI Archives).

Smith, General Francis H. *Superintendent's Annual Report*. Lexington, Virginia, July 1864 (VMI Archives).

Smith, Colonel George H. "More of the Battle of New Market." *The Confederate Veteran*, vol. 17.

Tanner, Robert G. *Stonewall in the Valley*. Garden City, New York: Doubleday and Co., 1976.

Turner, Edward Raymond. *The New Market Campaign, May, 1864*. Richmond: Whittet and Shepperson, 1912.

Vandiver, Frank E., Editor. "Proceedings of the Second Confederate Congress, First Session, Second Session in Part, 2 May/14 June, 1864; 7 November/14 December, 1864." *Southern Historical Society Papers*, vol. 51, 1958.

Wise, Henry A. "The Cadets at New Market, Virginia." *Confederate Veteran*, vol. 20, August 1912.

Wise, Jennings C. *The Military History of the Virginia Military Institute from 1839 to 1865*. Lynchburg, Virginia: J. P. Bell Co., 1915.

Wise, John S. *The End of an Era*. Boston and New York: Houghton Mifflin Co., 1899.

Wise, John S. "The West Point of the Confederacy." *Century Magazine*, vol. 37, January 1889.

Index